# THE TWO GREATEST IDEAS

## Soochow University Lectures in Philosophy

CHIENKUO MI, *GENERAL EDITOR*

The Soochow University Lectures in Philosophy are given annually at Soochow University in Taiwan by leading international figures in contemporary analytic philosophy.

*Also in the series:*

Duncan Pritchard, *Epistemic Angst*

Robert Audi, *Moral Perception*

Scott Soames, *What Is Meaning?*

Ernest Sosa, *Knowing Full Well*

# The Two
# Greatest Ideas

## HOW OUR GRASP OF THE
## UNIVERSE AND OUR MINDS
## CHANGED EVERYTHING

*Linda Trinkaus Zagzebski*

PRINCETON UNIVERSITY PRESS

PRINCETON & OXFORD

Published by Princeton University Press
41 William Street, Princeton, New Jersey 08540
6 Oxford Street, Woodstock, Oxfordshire OX20 1TR

press.princeton.edu

Library of Congress Cataloging-in-Publication Data

Names: Zagzebski, Linda Trinkaus, 1946– author.
Title: The two greatest ideas : how our grasp of the universe and our minds changed everything / Linda Trinkaus Zagzebski.
Description: Princeton : Princeton University Press, [2021] | Series: Soochow university lectures in philosophy | Includes bibliographical references and index.
Identifiers: LCCN 2021018386 (print) | LCCN 2021018387 (ebook) | ISBN 9780691199610 (hardback : acid-free paper) | ISBN 9780691211244 (ebook)
Subjects: LCSH: Philosophy of mind. | BISAC: PHILOSOPHY / History & Surveys / General | PHILOSOPHY / Ethics & Moral Philosophy
Classification: LCC BD418.3 .Z34 2021 (print) | LCC BD418.3 (ebook) | DDC 128/.2—dc23
LC record available at https://lccn.loc.gov/2021018386
LC ebook record available at https://lccn.loc.gov/2021018387

British Library Cataloging-in-Publication Data is available

Editorial: Matt Rohal
Production Editorial: Mark Bellis
Jacket Design: Felix Summ
Production: Erin Suydam
Publicity: Maria Whelan and Carmen Jimenez
Copyeditor: Molan Goldstein

Published in association with Soochow University (Taiwan)

This book has been composed in Miller

Printed on acid-free paper. ∞

Printed in the United States of America

10 9 8 7 6 5 4 3 2 1

Dedicated to Notre-Dame de Paris

This icon of human civilization was partially destroyed by fire on April 15, 2019, and is currently under restoration. That event reminds me of the fragility of our most vital cultural creations, whether they be buildings or ideas. Works of beauty and the ideas that ennoble humanity take centuries to build, but they can be destroyed in a flash.

# CONTENTS

## ACKNOWLEDGMENTS

THIS BOOK BEGAN as three Soochow Lectures, delivered at Soochow University, Taipei, in March 2018. I am very grateful to Professor Chienkuo Mi for his invitation and his gracious hospitality to me and my husband. I also want to thank the graduate students who served as my research assistants during the four years I was working on this book—Tyler Eaves, Raymond Stewart, Zachary Milstead, Zach Reimer, and Matt Budisin—as well as the students in my graduate seminar on the manuscript in spring 2018. My colleague Neal Judisch and his students in the capstone philosophy course at the University of Oklahoma wrote meticulous comments on a draft of the manuscript in spring 2020, and art history professor Rozmeri Basic at OU devoted much time to patiently responding to my ideas about the relationship between art and thought throughout Western history.

I presented versions of chapter 1, an overview of the book, as the Cardinal Mercier Lecture at the University of Leuven, Belgium, in October 2017, and the Claire Miller Lecture at the University of North Carolina in November 2017. A version of the first chapter was also a Last Lecture (a series in which the speaker is asked to give the lecture they would give if it was the last lecture of their life) at the University of Oklahoma in November 2017. A short version of the first chapter was also my Aquinas Medalist address to the American Catholic Philosophical Association in November 2017.

I want to think the anonymous Princeton reviewers, who spent a great deal of time writing detailed comments on previous drafts. Matt Rohal, my Princeton University Press editor, has been tremendously encouraging and more helpful than I ever thought possible. He shepherded the project from its beginning to its final revision, and his suggestions have greatly improved the book.

Finally, I owe a tremendous debt of gratitude to the University of Oklahoma, and especially to the Philosophy Department and its chair, Wayne Riggs, and former chair, Hugh Benson, who have given me everything I have needed in my professional life in the last twenty-two years. As I am about to retire, I thank them for helping me look back on those years with joy and satisfaction.

*December 20, 2020*
Santa Fe, New Mexico

# THE TWO GREATEST IDEAS

# CHAPTER ONE

# The Two Greatest Ideas: An Overview of the Narrative

*"The eternal mystery of the world is its comprehensibility."*

ALBERT EINSTEIN[1]

THERE HAVE BEEN two ideas in human history that underlie a vast number of cultural innovations in human civilization. These ideas are so simple, it is easy to overlook their tremendous power, and it is easy to forget that we did not always have them. One is the idea that the human mind can grasp the universe; the other is the idea that the human mind can grasp itself. I am going to tell a story about these two ideas and how their relationship changed from the dominance of the first to the dominance of the second. The ideas do not conflict and many societies have adopted them harmoniously, but in Western history they took the form of a clash between the idea that we grasp the world before the mind and the idea that we grasp the mind before the world. That clash has left us with intellectual confusion and

### The Word "Universe"

The word "universe" comes from the old French *univers*
(12th cent.) and the earlier Latin *universum*, which means
"all together, all in one, the whole of existing things." But
it is more commonly used to mean "the whole of physical
reality," or everything that came out of the Big Bang. This
ambiguity makes it tempting for people to identify all
of reality with all of physical reality, and Carl Sagan has
announced: "The cosmos is all that is, or ever was or
ever will be" (Sagan et al. 1980). But the issue of whether
everything that exists is the same as everything physical is
clearly not something that can be decided by the meaning
of a word. In this book I am using "universe" to mean
all existing things, whether physical or nonphysical.
Sometimes I use the word "world" to mean the same thing.

cultural discord. Looking back can help us look forward, and at
the end of this book I will offer some reflections on the prospects
for the ascendance of a third great idea and the unsolved problem of how to conceive of the world as a whole.

The first great idea might seem obvious because it is pre-
supposed by so many of our broad cultural practices—religion,
philosophy, natural science, mathematics. All these practices
attempt to discover something both deep and universal—the
numerical laws of the universe, its physical structure, the origin
and future of the universe, and possibly our ultimate destiny.
These practices require people to think of the universe as a unified whole rather than as a jumble of unrelated phenomena.
But the thought that the world is a unity is not forced on us,
and thousands of years of human progress did not rely on it.
From earliest times, all the societies of which we have evidence

had the ability to work with objects and manipulate them. But such achievements as mining metals and fashioning them into tools, developing building techniques, and cultivating crops and raising animals do not require the thought that the world is one unified whole; much less do they require the thought that the human mind can grasp it. Probably any invention relies on the belief that there are regularities in nature, but it is not necessary to think that the human mind can grasp the world as a whole to control fire or to make a pot or to plant crops. The same point applies to the decorative arts and the ability to tell a story. In fact, people could tell stories about the gods without thinking that they could grasp the universe, so the first great idea was not necessary for ancient mythology, and religion does not necessarily include the idea of the universe as one.[2] But in the most dramatic leap in the evolution of human thought, people began to think that we can comprehend the world as a whole. We can see through the plenitude of phenomena in our experience to see the world as one thing. Writers have occasionally raised the curious question of why philosophy, mathematics, science, and most of the great world religions were all started at approximately the same time, in the first millennium BCE.[3] I suggest that these achievements were all connected with the rise of the first great idea.

The first great idea might seem extravagant, but when I say that the first idea was an *idea*, I do not mean that it was necessarily a belief, although it probably is and has been a belief for many people. People can entertain an idea long before they believe it to be true, and even if they never believe it to be true. The first idea is the idea of a possibility—something the human mind possibly can do. For some people the idea functions as an aspiration or a hope rather than as a belief. For others it is clearly a belief, even a commitment. I will often treat the idea as if it is true because I believe it is true, but very little of what I will say in this book hinges on its truth. The power of the idea does not depend upon its being true.

When I describe the first great idea as the idea that the human mind can grasp the universe, I am leaving open the issue of whether the mind is aware of itself as grasping while it is grasping (or thinks it is grasping) the world. Some philosophers have thought that whenever the mind is aware of anything, it is aware of the act of awareness, so an awareness of anything outside the mind is always accompanied by an awareness of the mind grasping what is outside of it. That implies that in some sense, however vague, the mind is always aware of itself. I will return to this issue, but it is significant that the *idea* that the mind can grasp the world is different from the idea that the mind can grasp itself. Both ideas come out of the same mind, but historically they have been associated with very different ways of thinking about the relation between the mind and the world, and different ways of conceptualizing the human person.

In Western history, philosophy is almost always traced to the sixth century BCE with three philosophers who lived in the Greek city of Miletus in present-day Turkey, and who were probably among the first human beings to get the idea of the world as a whole. The first philosopher on record is Thales, and I am sorry to say that for decades I did not appreciate the significance of his proposal that water is the foundation of the world. In my experience, students generally find Thales silly, but his idea that there is some primary substance out of which the entire world is composed was genius of the first order. He and his successors, Anaximander and Anaximenes, had the idea that all of reality is one thing, an idea that has guided human intellectual and material advancement ever since. Anaximander's proposal that the origin and the principle of all things is the "Boundless" or "Infinite" (*apeiron*) was particularly impressive, not only for the content of the idea but for the fact that he attempted to demonstrate it by argument. Anaximander's urge to map reality extended to mapping the stars and drawing a map of the earth, making him one of the first astronomers and first geographers. When he mapped the stars and the earth and reasoned about the origin of the universe, he must have had the first great idea. He believed that everything that exists is connected in a structure, and since the structure can be mapped, the human mind can grasp it and communicate it to other minds.

Two very different pre-Socratic philosophers had the same idea. Parmenides lived in the Greek colony of Elea in what is now southern Italy around 500 BCE. What historians usually stress about Parmenides is that he was a pure monist. He argued that there is only one unchanging thing in existence, an extreme version of the first great idea. Parmenides is often contrasted with his contemporary Heraclitus from Ephesus, who taught that all things are in perpetual flux.[4] Yet Heraclitus is the author of one of the strongest and most vivid expressions of the first great idea: "Listening not to me but to the *Logos*, it is wise to agree that all things are one."[5]

The Pythagoreans expanded the first great idea in a way that integrated virtually all domains of human thought. Since they believed that the structure of the universe is numerical, they were able to connect the study of number (mathematics) with the study of number in time (harmonics), with the study of number on a grand scale in space and time (astronomy), with the study of harmony in the human soul (ethics) and in the state (political thought). The governing laws of the universe are the laws of harmony. That produced a unitary vision of the entire material and nonmaterial universe, an accomplishment unsurpassed in human history.[6] The idea that numbers are a deep feature of the universe spread throughout the culture of the West, and it will come up repeatedly in this book. Because of the Pythagoreans and the other pre-Socratic philosophers, the ancient Greeks created and left to us a legacy so close to universally acknowledged as to be invisible: that the universe in its entirety is rationally structured. Rationality is a property inherent in both the mind and the universe. Because the structure of the universe is rational, it is comprehensible to a rational mind. That was not just the basis for Greek philosophy; it was expressed in Greek politics, in Greek sculpture and architecture, and in Greek science. We still expect all areas of human thought and activity to be connected because we have inherited the idea that the entire universe is comprehensible, and it is comprehensible because it is, in a very important sense, one thing. We have never given that up. Evidence that we have not given it up is that we have never given up the word "universe."

I want to stress that the first great idea was not just the idea that there is a universe with a unified rational structure; it was the idea that the human mind thinks that it can *grasp* such a universe. The awareness of being able to grasp the universe as a whole transforms human consciousness. The first great idea was vast in scope, so it took a powerful mind to have it. The awareness of having a mind with such power must have been elevating. It led the Pythagoreans to the idea that the soul can rise to union with the divine, an idea that occurs repeatedly in the major world religions. We see it in the Hindu Upanishads, in Buddhism, in Neo-Platonism, and later, in the great metaphysical systems of the West such as those of Aquinas and Spinoza. The first great idea gave human beings a sense of harmony with the universe, and that led them to a view of morality that has persisted through long periods of history in many cultures as well as in the West: the idea that morality is living and feeling in accord with the world.

There is another way in which the first idea led to morality. Grasping the human place in the universe as a whole not only leads to the aspiration to an afterlife or union between the individual mind and the highest power, but also to a sense of responsibility to God or the highest power. When the members of our species came to regard themselves as important, they realized that their actions are serious. Moral laws are not just rules to get along with a minimum of violence; they are the laws demanded of beings whose grasp of the universe makes them answerable *to* the universe.

So before Socrates, Greek philosophers had managed to both originate and connect metaphysics, natural science, mathematics, musical theory, morality, and a type of religious vision that did not appear in the Greek religion. Elsewhere in the world, the first great idea took the form of the beginning of a world religion—Hinduism, Buddhism, Zoroastrianism, Taoism, Judaism—but in Greece it was philosophy rather than the Greek religion that initially expressed the first great idea, making the Greeks unique in the history of that idea. The first idea transformed human consciousness, making possible the experience of conversion.[7] Humans were able to perceive themselves as exalted beings, a perception that raised human consciousness to a level that, as far as we know, has never been reached by any other kind of creature. But there are instances of the first great idea that are not transformative, as we will see.

Monotheism is one of the most important and enduring ideas in human history. It was explicitly adopted by the Jews no later than the seventh century BCE, a century before the school of Pythagoras flourished in southern Italy. Monotheism in the Hebrew scriptures raised the first great idea to the level of the personal. What made it personal was partly that it included the idea that the whole natural universe comes from the choice of a personal being, and partly that it included the idea that a human being can have a personal relationship with the Creator. The paramount expression of Jewish monotheism appears in Deuteronomy (6:4–5): "Hear, O Israel: The Lord our God, the Lord is one. Love the Lord your God with all your heart and with all your soul and with all your strength."[8] This is the definitive statement of Jewish identity, and it is especially remarkable because it expresses both a metaphysical claim about God and a claim about the Jewish people's relationship to God. It is a version of the first great idea in which personhood is at the core.

The idea that the physical universe was created by the choice of a personal deity had some important implications. It meant that although the universe is comprehensible, it did not come into being out of necessity, and therefore it could not be comprehended by rational reflection alone. Since the features of the universe are contingent, they need to be discovered. The belief in the contingency of the world is one of the metaphysical presuppositions of modern science, and it has been argued that the ancient Jews set the stage for the eventual rise of science since they were unique among ancient peoples in thinking of the universe as contingent rather than necessary and as linear rather than cyclical.[9]

Monotheism was also connected with the idea that there are moral laws that apply to all human beings. Even before the Jews were clearly monotheistic, they had a covenant with God, who required of them that they obey his moral prescriptions, but at some point they began to see some of those prescriptions as universal. There are hints of this idea as far back as the early eighth century BCE at the beginning of the book of Amos, where monotheism is connected with a moral law that is not tied to a particular culture. Amos declares that not only the Israelites but also the inhabitants of neighboring kingdoms will be judged by God for their evil acts. The Israel-ite neighbors could not use the excuse that their behavior was endorsed by their local gods. That was a significant move in the development of the belief that there are moral prescrip-tions that cross the boundaries of individual societies, and the logic of that belief eventually led to the view that there are uni-versal moral laws.

An even more interesting extension of the first great idea appears a century later in the book of Jeremiah, in which God invites people to see their faithlessness from his own perspec-tive. In one passage God says: "How can I pardon you? Your children have forsaken me and sworn by those who are no gods. When I fed them to the full, they committed adultery and trooped to the houses of prostitutes" (Jer. 5:7).[10] Imagine what it does to an intelligent creature to think that there is a single personal Creator with whom they have a relationship, and now they are invited to see themselves from his point of view! The awareness of having such a view must have been transforming to the Jews,[11] just as the Pythagoreans were transformed by the sense that their mind could grasp the mathematical struc-ture of the universe. What I find so intriguing about verses like the ones in Jeremiah is not *what* God tells the Jews, but the fact that they thought that they could see into the mind of the being who sees all things.

The incipient idea of a natural law that we see in many ancient peoples, and especially in the Stoics, was developed many centuries later by Aquinas into the idea that there is a single Eternal Law of God that is expressed in the created world in both a universal moral law and a universal physi-cal law. The idea of a universal moral law is a condition for the modern idea of universal human rights, and the idea of a universal physical law is a condition for the development of modern science.[12] So in Western history we see a connected move from early physics and metaphysics and mathematics to ethics, and then eventually to modern natural science and international law, all of which have roots in the first great idea.

But the form that the first great idea took in the West faltered. After more than two thousand years of dominance, the first great idea declined in importance and the second great idea overtook it. The pivotal period in the confrontation of the two great ideas began in the Renaissance in art and literature, and the seventeenth century in philosophy and science.[13] And here my story takes a turn.

The second great idea, that the human mind is capable of grasping itself, probably arose at about the same time as the first. Of course, people were aware of their minds long before that, but I am referring to the rise of the *idea* that the human mind can grasp itself. For millennia, the second idea was secondary to the first. That does not mean that people did not reflect on their minds. In fact, in both the East and the West there were highly developed practices of prayer and meditation that focused on the mind, but the purpose of these practices was usually the desire to grasp something else—God or Brahman or the Tao or the One. The individual mind was not thought to be important in itself. What human beings thought of their own minds derived from their idea of the place of the mind in the totality of reality. Since human minds are a component of the world as a whole, the first great idea that the human mind can grasp the world included the second great idea that the human mind can grasp itself. In the West that meant there was a distinct order of knowing. Human beings know themselves primarily through knowing the world. We grasp the world first, and because we can grasp the world, we can grasp ourselves. One's own mind is not transparent to oneself, and it is not the primary object of awareness. The oft-repeated Delphic maxim "Know thyself" was not an invitation to make introspection of one's mind primary, and it was certainly not an expression of the importance of the individuality of the mind. It would never have occurred to Socrates to replace the first great idea with the second. What Socrates taught us is that we have to find out our nature, and we find it out by following the Socratic method in application to the world, not by an examination of our inner conscious states.

When the first great idea dominated, the distinctiveness of consciousness was not an issue, and the distinctiveness of an individual consciousness was certainly not an issue, although Saint Augustine's brilliant sense of interiority might have been one of the exceptions.[14] People probably noticed that there is something different about grasping one's own mind than grasping minds in general, but there was little or no attention to the idea that the mind's grasp of itself differs *in kind* from the mind's grasp of the universe, even that part of the universe that contains minds. When a human mind grasps itself, it grasps something that is unique, but I do not see any indication that the uniqueness of individual consciousness was treated with any more importance than the uniqueness of the human body for most of human history. It seems to me that love is always directed towards the uniqueness of a person, and so personal uniqueness would have been experienced, but love is not part of human thought.[15] In any case, the idea of the individuality of consciousness did not change anything in the way philosophers thought of the place of the human being in the universe. Nor did it change the practice of religion. Nor did it change the practice of morality. In Christianity, human personality became more interesting with the doctrine of the Incarnation, which directly connected human persons with the Godhead, and we see the importance of the human individual in Gospel passages in which Jesus says that God knows even the number of hairs on your head (Luke 12:7;

Matt. 10:30), and the parable in which God is compared to a shepherd who will search for a single lost sheep (Luke 15:4–7). But the description of the mind of Jesus in the Gospels is meager in its particulars and is focused more on his teaching of truths that reveal what human beings need to learn about themselves, not the unique personality of the most important person in Christianity. There are roots of the idea of subjectivity in early Christianity, but Christianity never attempted to make the second idea dominate the first.

It is commonplace to observe that the early modern period was important, and I dislike repeating something commonplace, but I am convinced that the second most dramatic event in the history of human thought really did happen around the seventeenth century in Europe. The idea that the human mind can grasp itself took on a degree of importance that separated it from the idea that the human mind can grasp the universe. Starting with Descartes or thereabouts, the second great idea began to supersede the first.

There are a couple of things to note about this historic change. First, the second idea would not have risen to such importance if the first idea had not faltered. The unity of the study of nature and human destiny and morality started to fall apart. Descartes would not have made the second idea the starting point of an entire method of philosophy if he had been satisfied with the first. He says that explicitly.[16] The Reformation of the sixteenth century had broken the unified authority of the Christian religion in expressing the version of the first great idea that virtually everyone accepted. Since morality had been connected with religious authority, the undermining of religious authority led to the undermining of the conception of morality as obedience to authority, the voice of God expressed in human institutions, preparing the way for a new foundation of morality in the individual. Aristotelian natural science, which had long been a component of the medieval worldview, was found to be defective and was replaced by the new empirical science. The religious wars and the Black Death dismantled the medieval economy and the social and political structures that had embodied a common expression of the first great idea. Of course, the disarray in a particular version of the first idea is no reason to give up the first idea itself, and the first great idea continued to fare well in Eastern thought; but in the West, the effect of philosophy and historical events on the first idea was devastating. Eventually, in the minds of many, the only version of the first great idea left standing was the conception of the world produced by natural science.

Before Descartes, the rise of the second great idea had already started with advances in a number of fields. Discoveries in perspective geometry by the Arabs were brought to Florence in the fifteenth century, making it possible to depict visual works from a consciously chosen point of view. The discovery of perspective not only led to the glorious art and architecture of the Renaissance, it produced innovations in optics, navigation, and astronomy, so its importance went well beyond its usefulness in depicting an object in three-dimensional space on a flat surface. The ability to depict points of view did not simply make painting more realistic; it led to greater awareness of the existence of different points of view and the individual minds that possess them. Literature was revolutionized at the same time as art with the invention of a form of literature in which the point of view of the characters is the focus of the narrative. Thirty-six years before Descartes published the *Meditations*, Cervantes published the first part of *Don Quixote*, universally regarded as the first modern novel and one of the most influential works of fiction ever written. What made *Don Quixote* revolutionary was the invention of *characters*, who are not just types but are like real people with worlds of their own and unique points of view.[17] We are so used to the second great idea that we often do not pay attention to the origin of its supremacy, but its rise required a revolution on many levels.

I think that it is important to see that the two great ideas are not in conflict, but they were interpreted that way when the second idea superseded the first. What was dramatic about the ascendance of the second great idea was the shift from the view that the human mind grasps itself through grasping the world to the idea that the human mind grasps the world through grasping itself. People began to think that one's consciousness is the gateway through which all knowledge of the world must pass. I know many philosophers who find this idea so obviously true as not to require argument, but actually it is not obvious at all. When an idea becomes so widely accepted that it appears trivial, it is easy to forget and to misread the millennia of work by writers who did not accept it.

When the first great idea dominated, philosophers thought of the mind as an open window to the universe. Theories of perception in this period were typically forms of direct realism—what you perceive is what is there in the world. When the second great idea dominated, philosophers thought that we need to construct our idea of the world out of the contents of our own minds. The mind has a boundary, so the relationship between mental contents and the world outside became critical. Perceptual theories were either forms of indirect realism—what you perceive is a copy of what is in the world, or idealism—what you perceive is an idea, and the world is a world of ideas. Either way, the grasp of the mind comes first. The mind takes in perceptions, and then needs to figure out what kind of world would produce those perceptions.

Similarly, when the first great idea dominated, semantics was what we now call externalist: the meaning of a word is partly outside the mind. In contrast, when the second great

**The Big Shift**

| Era of the primacy of the first idea | Era of the primacy of the second idea |
|---|---|
| The mind is an open window to the world. | Contents of the mind "represent" the world. |
| The mind does not have a fixed edge. | The mind has a fixed boundary. |
| Perceptual theories are forms of direct realism. | Direct realism about perception abandoned. |
| Philosophy begins with metaphysics. | Epistemology becomes "first philosophy." |
| Focus on persons as having a place in nature. | Focus on the self and its subjectivity. |
| Morality is living in harmony with the universe. | Morality is grounded in self-governance—autonomy. |

idea dominated, semantics was what we now call internalist: a meaning is an item in the mind that corresponds to something in the world. When philosophers divided the individual mind from the rest of the world, the issue of how language connects each mind to the world and whether a language is the same for all users of the language became critical.[18]

There were other important shifts in philosophy. No longer did philosophy begin with metaphysics, the study of being *qua* being. That status went to epistemology, the theory of knowledge. The metaphysical study of human beings shifted from a focus on the *person*, a being defined by its place in the world, to a focus on the *self*, the bearer of individual subjective consciousness. The consequence was a dramatic shift from the idea of morality as living in harmony with the universe to the idea of morality as grounded in autonomy, or self-governance, and the ultimate bearer of authority became the self.

The dominance of the second great idea led to far more skepticism about the human ability to comprehend the universe than an approach that made the first idea basic.[19] If you have to start with the contents of your own mind and then try to figure out how to combine those contents in a way that allows you to infer what the universe outside your mind is like, you have a job that might be insurmountable at the first step.[20] And even if you can get beyond the skeptical threat, you will find it difficult in the extreme to construct a view of the world with anything like the comprehensiveness of the great religions or the great metaphysical systems of the past. Consequently, the dominance of the second idea had a deflating effect on traditional metaphysics and theology and any attempt at a grand worldview.[21]

The second idea did not destroy the first idea in all forms. One of the most important philosophical forms of the second great idea was the British empiricism of the eighteenth century—not the kind of empiricism of Aristotle where you look around you and investigate, but the only kind of empiricism possible when you have to construct the materials of the world out of your perceptual states. That made empirical science foundational. It also made it possible to treat the universe of mental states as a complete universe, so it is not surprising that the rise of the second great idea led to the empirical idealism of George Berkeley, in which all objects are in minds, and by a different path to the idealism of Hegel, in which the history of the world is the history of consciousness. The clash between realism and idealism became important once the second great idea rose to prominence. Prior to its rise, there was no idealism with which to contrast realism.

We see, then, that the dominance of the second idea was accompanied by and partly caused by the rise of modern science and its breathtaking success in improving human lives as well as advancing our knowledge of the physical world. In the minds of many, the combination of trust in science and lack of trust in the Christian worldview led to the idea that science is capable of giving us a theory of everything. That reduced the first idea to the product of empirical science. But science did not transform human consciousness the way the first idea had done. Earlier I wrote that the first idea gave human beings a sense of importance in the universe. When it diminished, the beliefs that had given people meaning were gone, and what was left was the idea of scientific and technological progress. By the twentieth century, Max Weber famously declared that science undermines religion, not only theology, by revealing a reality devoid of meaning and value, bereft of the presence of God, and therefore "disenchanted."[22] Volumes have been written arguing that there is no conflict between science and religion, but some science triumphalists like Daniel Dennett embrace the disenchantment of the world that results from the dominance of the view that science gives us a theory of everything.[23] The disenchantment that comes from the reduction of the first idea to natural science can therefore be seen as a good thing, but it seems to leave modern people with no sense of what connects *them* to the universe, an objection expressed by Thomas Nagel (2009) in a frequently cited essay.[24] Nagel observes that not everyone has what he calls "the religious temperament," and I would agree that not all people long for a view of the world as a whole in which their own lives play a significant role, but it is worth noticing the difference between those products of the exercise of the first great idea that are satisfying in this way and those that are not.[25]

The rise of the second great idea has had many welcome consequences. When the mind reflects on itself, it is aware of directing itself in thought and action, so the rise of the second great idea led to the idea that self-governance is the primary bearer of authority over any individual person, whereas previously the mind looked outside itself for authority. The acceptance of self-governance is the greatest block to tyranny human civilization has ever produced, and the focus on the value of the human being as an individual rather than as a member of a social group was critical for the recognition of individual human rights, one of the greatest achievements of the modern era.[26]

Another important consequence of the second great idea is that we now value the uniqueness of each person's subjectivity, and that has had enormous implications for the way we treat individual differences. It has affected virtually every aspect of culture and social life. We enjoy people who are unlike other people. We appreciate human variations. We celebrate the differences between individual points of view and attempt to understand them. We recognize the value of persons whose differences make them less able to perform ordinary human functions than the norm. We would not have cared about that were it not for the power of the second great idea.

The first great idea never disappeared, and both of the two great ideas exist in the way we think about human beings. A human being is a person and a human being is a self, and there is an important difference between a person and a self. A person is a being in the world seen as a whole; a self is a being as seen from inside its own mind. A person has dignity because it possesses *rationality*, identified as the distinctive property of human beings and the ground of our value during the entire premodern era. In contrast, a self has dignity because of the value of its unique subjectivity, making autonomy in the sense of self-governance a political and moral ideal.[27] I believe that Kant should get credit for trying to give equal importance to both of the great ideas, and the two ideas confront each other in Kant's work—particularly, in his attempt to make autonomy both the value of an individual's self-direction and the universal value of rationality. But it seems to me that in Kant's work the second great idea is ultimately victorious. As much as he wanted to retain the first great idea, he thought that he had discovered that what we grasp when we think we grasp the universe is not the universe in itself, but the universe as an object of possible experience. For many philosophers, that was the final nail in the coffin of the first great idea.

The discovery of subjectivity created a major problem in the history of both of the great ideas. First, it meant that people in the premodern period must have made a mistake when they thought that they had successfully grasped the world as a whole. They had not. Their idea of the whole of reality was missing subjectivity, and if subjectivity is real, it was missing something real. It is even possible that what it was missing was the most important part of reality. But in the centuries since the modern period began, people have been unable to integrate subjectivity into a conception of the entire universe. The discovery of subjectivity brought with it the dichotomy between the subjective world—the world of your unique conscious experience—and the objective world—the world without conscious experience. Combining them into a conception of the whole has proved to be a daunting task. A view of the whole based on the scientific description of the objective world is popular in many quarters, including much of professional philosophy, but so far it has been unsuccessful. Neither the era dominated by the first great idea nor the era dominated by the second has succeeded in forming a conception of the whole of reality.

During the twentieth century the second great idea started to fracture. One direction of attack appeared with the discovery of the subconscious by Freud and the subsequent emergence of the idea that the part of the mind that the mind can grasp is severely limited. Later in the century there arose the idea that the self is socially constructed and shaped by the outside world, and Foucault argued that the process by which the mind grasps itself is just as complex and problematic as the process by which the mind grasps the world.[28] The result is that both ideas are objects of skepticism, yet they both persist. Two decades into the twenty-first century, we are still struggling to find a way to think of the world as a whole and the place of our individual minds in it.

It is important to see that since the two great ideas are not in conflict, it ought to be possible to put them together. However, their dominant historical expressions *were* in conflict. The premodern idea that our grasp of the world precedes our grasp of our mind conflicts with the modern idea that our grasp of our mind precedes our grasp of the world. That has left us with both practical and theoretical problems. Many of our cultural conflicts can be traced to whether we think of ourselves primarily as persons or as selves, and so we have inherited the apparently conflicting values of harmony with the world and the autonomy of the self. This problem will be the topic of chapter 4. The theoretical problem of attempting to form a conception of the whole by combining our idea of the subjective world with the idea of the objective world will be the topic of chapter 5.

When we think of the two greatest ideas together, we will notice something missing. There is another idea that ought to be significant, but it is not yet among the greatest ideas: the idea that the human mind can grasp another mind. Grasping the world is one thing, grasping one's own mind is another, and grasping other minds is something else again. What made each of the first two ideas a *great* idea was that it led to cultural innovation and sometimes upheaval, and it was expressed at great length in more than one cultural form—in art, science, literature, and philosophy—and it had long-lasting effects. These changes will be the topics of chapters 2 and 3. The third idea is critically important, or at least it ought to be, but it has not yet had deep cultural effects equal to the effects of the first and second great ideas. I think that we need a new science of subjectivity, a science that would have to be completely different from empirical science, the study of the physical world, and different from any field of study of the objective world. I will discuss the need for that in chapter 6.

The individual human mind has infinite powers of inclusion. That is the genius of the first idea. But it also is excluded from everything else. We get that from the second idea. Each individual consciousness has a uniqueness that resists incorporation into any full description of the universe anyone has ever offered. Until we can get that to make sense, we will not have a comprehensive view of reality. We will not even understand our own minds.

---

**A Vignette of Two Ideas in Two Buildings: The Roman Pantheon and Gehry's Guggenheim Museum**

The Pythagorean cosmos is stunningly represented in the best-preserved building from ancient Rome—Hadrian's Pantheon, completed in 126 CE. The temple is laid out as a circle, the symbol of pure unity, with a magnificent dome, originally covered with sheets of gleaming bronze. At the top of the dome is an open oculus, eight meters in diameter, representing the Pythagorean monad—the number one, the source of all numbers and the origin of all things.

Every person who enters the Pantheon is drawn to the oculus. As the rays of the sun stream through the hole, they irradiate the interior of the temple, so it is unsurprising that the oculus also represents the sun-god Apollo. The central axis and the alignment with the four cardinal directions express the Pythagorean view of the order of the universe. The twenty-eight ribs extending from the oculus represent the twenty-eight months in the Pythagorean lunar calendar. People who

FIGURE 1. The Roman Pantheon. Mikhail Malykh, via Wikimedia Commons.

FIGURE 2. Frank Gehry's Guggenheim Museum, Bilbao, Spain. Steppschuh Photography.

enter the Pantheon may be unaware of the cosmic significance of these numbers for the Pythagoreans, but the preoccupation of the building with order and symmetry is obvious. Perhaps Hadrian's passion for mathematics explains the many Pythagorean features in his Pantheon, and while we do not have direct evidence of his intent, it is said that he kept a secret collection of Pythagorean teachings.* The Pantheon is a magnificent expression of one of the most abstract examples of the first great idea.

A striking contrast with the Pantheon, and a work of art that succeeds brilliantly in expressing the modern sense of subjectivity is Frank Gehry's Guggenheim Museum in Bilbao, Spain. Gehry's building is a mass of curving titanium forms that remind me of the scales of fish in an animated film. The shape of the museum is unlike anything recognizable, although it might be similar to a futuristic ship. It appears to shatter traditional forms in an anti-Pythagorean outburst and magically reassemble them. Still, flights of fancy are not enough to make a building. It had to stand up, and it required extensive technological innovation to handle the engineering and construction challenges that Gehry could not have managed before the era of advanced computer technology. Of course, the city of Bilbao and the Guggenheim Foundation did not say anything about the two great ideas, but they wanted something daring and they got it. The response from both the critics and the public when it opened in 1997 was ecstatic.

Gehry's Guggenheim Museum and the Roman Pantheon are a visual testament to the contrast between the two great

---

*See Joost-Gaugier (2006), chap. 10, "The Pythagoreanism of Hadrian's Pantheon," esp. 176–177.

ideas. Both buildings are architectural and engineering
marvels that are among the most advanced of their
respective ages. The Pantheon was built at the center of
an empire and commissioned by the emperor. The Bilbao
Guggenheim was built in a dilapidated Basque steel
city looking for a way to renew itself. The dome of the
Pantheon was originally gilded as befits the home of all the
gods, and it was surrounded by magnificent buildings and
an enormous open square. The Guggenheim shimmered
in the midst of sooty, forgettable buildings on the edge of a
dirty river. When I see the Pantheon, I want to enter it and
sit and contemplate it. My reaction to the Guggenheim
Museum is to walk around it and view it from every angle.
The Roman Pantheon was designed for the Romans to
honor the Olympians gods, with attention both to its
interior and to its position in the grand city of Rome.
The Bilbao Guggenheim is intended to be a museum to
hold art, but the museum itself is much more interesting
than the art it contains. It could just as well hold plants
or books or nothing at all, and I think it would be fair to
say that the museum was built for itself. Gehry could have
built it anywhere. The museum catapulted Bilbao into the
post-industrial age, which it did spectacularly by defying
its surroundings and leading to their revitalization. Bilbao
clearly wanted something that did *not* fit the landscape.
The building owes nothing aesthetically to the past
and not even to the present. It is a flight of one person's
imagination.

# CHAPTER TWO

# The World Precedes the Mind: The Primacy of the First Great Idea

## (FIRST MILLENNIUM BCE TO THE RENAISSANCE)

### The Two Great Ideas in a Narrative

Human beings are conscious, like many other animals, but there must have been a moment in our evolutionary history when we became conscious of being conscious. We became aware of our own awareness. It is natural to distinguish our awareness of our awareness from our awareness of the world, and babies are apparently able to make that distinction not long after birth.[1] The idea that we can grasp the whole world is a natural extension of the idea that we can grasp part of the world—our immediate surroundings—and the idea that we can grasp our whole mind is a natural extension of the idea that we can grasp part of our mind—the part that is aware at any given moment. The two great ideas are extensions of natural powers of the mind that we exercise all the time. In ages of history more optimistic than our own, people had confidence that these two ideas expressed actual powers of the mind, but even when confidence in one or both powers diminished, the ideas survived as aspirations. In spite of millennia of cultural upheavals of every kind, the two great ideas have never disappeared.

I proposed in the first chapter that there have been two major revolutions in human intellectual history. One marked the rise of the first great idea, which gave us within a short period of time the origins of mathematics, metaphysics, science, religion, and moral theory, followed by an era dominated by the human passion to grasp the structure of the world. This era did not lack the desire to grasp the mind that grasps the world, but it was taken for granted that the primary object of our awareness is the world. The first revolution occurred in many parts of the world, but the West had a second revolution, which marked the ascendance of the second great idea and the belief that our primary object of awareness is our own minds. During that era the belief that we can grasp the whole of reality faded in social consciousness for at least two reasons: decline in trust in the authorities that had produced and preserved the medieval Christian version of the first great idea and, even more seriously, decline in trust in the power of the human mind to get very far beyond its own subjective perceptions. There remained the idea that the mind aims at grasping as much of the world as possible, but there was a striking shift in the answer to the question, What is the primary object of awareness—the world or the self?

What reason would there be to tell the story of human history this way? Can we learn anything from it? Historians of philosophy tell their story differently from art historians, and both differ from historians of religion or historians of science, but all of them like to identify milestones. Ever since the nineteenth-century historian Jacob Burckhardt's (1954) famous invention of the term "Renaissance" for the stunning artistic revolution in fifteenth-century Italy, it has been common for that era to be identified as a turning point in art and architecture, whereas the Scientific Revolution is usually dated to the sixteenth century, the same century in which the Reformation created an upheaval in Western religion. Philosophers usually date the beginning of modern philosophy to Descartes in the seventeenth century, accepting Descartes's interpretation of his own work as a new beginning. Changes in political institutions were no less groundbreaking, and the modern nation-state gradually emerged at the same time as these other revolutions, from the fifteen to eighteenth centuries.[2] As historical research proceeds, these dates tend to get pushed backwards,[3] but my purpose here is not to give precise dates, which clearly can be contested, but to observe that these cultural breaks with the past occurred quite close together. In fact, their proximity to each other is so remarkable it cannot be a coincidence.

The idea that there are connections among the art, literature, philosophy, and political structure of a given period of history is certainly not new. One period of Western history that has been so thoroughly researched that these connections are apparent is that of ancient Greece. Historians often observe that an important feature of ancient Greek culture was the idea that the universe is rationally ordered.[4] In the Greek view of the world, reason is not just a human faculty for drawing inferences; the universe is structured in a rational way. We see that in Greek philosophy, but also in Greek sculpture and architecture and Greek political institutions.[5] Rational principles determine what is beautiful, what is harmonious, what makes a life good, and what makes a polis just.

There are other eras in which the connections among distinct areas of the culture have been well documented, such as medieval Christian Europe, the Italian Renaissance, ancient China, and medieval Islam. In these periods and many others, a study of the religion, the philosophy, the art, the science, and the political institutions reveals common ideas that run like a thread through the culture.[6] Sometimes it is hard to see the thread until it breaks, as the thread of the first great idea broke in the West in the period between the medieval and modern ages. I think also that it is harder to see the common thread in the cultural products of a given era if we examine the history of each area of culture independently of the others. In this chapter and the next I want to highlight the two great ideas by looking at what the art, literature, philosophy, moral thought, and religion had in common in the ancient and medieval periods, which became noticeable when the thread broke and a new one emerged in the modern era, the topic of chapter 3.

There are many other ways to tell the history of human culture. It can be told in a sequence of artworks with little commentary on their connections, a method that gives maximum attention to the individuality of the creative work. Similarly, it can be told in a sequence of literary works or works of material culture and technology. It can be told as a sequence of military events, or philosophical ideas. The suspicion of "grand narratives" made famous by Lyotard (1984) has led to an emphasis on small local stories, each of which would have remained untold if, as postmodernists maintain, grand narratives tell a story to legitimate a master viewpoint or to protect the status of the politically powerful. My story is not constructed to defend one of the two ideas at the expense of the other, and I doubt that it maintains the social status of any group, but it must be acknowledged that stories are always selective. Some things are said and some things are left out. Of course, the shorter the story and the longer the period of history a story encompasses, the more there are important things left out. What can we possibly hope to learn from a story when very different stories could be told instead, or no story at all?

I think it is significant that we always have stories about the past in mind when we reflect upon the future. We have personal stories; we have national stories. We have stories that highlight past injustices, or cultural triumphs. A story shapes our self-concept and our self-concept shapes the story, but we tell the story to others because we hope it can help our joint reflection upon the direction we take in the future. I believe that ideas have power in the world. Material conditions are not the only things that direct human history. My aim is to identify a common idea that runs like a thread through a long period of history, then breaks, but continues to exist in pieces. Another thread became dominant, but that also is becoming tattered, and when we look at the whole fabric, we see many frayed edges and disintegrating patterns. My story will miss many significant cultural moments, but an advantage of approaching human history from the abstract viewpoint I am adopting is that abstraction gives us a degree of emotional detachment that can make it easier to see our history through the eyes of others, and that can soften cultural controversies such as those we will discuss in chapter 4.

I believe that both of the two great ideas are universal, but I propose that thinking of Western history as a narrative of the switch from the dominance of the first idea to the dominance of the second can illuminate our understanding of the past and give us perspective on current problems. The two great ideas are compatible, but their dominant historical expressions conflicted. When the first great idea dominated, people thought that they grasped their mind through their grasp of the world; when the second great idea dominated, it was the reverse. That makes it difficult to see how to put them together in a way that respects the power of both ideas in our history, but I propose that the way to begin is to look at that history with the aim of identifying what the change was and why it arose.

In this chapter we will look at the rise and development of the first great idea in the premodern period—in the mathematics, metaphysics and science, the arts and literature, and the moral thought of the era. The first great idea was sometimes a presupposition and sometimes a driving force. Sometimes it was conscious, but more often it was unconscious. The philosophy in an era is more likely than the art or the literature to make the idea conscious because that is what philosophers are supposed to do. We are supposed to make implicit ideas explicit so that we can see both hidden similarities and hidden differences between one person's cultural creations and those of another, and that is one way to help us understand each other. In the next chapter I will tell the story of the second great idea from the Renaissance through the twentieth century in the same way.

## The Origin of Mathematics, Science, and Metaphysics

Many decades ago, Karl Jaspers (1953) called the historical period from roughly 800 BCE to 200 BCE the deepest dividing line in human history. He named it "the Axial Age." Before this period, language was invented, great technological innovations were made, and societies were formed with functioning governments. But, Jaspers argues, there was a transformation in human consciousness in the Axial period that determined human understanding of the self and the universe ever since. Independently in three regions of the world—China, India and Persia, and "the West" (Palestine and Greece), the great world religions and philosophies began,[7] but in spite of the obvious differences among early Hinduism, Buddhism, Jainism, Zoroastrianism, Taoism, Judaism, and Greek philosophy, they had something very interesting in common.[8]

> What is new about this age, in all three areas of the world, is that man becomes conscious of Being as a whole, of himself and his limitations. . . . He asks radical questions. Face to face with the void he strives for liberation and redemption. By consciously recognizing his limits he sets himself the highest goals. He experiences absoluteness in the depth of selfhood and in the lucidity of transcendence. (2)

Jaspers claims that after the Axial Age, there were no more great spiritual innovations in the world.

If Jaspers is right, both the two great ideas burst into human consciousness at the same time in different parts of the world. Jaspers focuses on the rise of the great religions and philosophy, but there were revolutions in mathematics and science at the same time. We know that practical mathematics preexisted the Axial period since arithmetic, algebra, and geometry had been used in the Mesopotamian states from around 3000 BCE and by the Egyptians from 2000 BCE for commerce and to plot the stars and to create calendars. But in the sixth century BCE, the Pythagoreans turned mathematics into a theoretical discipline, and Euclid's systematization of geometry in the fourth century BCE is still standard textbook geometry. Even its twentieth-century non-Euclidean forms are a modification of Euclid. That suggests that we can interpret Jaspers's Axial Age as pivotal not only in the history of religion and philosophy but also in mathematics, and since mathematics was a powerful tool for the measurement and prediction of natural phenomena, the Axial Age was pivotal for astronomy and other sciences.

I mentioned in chapter 1 that it is significant that some of the same people who were pioneers in mathematics and science were also among the first philosophers. The sixth-century BCE philosopher Thales is often credited with being both the father of science and the father of philosophy. He and his Milesian successors believed that everything derives from the existence of a single ultimate substance, and his ability to connect mathematics, scientific observation, and metaphysics was one of the earliest expressions of the unity of human knowledge. Aristotle repeats a piece of historical gossip about Thales that shows in an amusing way that the unity of knowledge can even reach into the domain of practical economy. According to Aristotle, Thales was reproached by people who said that his poverty proved that philosophy is useless, so Thales used his knowledge of the stars in winter to predict that there would be a great olive harvest in the coming year and he made deposits on all the olive presses. When harvest time came and many presses were wanted for the large harvest, Thales rented them out at a rate of his choice. His supposedly useless knowledge made him a great deal of money (*Politics* 1259a).[9]

What made Thales different from the thinkers who went before? It is often observed that instead of giving mythical accounts of natural phenomena, he looked for naturalistic explanations, and that permitted an explosion of scientific and practical knowledge. That is true, but it does not necessarily mean that if we want to grasp the whole of reality we must move beyond mythical thinking. Thales did something important, but a closer look at pre-philosophical thought reveals features that are still components of our idea of the whole of reality.

At almost the same time as Karl Jaspers was writing about the Axial Age, Henri and Henriette Antonia Frankfort invented the term "mythopoeic" for a form of thought in which the world was seen primarily in terms of myths, and which preceded what they called "speculative thought," originating with the Greeks and still the dominant form of thought in the West (Frankfort et al. 1946). The Frankforts tied mythopoeic thinking to ancient Egypt and Babylonia, and that has been criticized,[10] but their most important point is that mytho-poeic thinking is a very different form of thought than the speculative, and that is significant because it forces us to think about what it takes to have the idea that the mind can grasp the world. Does it require organizing the world under very abstract concepts? Does it require ignoring the personal?

Mythopoeic thinking understands the world in the form of stories about personal agents. It is natural for contemporary Westerners to think that the stories are not true, but if we think of truth as a proper contact between the human mind and reality, there is another way to be in touch with real-ity than the cognitive. In mythopoeic thought, the contact is emotional and personal. They were not simply observing and describing nature; they were interacting with it. The myths of the Babylonians and the Egyptians were intended to explain some of the same concepts later addressed by the Greek philosophers: time, space, number, causality, human destiny. They reasoned with these categories, but the materi-als with which they reasoned were personal. They thought of their relation to the world in terms of *I* and *Thou*, a relation between subjects, whereas in speculative thought the rela-tion is between *I* and *It*, a relation between subject and object (Frankfort et al. 1946, 16). That change allowed civilization to advance, but it also created problems that we will see many times in this book.[11]

The world of scientific investigation is a world of general laws that apply to repeatable events, which makes the events predictable. In contrast, Thou has individuality and, for that

reason, is unpredictable. Causality is as important in mythopoeic thought as in speculative thought, but personal causality exists in intention, not in the following of a general law.
As the Frankforts observe, Newton's discovery of a connection between the planetary motions, the movement of the
tides, and falling objects requires a way of thinking that links
together very different and widely separated phenomena that
would not be possible in mythopoeic thinking. The ancient
Babylonians and Egyptians were looking for a *who*, not a *what*,
in causes. The Nile decides to rise (Frankfort et al. 1946, 24).
Death is willed by somebody. We think that they were deluded
because we know that the Nile is not a person who decides to
rise, and we realize that their perception of the world around
them as personal inhibited them from being able to accurately
predict when the Nile would rise. They could not subsume
natural phenomena under the category of personal causation. But we have the opposite problem. We cannot subsume
personal phenomena under the category of natural causation,
although many of us try. The problem is that we do not fully
understand another person by what makes her the same as
other things in nature; what is critical is often what makes
her different. The advantage of speculative thought is that it
extends so widely, attempting to encompass all of reality in its
scope. The disadvantage is that it leaves the personal behind.

Chapter 4 will investigate the way we humans can either be
conceptualized by our place in the world as a whole or by our
individual subjective life. Greek thought heavily influenced
subsequent Western philosophy with its emphasis on our common human nature, and individual personality did not acquire
the status of philosophical importance until late in our history
after the rise of the second great idea. But it is worth noticing
that the first great idea in the Greek form of grasping a world
of objects left out the world of subjects. I interpret mythopoeic

thought as a world of subjects. When we look at the history of ideas, we see that the turn from mythopoeic thinking to speculative thinking produced philosophy, but it also produced philosophical problems. The ancients' ability to see mind in the world is something that Western civilization lost.

Mythopoeic thought organized reality into categories, but the categories resisted generalization and that is why there could not be a Pythagoras or a Newton in the mythopoeic era. The myths of the ancient Sumerians, Babylonians, and Egyptians made all known facts fall into place (Frankfort et al. 1946, 28), and in that way it was probably a precursor to the first great idea or an early form of it. Their categories of reality foregrounded the emotional recognition of values that were set aside when the first great idea emerged in Greece, dominating Western thought into the modern age. Mythopoeic cultures also gave us the gift of the idea of the unity of human beings with nature, an idea that faded from moral thinking in the West for many centuries. There are signs of its return in environmental ethics, which we will look at in chapter 4, and in the belated interest in Native American philosophy by Western philosophers.[12] I think that mythopoeic thought deserves attention, not only because of its historical interest, but because its strengths are weaknesses in the version of the first great idea we inherited from the Greeks.

Thales, Anaximenes, and Anaximander were the first Western philosophers of record and some of the earliest scientists and mathematicians. There is no doubt that they all were thinking about being as a whole, so they must have thought that there *is* such a thing as being as a whole. Reality is not just an assemblage of disconnected phenomena; it is unified. Their underlying idea is a perfect expression of the first great idea: *There is something that everything is.* There is an *arche*, or principle, underlying all things, and the human mind can discover it. It is possible to give a systematic account of the entire universe.

One of the most impressive versions of the first great idea in human history was created by Pythagoras (570–495 BCE), and I want to look more closely at his philosophy because its influence will appear many times in this book, and it is perhaps the most important instance of the first great idea in the history of the world. Pythagoras was born on the island of Samos near the coast of Turkey, close to the area where Thales and Anaximander lived, and he was possibly a student of Anaximander.[13] Pythagoras is credited with being the father of mathematics and the father of geometry as well as the father of music. He discovered the mathematics of harmonic frequencies and connected the mathematics of harmony to his study of astronomy, and there is a legend that he could hear the music of the spheres. That is admittedly a stretch, but I mention it for its expression of a breathtaking link between musical sound and the physics of motion on a large scale. We can hear vibrations on a small scale in a short span of time, but the idea that the physics of sound is the same on a large scale over a long span of time was brilliant. It was a version of the first great idea that helped Kepler formulate his laws of planetary motion and made its way into contemporary string theory. I will give a story about that in the vignette at the end of this chapter.

Pythagoreanism developed over many centuries and had many variations, but I would like to highlight two main features: (1) The Pythagoreans believed that everything that exists is numbers, or in a weaker version, everything exists with a form that can be expressed numerically. (2) Numbers and their relations are beautiful. It might seem bizarre to say that everything is numbers until we add two more features of their teaching: everything that exists is knowable, and everything knowable is numerical.[14] The idea that the mind grasps numerical form *is* intuitive,[15] and the idea that what the mind can grasp is the same as what exists is just a variation of the first great idea. The idea that numerical relations are beautiful follows from the physics of harmonics, and the Pythagoreans thought also that what is pleasing to the ear is pleasing to the eye; and Pythagorean principles were used to great effect in Greek architecture and sculpture, most famously in Phidias's breathtaking design for the Parthenon and its sculptures. The Pythagoreans also prescribed music as medicine, using the harmonic frequencies to heal the human body and mind. I cannot say how well it worked, but the idea persisted for many centuries and appears in many other cultures.

Let me stress that in the Pythagorean view of the universe, numbers are not only significant as symbols of something else such as the lunar calendar, the gods, and the heavenly bodies. Rather, numbers or numerical relations *are* the basic structure of the universe. The discovery of numerical formal relations and mathematical laws was one of the most important driving forces in the history of civilization, and the connection between number and the formal features of the world that the mind can comprehend has never disappeared. It dominated Greek philosophy throughout antiquity, and through Saint Augustine's fascination with Pythagorean number theory, it spread to the philosophy of the Latin West.[16] Like Pythagoras, Augustine identified numerical form with the knowability of everything that exists. And by identifying number with form and form with knowability, Augustine was able to connect the mind's capacity to grasp form with the existence of God:

Whatever changeable thing you may look at, you could not grasp it at all, either by the sense of the body or by the contemplation of the mind, unless it had some form composed of numbers, without which it would sink into nothing. Therefore, do not doubt that there is an eternal and unchangeable form that sees to it that these changeable things do not perish, but pass through time in measured motions and a distinct variety of forms, like the verses of a song. This eternal form has no bounds; although it is diffused everywhere, it is not extended in place, and it does not change in time. (Augustine 1993b, bk. 2, sec. 16)

To Augustine, the eternal form was God, and the idea that God impressed numbers into the physical and moral order of the universe was influential throughout the medieval period. Many philosophers believed that numerical structures tie the universe together and connect the divine with the order of nature. God, nature, beauty, health, musical harmony, architecture, and morality are conjoined by numbers. Numerical relations are the form of the entire physical and nonphysical universe, and it is because of numerical form that the universe is knowable.

The classical Greek and medieval notion of form disappeared in the early modern era and was replaced by a different conceptual system that we will discuss in the next chapter, but formal structure in logic and mathematics has endured throughout the era of the second great idea as well as the first. The dominance of one science over another varies over time, but mathematics has never lost its prestige. Mathematics can be treated as the study of forms or patterns, and if so, it describes one of the most important ways in which the universe has structure—possibly *the* most important way.[17] That is why in the *Republic* Plato maintains that the study of mathematics prepares the person for apprehension of the eternal Forms or Ideas.[18] The world we see and the world we grasp with our minds are linked through mathematics, and in the *Timaeus* Plato (1997) tells us that the path from the beginning of scientific observation to the beginning of philosophy goes through mathematics:

> [H]ad we never seen the stars, and the sun, and the heavens, none of the words which we have spoken about the universe would ever have been uttered. But now the sight of day and night, and the months and the revolutions of the years, have created number, and have given us a conception of time; and the power of inquiring about the nature of the universe; and from this source we have derived philosophy, than which no greater good ever was or will be given by the gods to mortal man. (*Timaeus* 47c)

## Art and Architecture

Tens of thousands of years before the invention of writing, drawing and painting were representing the contents of human consciousness,[19] so it would not be surprising if examples of the two great ideas appeared in art long before they did in philosophy or literature. The earliest possible examples of the first idea that I have seen are jade *bi* disks and *cong* tubes from the Neolithic Age in northeastern China, some dated to 3400 BCE in the Liangzhu culture, well before the invention of writing in China.[20] By that period, jade objects were no longer limited to tools but were created to represent the cosmos, and jade was thought to have supernatural power. Heaven is round and the earth is square; the bi disk represented heaven and the cong tube represented the earth. For the same reason, altars were round and tombs were square. The Liangzhu people thought that cong tubes and bi disks were able to carry the mystical code between mortals and the deities. Much later, by

FIGURE 3. Bi disk from Liangzhu culture, China,
3rd millennium BCE. Museum Angewandte Kunst (2006),
via Wikimedia Commons.

the time of the Warring States period and the dynasties of Qin
and Han (3rd cent. BCE), the cosmology of round and square
was interpreted as the movement of yin and yang energy in the
universe. The yang energy circles the round orbit, while the yin
energy follows the square path. Since jade is a very hard stone,
bi disks and cong tubes had to be laboriously crafted, requiring
many material and human resources to make them. We may
not be able to tell what the creators of these artifacts thought
about the universe as a whole, but they must have thought that
a major part of it has a structure that can be depicted in a way
that is both beautiful and sacred.[21]

The desire to represent the cosmos in art may be universal. More than five thousand years after the Liangzhu and in
a distant part of the world, there are people in the Amazon
today who paint the body to reflect the triple-tiered cosmos.
The headdress depicts the most powerful birds who dwell in

FIGURE 4. Jade cong tube from Liangzhu culture, Lower Yangzi, China, 3300–2200 BCE, via Wikimedia Commons.

the upper levels. The middle part of the body is decorated with beads and the skins of animals of the earth. The decorations on the legs depict reptilian beings of the underworld. The people in this culture make their bodies a map of the universe and they have arranged their physical environment in the form of a map. Their bodies, their possessions, their huts, their villages, and the clusters of villages around them form a series of concentric circles that represent the universe as they understand it. Like a medieval *mappa mundi*, the world of the Amazon jungle is laid out in circles, and everyone knows their position on the map (Hallam 2017). The idea is simple but elegant. Imagine living in a world where there is little or no information about the outside world, yet these people have an image of the world as a whole. It is centered on themselves, as most conceptions are, yet it extends farther and farther outward in a way to which many modern Westerners aspire. I cannot talk to these people and find out what they think about the first great idea, but their creations and the creations of the ancient Liangzhu people suggest something interesting about the connection between cosmic ideas and the urge to create art. Artworks express many different features of their creators' consciousness, but when the artwork depicts the whole of reality, or reality as far as the creator's imagination can go, the creator sees herself as having an active part in that world and often uses the objects in sacred rituals, as both Liangzhu people and people of the Amazon do. The artist is not just an observer, but a participant in the world depicted.

In the vignette at the end of chapter 1, I mentioned one of the most impressive buildings from ancient Rome, the Pantheon, which does not merely symbolize Pythagorean ideas but *uses* them in following the Pythagorean view that numbers are the form of the universe, and form is pleasing to the senses. The building is beautiful, but the Pythagoreans believed that they knew the reason why it is beautiful. It is the same reason that musical harmonies are pleasing. Mathematics, beauty, and harmony in the human body and soul are all connected.

The Pythagorean view of the universe is probably the most vivid example in human history of the way the grasp of the universe as a whole can be displayed in so many areas of human culture, but the idea that the art and the thought of an age are connected did not become the focus of academic study until the nineteenth and twentieth centuries in the modern field of iconography. The great art historian Erwin Panofsky (1892–1968) was probably the most influential in the field. Panofsky maintained that there are layers of meaning in art that reveal the religious or philosophical perspective of an entire nation or historical era.[22] That insight brought the connection between art history and intellectual history closer together, and although the two great ideas are abstract, I have been suggesting that they form the conceptual backdrop of many cultural products other than philosophy, reaching deep into the artistic imagination.

The medieval cathedral is a classic case study for the field of iconography because the medieval vision of the universe was expressed in a particularly direct manner, in stone and glass and painting. My understanding of medieval cathedrals is drawn from Emile Mâle's (1972) classic work on the thirteenth-century cathedral, which Mâle describes as a microcosm of an entire worldview.[23] The leaders of the church understood the way art expresses and cultivates a perspective on the world, and so the church was the conscious guardian of artistic imagery. At the Second Council of Nicaea in 787, the bishops declared that the composition of religious imagery was not up to the artist but should be formed upon principles laid down by the church. The artist knew how to execute the work in a way that captivated the viewer's emotional attention, but the subject matter belonged to the church fathers (Mâle 1972, 392). The bishop supervised the construction of the cathedral, which was attached to a cathedral school where the most eminent teachers of the day met and could observe the progress of the building. A cathedral was an image of the creation. It depicted the beginning of the world and its end, portrayed the major figures of human history, and displayed the grand narrative of Redemption. Even the orientation of the church had a cosmic significance. By the thirteenth century there were precise directions. The head of the church was required to lie exactly to the east, to the part of the sky in which the sun rises at the equinox (5). The western facade, where the sunset lights up the evening of the world, almost always portrayed the Last Judgment. The Old Testament was generally depicted in the north, the region of cold and darkness, while the New Testament was bathed in the sunlight of the south.

Because the purpose of art was to portray a common vision, art was never the exclusive creation of an individual talent but was the product of what Mâle calls "diffused genius" (4). Artists and architects involved in the creation of a cathedral were participating in a communal project lasting longer than the lifetime of any of them, and intended to portray human history as part of an eternal story. The personal point of view of the artist was of no interest, not even to himself. What was important was the part played by artist, workman, worshipper, and church leader in expressing, appreciating, and perpetuating one magnificent version of the first great idea, and the result was captivating. The cathedral drew from all the known arts and sciences to create the sum of revelation. Painting, music, sculpture, stained glass, architecture, even the fragrances the faithful breathed in upon entering the cathedral combined to give them a sense of the unity of their being with the divine spirit that infuses the universe. The meaning of a cathedral was accessible to anyone, unlike the pedantic theology and philosophy of the period, and since the viewer knew how to interpret it, it aroused powerful emotions. Even today, a modest artist can achieve a strong emotional reaction in others if those emotions have been acquired in a lifetime of emotional learning.[24]

The same point applies to the icons that have been created by Eastern Christians for more than one and a half millennia. The icon maker is said to "write" an icon rather than to paint it. The colors have meanings; the poses have meanings; there are standardized ways to depict Jesus, Mary, and the saints. The ego of the icon maker is irrelevant, and for over a thousand years icons were unsigned. When we look at an icon, we see the universe as told in a visual language, and we read a prayer that connects us with that story. For people living in the Middle Ages the function of art as understood at that time was probably unnoticed because there was no alternative function with which to compare it, but icons are still written, and to us, the contrast between the intention of the icon maker and the intention of a painter of contemporary art is obvious.

Art makes a statement as much as philosophy does and as much as literature does. Statements take many cultural forms, and they are not independent of each other. The features that they have in common are easier to see when we compare the products of one period of history with a later time, and we notice that different areas of human culture change together or in a related sequence. I have mentioned five examples of art or architecture, spanning many centuries in different parts of the world: jade carvings from Neolithic China, body painting in the contemporary Amazon region, the Roman Pantheon of the second century CE, medieval cathedrals, and Byzantine icons from the fifth century CE until the present. I propose that they have something in common, and what they have in common is something that significantly diminished after the modern period began. The people who created them depicted the world and their place in it as they saw it in common with others. The individual was not important as an individual but as a part of a whole.

Art and ideas have always been connected. Sometimes ideas guide art, and sometimes art guides ideas. Both art and ideas are constrained by material conditions, but the human imagination reaches further than material constraints. In the Renaissance, material conditions permitted the imagination to be released in a particularly explosive way, and art took the position of cultural leadership. We will look at that in the next chapter.

## Epic Poetry

Imaginative literature has the power to describe an enormous number of other possible worlds and possible persons. Most of us are used to thinking of imaginary persons as populating a fantasy world with little philosophical import, but Aristotle thought that imaginary persons tell us what is universal, and he distinguished the writing of history (what in fact happened) from poetry (what might have happened but did not), claiming that poetry represents something more philosophical than historical events:

> From what we have said it will be seen that the poet's function is to describe, not the thing that has happened, but a kind of thing that might happen, i.e. what is possible as being probable or necessary. The distinction between historian and poet is not in the one writing prose and the other verse—you might put the work of Herodotus into verse, and it would still be a species of history; it consists really in this, that the one describes the thing that has been, and the other a kind of thing that might be. Hence poetry is something more philosophic and of graver import than history, since its statements are of the nature of universals, whereas those of history are singulars. By a universal statement I mean one as to what such or such a kind of man will probably or necessarily say or do—which is the aim of poetry, although it affixes proper names to the characters; by a singular statement, one as to what, say, Alcibiades did or had done to him. (*Poetics*, beginning chap. 9)

This passage is interesting as much for what it implies about the nature of imaginative literature as for Aristotle's praise of it. Aristotle thinks of characters in poetic discourse as universals with proper names attached, not as individuals in the modern sense. The kind of person Achilles is, or Odysseus, or Clytemnestra, is revealed through the character's words and actions, each of which is a component of a unified plot with a causal structure that explains each event (*Poetics* 1451a16–20). No extraneous event that is not part of an interrelated causal sequence should be contained in the work, he says (1451a30–35). Details that do not depict causal relations are unnecessary, and that includes all the details about the character's unique features that would be interesting to the modern reader. Poetry is imitation (1447a14), but "the objects the imitator represents are actions, with agents who are necessarily either good men or bad—the diversities of human character being nearly all derivative from this primary distinction" (1448a1–4). The individual is important for what he or she reveals about something that could happen to someone else. The individual as such is not interesting.

When Aristotle speaks of poetry he is thinking of the play or the epic poem, both well suited to expressing characteristics of types of human beings and the effects of their acts. Neither genre is well suited to expressing states of mind as experienced from within, and neither attempts to get the reader or viewer to identify with a character. "The characters are for the sake of the action," as Aristotle says. In his essay "Forms of Time and of the Chronotope in the Novel," Mikhail Bakhtin argues that for the Greeks every aspect of human existence could be seen and heard (1981, 134). The Greeks did not distinguish what we call the internal from the external. "Our 'internal' was, for the Greeks, laid out on the same axis as our 'external,' that is, it was just as visible and audible and it existed on the surface, for others as well as for oneself" (135). For them, an autobiography is the same as a biography; both are public (136).

> The individual's consciousness of himself . . . relies exclusively upon those aspects of his personality and his life that are turned outward, that exist for others in the same way they exist for the individual himself; in those aspects alone can self-consciousness seek its support and integrity; it knows of no aspects other than these, aspects that might

be intimately personal, unrepeatably individual, charged with self. (137)

In Greek literature there are no deep soliloquies,[25] and no attention to individual uniqueness even in external descriptions; no attention to personal idiosyncrasies, not even a description detailed enough that we would call it a portrait. The difference between inner subjectivity and the outer person, the core and the shell, appeared later.

Bakhtin's 1981 essay "Epic and Novel" contrasts the dominant literary form of ancient Greece and the Middle Ages with the dominant literary form of the modern era, and Bakhtin argues that that difference expresses a transformation in human consciousness that I believe is a good illustration of the difference between the dominance of the first great idea and the dominance of the second. One of the most important contrasts Bakhtin notes is in the treatment of time. In the epic poem the subject is a "completed past," long before the time of the telling, and given as part of the memory of an entire culture. Time in the epic is an organic whole, transmitted by tradition over an absolute distance separating the epic world from the world in which the epic is recited. In contrast, the subject of the novel is the present, or it is treated as if it is present, and time moves forward into a future not yet completed (1981, 13). The novel invites a contemporary perspective on the novel's subject, and there is no common tradition in the telling. There are instead multiple perspectives (13). In the epic we know what happened, whereas in the novel we are not sure what happened and what did not. Bakhtin links this feature of the novel with the fact that epistemology became the dominant discipline shortly after the genre of the novel appeared (15). Philosophers are used to linking the rise of epistemology with Descartes, but we should not be surprised if Bakhtin is right also. When different cultural domains change in the same direction and at approximately the same time, there is bound to be something that connects them.

Bakhtin says that in the epic the consciousness of the individual characters is not as relevant as the action—a point consonant with Aristotle's interpretation of poetry—and the consciousness of the listener or teller of the story is not relevant at all. In the novel, the consciousness of the character is not only highly relevant, it is sometimes the whole story. The reader's consciousness is intentionally engaged by the author. We can identify with the characters in novels and experience their lives with them. Nothing like that happens with epic characters (32).

Bakhtin writes that the features he identifies in the epic continued into the high genres of the Middle Ages. He does not discuss Dante's fourteenth-century masterpiece, *The Divine Comedy*, but it is a particularly powerful expression of the first great idea in imaginative literature, and it conforms to Bakhtin's observations about the premodern literary mind. Dante's poem is simultaneously a journey through the world of hell, purgatory, and heaven, and an allegory of the soul's journey to God—both a metaphysical treatise and a personal voyage. Dante describes a universal community composed of everyone who has ever lived, a world that is grandly unified under the Creator. The individual must not change God's order, but must honor it and represent it. In describing the whole universe, Dante combines a strong sensitivity to the human condition and a penetrating eye for the details of nature with the ability to grasp abstract ideas and a spectacular vision of the supernatural world. Dante was another major figure who was fascinated by Pythagorean numerology, and the poem is encoded with a system of numbers and symbols.[26] Like the medieval cathedral, Dante's poem expresses the religious worldview of the time, but with much greater theological detail than a cathedral. In fact, *The Divine Comedy* owes so much to the theology of Aquinas that it has sometimes been called "the *Summa* in verse." That does not mean, of course, that it does not have the stamp of Dante's personality. All artworks, and particularly the works of genius, express the individuality of the artist, but before the modern age it was not deliberate. Rarely did artists intentionally represent their inner life.

The artists, poets, architects, philosophers, theologians, mathematicians, and scientists of the era of the first great idea created works that expressed many ideas, as humans always have, but there was a commonality in these works that is difficult to see until it changed—quite suddenly, from a historical perspective. What they had in common was the thought that the world is a unity, an organic whole. We can see it and admire it and play our part in it, but we cannot change it, nor would we want to. We know ourselves through knowing the world and what everyone knows about it. The world has form; it has purpose. Goodness and beauty are built into the nature of things. The creators of cultural products of all kinds agreed on most of that, and when we see or read these works, we are bound to be impressed because they are enthralling, but we are bound to be impressed for another reason: we have rarely seen anything like them in the West for hundreds of years.

## Morality as Harmony with the Universe

The idea that the entire material and nonmaterial universe is a unity led to a conception of morality that lasted from the time that moral thinking became systematized to the beginning of the modern age. Human societies have always needed rules of behavior that constitute a rudimentary form of morality, and even other primates observe social norms and have a sense of reciprocity,[27] but at some point people expected the rules to come with a system of justification based on an idea of justice. Early in the second millennium BCE in Babylon and much earlier than Jaspers's Axial Age, Hammurabi dictated a large number of laws applying to all the people in his vast empire.[28] In his prologue, Hammurabi says that his code was decreed by the gods in order to establish righteousness and bring about the well-being of humankind, and he declared his laws to be the ones that should live on forever. He says that as his conquests spread to the north and to the south, the gods decreed that he should spread the laws of justice to the lands he conquered.[29] And in the epilogue, he says, "In the days that are yet to come, for all future time, may the king who is in the land observe the words of righteousness which I have written upon my monument! May he not alter the judgments of the land which I have pronounced, or the decisions of the country which I have rendered" (Harper 1904, 101). Hammurabi declares himself the emissary of the gods, which obviously supports his authority and the power he intended to exert, but to me what is interesting about his statement is that it implies the possibility of a moral code that applies universally.

In chapter 1 I mentioned the connection between monotheism and the idea of a universal morality. The prophet Amos declared that God would judge the neighbors of the Israelites for their evil acts, implying that those people could not use the excuse that their behavior was accepted by their own gods (Amos 1). The logic of this exhortation is intriguing because it does not make sense unless there is a moral code that transcends local boundaries. The connection between monotheism and the idea that morality or some important part of it applies universally meant that when a monotheistic worldview ceased to be universally shared in the early modern period, a new foundation had to be found. The response was to ground morality in the authority of the self over itself, as we will see in the next chapter, but Jewish monotheism was not the only source of the idea of a universal morality in the West. The other source was Greek.

The ancient Greeks left to us a magnificent sense of the order of nature, one in which morality is built into its structure. The Pythagorean idea that natural laws of harmony apply to the whole universe, including the human soul and the state, linked individual morality with the proper ordering of the state, so this idea was already part of Greek consciousness before Plato turned it into one of the most famous ideas in philosophical history in his *Republic*. Morality exists because the interior of a person follows the same principles as the cosmos.

In the *Republic* Plato makes explicit the idea that the structure of society is isomorphic with the structure of the individual psyche, and Socrates proposes that the polis is the individual soul "writ large" (*Republic* 2 in Plato 1997, 358c7–369a3). To understand what justice is in the soul we should first look at justice in the political state, because there it is easier to see. Socrates does not go on to say that justice in the polis is isomorphic with something larger, such as justice in the cosmos, but in the creation myth in *Timaeus* 29, the universe is a living being, and it is good because it is a copy of the eternal patterns or Forms. Plato says that the individual soul's revolutions were thrown off course around the time of birth (43a6–44b1), and the goal is to realign those revolutions with those of the cosmos (90d3). The realignment is aided by a study of astronomy, and when that is achieved, the soul is fulfilled by being restored to its original condition.

The *Timaeus* was easy to harmonize with Christian cosmology and ethics, and its influence extended to a long line of medieval Christian philosophers who maintained that the goodness of everything comes from the cosmic order, and that

our grasp of the Good comes through a sequence of educa-
tional steps culminating in astronomy and mathematics, with
the ultimate aim to see God, which Christian philosophers
easily substituted for Plato's Form of the Good.[30] It is amazing
to think of the thousands of years in which the study of astronomy and mathematics were the last steps in gaining moral
knowledge, a knowledge of the metaphysical good from which
all things come. Most people these days would think that
astronomy and mathematics are as far from moral thought as
it is possible to get, and when students first study Plato, they
usually find his view of moral education startling, but when
they see how everything fits together, they usually like it. It is
exciting to contemplate an idea in which the moral structure
of the universe is closely connected with its physical structure,
and the grand unity of the universe is beautiful as well as good.

An implication of the Greek view that everything has a unified structure is that it can be systematized by someone with
the patience and the talent to map that structure. At about
the same time as Euclid was systematizing geometry, Aristotle
was giving the first systematic treatment of ethics in human
history. Aristotle introduced to Western history a way of inter-
preting morality that survived throughout the rest of the era of
the first great idea and has reappeared in recent decades: the
idea that morality is about achieving *eudaimonia*, or human
flourishing, and that the kind of life that constitutes flourishing is determined by human nature, a component of nature as
a whole. The goal of human life is determined by nature, just
as the flourishing of a cat or a fish or a tree is determined by
the nature of each. The distinctive place of humans in nature is
given by the exercise of reason, which separates humans from
other animals, so it is nature that determines that reason governs human beings and enables them to flourish. The qualities
a person must have in order to flourish are dispositions to feel
and act as reason dictates. These qualities are the virtues (*NE*

bks. 1–2). To live morally is to cultivate the virtues, and the virtues are defined by the distinctive place of human beings in nature. What is good is not determined by human preference, but by the structure of the universe. Contemporary people are used to thinking of the structure of the universe as evaluatively neutral. It is neither good nor bad; it just *is*. But that was not the view almost universally accepted from antiquity until the modern era—the idea that goodness is a fulfillment of the nature of a being, whether human or nonhuman. We are fulfilled by adapting to the way the universe is, not by making the world adapt to us.

Perhaps Aristotle's most striking idea is his view that contemplation of the universe is the ultimate good to which humans can aspire. That makes the highest good an intellectual act—contemplation of eternal things, and in *Eudemian Ethics* 8.3 he says that God is the preeminent object of contemplation. For Aristotle, then, the first great idea is an idea of the highest human good. Both Plato and Aristotle link the moral life directly to the first great idea, and for almost two more millennia, morality was derived from the place of human persons in the world, and in its Christian version, with the place of human persons in the divine plan. The authority of morality came either from the natural authority of reason—the view of the Greeks, or the authority of the Creator over the Creation—the view of medieval Christians, or from both—the view of Aquinas, who argued that there is an Eternal Law of divine reason for governing the entire universe (*ST* I–II q. 91 a. 1 corpus).

The central place of reason in the universe is one of the dominant themes of the ancient and medieval period. Reason is the supreme governing force, a metaphysical insight that also created mathematics and science, was linked to Christian theology, and was expressed in the art and literature of the period. A second theme of the thought of the premodern period was the idea that the universe is a unity with a structure of forms that permeate the physical and nonphysical universe and can be expressed mathematically. As we will see in the next chapter, both themes changed in one way but not another. Reason maintained its importance as the source of authority, but it changed from a governing force in the universe to a governing force in the individual will. The idea of the mathematical structure of the physical universe was retained, but the idea that it is mirrored in the structure of the human soul and society was given up. Both changes required a reexamination of the nature of morality.

## The Transcendence of the Mind

The first great idea gave human beings a sense of supremacy because it meant that our minds can extend to enclose the universe. That implies something about the human mind; it also implies something about the universe. The universe can be encompassed by a finite mind because everything that exists is in some sense a magnificently unified thing, and there is a natural affinity between the human mind and the universe. It lies in the nature of the mind to grasp reality, and it lies in the nature of reality to be grasped by the mind. In a sense the boundary of the human mind is the same as the boundary of reality.

The idea that grasping is unity with the object grasped appears many times in the traditions that emerged with the first great idea in the East as well as in the West. In Hinduism all reality is ultimately one, and the human soul is one with it.[31] The predominant teaching in the Upanishads, begun around 700 BCE, is the spiritual identity of the soul (*Atman*) within each human being with the soul of every other living being, and with the supreme, ultimate reality, *Brahman*. My interpretation of that is that enlightenment comes in realizing that the two great ideas are in fact the same idea. This ancient tradition is important to remember since I will later discuss the difficulty in putting the ideas together. In the West we take for granted that the subjectivity of each individual mind is distinct from the subjectivity of every other mind and that both are a part but not the whole of reality. In contrast, Hinduism interprets mind as part of *Maya*—illusion. The two great ideas are separated only in the illusory world. When the attempt to put them together ends in the discovery that one's true self (*Atman*) is identical with all of reality (*Brahman*), the mind disappears. This contrast with Western philosophy shows us that what is universal about the two great ideas is the *ideas*, not the way they are related.

The Greek idea of *henosis,* or mystical unity, became prominent in the Neo-Platonist schools, beginning with the writings of Plotinus (204/5–270 CE), who through Augustine and the mysterious late-fifth-century Pseudo-Dionysius influenced Christian philosophy until at least the Renaissance. Plotinus, like the Pythagoreans, combined metaphysics with mystical practice. He believed that everything that exists emanates from the One, with the material world being the last emanation. But in consciousness the human soul can reverse the emanations and can grasp or merge with the One. Towards the end of the *Enneads*, Plotinus (2018) writes:

> We are in search of unity; we are to come to know the principle of all, the Good and First; therefore, we may not stand away from the realm of Firsts and lie prostrate among the lasts: we must strike for those Firsts, arising from things of sense which are the lasts. Cleared of all evil in our intention towards The Good, we must ascend to the Principle within ourselves; from many, we must become one. (*Ennead 6*, 9.3)

He personally had had such an experience, which he describes in the *Fourth Ennead*:

> Many times it has happened: Lifted out of the body into myself; becoming external to all other things and self-encentered; beholding a marvelous beauty; then, more

than ever, assured of community with the loftiest order;
enacting the noblest life, acquiring identity with the
divine; stationing within It by having attained that activity; poised above whatsoever within the Intellectual is less
than the Supreme; yet, there comes the moment of descent
from intellection to reasoning, and after that sojourn in
the divine, I ask myself how it happens that I can now be
descending, and how did the soul ever enter into my body,
the soul which, even within the body, is the high thing it
has shown itself to be. (*Ennead 4*, 8.1)

At the moment of death, Plotinus is reported to have said to a
friend: "Now I shall endeavor to make that which is divine in
me rise up to that which is divine in the universe" (Porphyry
2018, 18).

In Plotinus and other Neo-Platonists like Porphyry and Iam-
blichus, the boundary of the human soul is the Unity from which
it emanates. Again, this implies something about both the nature
of the universe and the nature of human consciousness. It lies in
the nature of the human mind to unite with God or the One, and
it lies in the nature of the One to be grasped by the human mind.

We get the same conclusion from a completely different
direction in Aristotle and Aquinas. Aquinas argued that it is
because human beings are endowed with spirit that we can
grasp the whole of things, and he quoted Aristotle's oft-repeated
line in *De Anima*: "the soul is in a way all existing things"
(3.8.431b20). Aristotle makes this tantalizing remark by exam-
ining the implications of the fact that all existing things are
either sensible or thinkable (ibid.). In perception, he says, the
object acts upon the mind's capacity to receive the form of the
object by imprinting the form on the mind, making the mind
isomorphic with the form of the object. It does that the way a
signet ring takes on an impression (2.12.424a19–23). Likewise,
when thinking, the mind thinks of an object by becoming isomorphic with its form. Aristotle says, "The thinking part of the

soul must therefore be . . . capable of receiving the form of an object; that is, it must be potentially identical in character with its object without being the object" (3.4.429a14–17). Since the soul has the capacity to receive the forms of all objects that can be either sensed or thought, it *is* in a sense all objects that can be either sensed or thought, since the only aspect of an object that is not sensed or thought is its matter. Given that all existing objects can be either sensed or thought, Aristotle's conclusion follows: the soul is in a way all existing things.

Aquinas extends this view all the way to knowledge of God and the highest human good:

> [S]omething is known by a knower by reason of the fact that the thing known is, in some fashion, in the possession of the knower. Hence, it is said in *The Soul* [*De Anima*] that the soul is, "in some manner, all things," since its nature is such that it can know all things. In this way it is possible for the perfection of the entire universe to exist in one thing. The ultimate perfection which the soul can attain, therefore, is, according to the philosophers, to have delineated in it the entire order and causes of the universe. This they held to be the ultimate end of man. We, however, hold that it consists in the vision of God; for, as Gregory says: "What is there that they do not see who see Him who sees all things?" (*De Veritate* q. 2 a. 2)

When the soul enjoys the Beatific Vision in heaven, it unites with the being who sees all of reality, and by doing so, a human being satisfies the deepest desires of the human heart—union with God through whom a human being can achieve union with all of reality.

When the second great idea superseded the first, there was a noticeable decline in the idea that the human mind can reach union with God or all of reality, but the idea did not

disappear, at least not immediately. One of the most important seventeenth-century philosophers was Baruch Spinoza,
and his idea of the intellectual love of God (*amor dei intellec-
tualis*) is an important example. In Spinoza's ontology, God is
an infinite substance, the greatest thing that can be conceived.
All things other than God are modes of God and can neither
exist nor be conceived without the substance of which they are
modes. So nothing can be or be conceived apart from God. The
same thing applies to what we can love as well as to what we
can think. In the intuitive love of God, the ideas constituting
the mind become identical with the ideas in God's mind, and a
human person unites with God under the attribute of thought.
Knowledge of God is the mind's greatest good (*Ethics* 4, P28).

It is remarkable that with a metaphysics completely different from that of Aquinas, ancient Hinduism, and Neo-
Platonism, Spinoza reaches a very similar conclusion. There
are obvious differences in the way these philosophies and
religions interpret the One or God or the whole of reality, but
what they all have in common is an interpretation of grasping
as union and an aspiration that is driven by the first great idea.

The belief that the human mind can achieve its greatest
good by union with all of reality has faded in the last few hundred years, but it never disappeared, and it can sometimes be
found in unexpected places. Consider, for instance, the last sentence of Bertrand Russell's *The Problems of Philosophy* (1959):
"Philosophy is to be studied . . . above all because, through the
greatness of the universe which philosophy contemplates, the
mind also is rendered great, and becomes capable of that union
with the universe which constitutes its highest good." Russell is
no doubt writing this more for dramatic effect at the end of a
book rather than out of earnest commitment, and the atheist
Russell was by no means a Plotinus or an Aquinas or a Spinoza.
Still, it is fascinating that the idea that the human mind can

grasp the universe and that doing so is a great human good has persisted from the origin of the first great idea to the present. It has persisted through enormous changes in metaphysics, epistemology, and religious belief. It is also fascinating that for so many philosophers in many parts of the world and in many eras, grasping was interpreted as union with the object grasped. When a mind grasps the universe, it is not like a hand grasping a doorknob, or one body clasping another in an embrace. The mind has no edge. It extends to encompass the reality it grasps. That is the power of the first great idea.

From the Greeks we got the idea that the universe is one, and it is rationally ordered. From both the Pythagoreans and the great religions we got the idea that there is a transcendent reality, and the human mind may hope to reach union with it. From the ethics of the era we got the idea that morality is living in harmony with reality, an idea that appeared before the Greeks in mythopoeic thought and all the way through the thought of the period. In architecture and literature, we see that harmony and rational order can be beautiful. The first idea declined in the West when people lost confidence that their minds can grasp a transcendent reality that is more important than they are. But they did not lose confidence in the power of reason. It just changed its place. We will look at that in the next chapter.

---

### A Vignette of the Unity of Knowledge: Pythagoras, Kepler, and String Theory

On July 19, 1595, while he was teaching a class in Graz, Johannes Kepler had the sudden insight that there is a connection between the planetary movements and musical ratios. The laws of harmony underlie the motions of physical objects, from the level of a single vibrating string to the motions of heavenly bodies. That insight guided

Kepler through many years of investigations and measure-
ments, leading him to his monumental discovery of the
three laws of planetary motion, and revealing the power of
the mind to connect reasoning in one domain with that of
another. According to Kepler, it follows from the physics
of motion that the movement of each planet makes a
sound, with faster movement playing a higher pitch, and
slower movement playing a lower pitch. The lowest note
of a planet's orbit corresponds to its largest distance from
the sun—the lowest orbital velocity, and the highest note
corresponds to its shortest distance from the sun—the
highest orbital velocity. Each planet's orbit is therefore
a different harmony. According to Kepler's calculations,
Saturn plays a major third, Jupiter a minor third, and
Mars a fifth. Earth plays a minor second. (See fig. 5.) In the
epilogue of *Harmony of the World*, Kepler conjectures that
a mind in the sun sees and hears it all.

What Kepler realized at the dawn of the seventeenth
century was a component of the Pythagorean system over
two thousand years earlier in which arithmetic (the study
of number) was connected with geometry (the study of
number in space), with harmonics (the study of number in
time), with astronomy (the study of number in space and
time), and with ethics (the study of harmony in the human
soul). Everything that exists can be explained by numbers
and their relations.

Stephon Alexander, a Brown University astrophysicist,
jazz musician, and innovator in string theory, credits
his knowledge of the waves that make up sound to the
development of his hypothesis that the physical universe
is one enormous vibrating string, oscillating from Big
Bang to Big Bang in a continuous rhythmic movement,
creating the purest tone the universe can play (Alexander

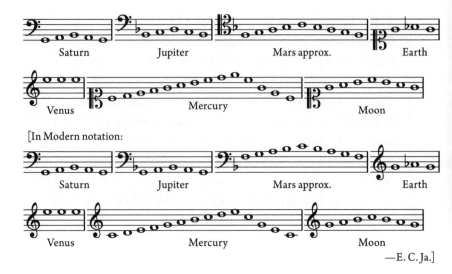

FIGURE 5. Kepler's notation for planetary harmonies. Kepler ([1619] 2014),
*Harmonies of the World*, 42.

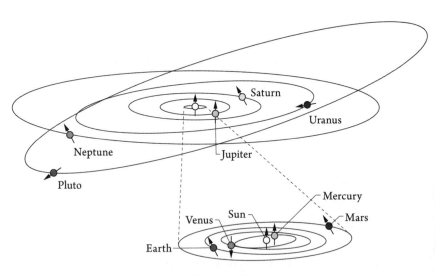

FIGURE 6. Planetary orbits. NASA.

2016, 208–209). Alexander says that he was inspired by Pythagoras and Kepler to think of the universe as playing music. There are recordings of the music Kepler believed that a superior being hears when the planets orbit. It would take a while to hear the complete orbits of all nine planets (264 Earth years), but in 1979 Yale music professor Willie Ruff and pianist John Rodgers, with the assistance of computer scientists, synthesized the music of the spheres based on Kepler's calculations. The speed of the synthesized celestial song has been greatly increased, with five seconds representing one Earth year, so that the human ear can perceive it (Ruff and Rodgers, 2011). The sound is not what you and I would call melodious. Mercury whistles, Earth moans, Pluto produces a strong bass rhythm, planets with irregular orbits move up and down like a police siren. The effect is haunting.

What we learn from Pythagoras and Kepler and Alexander is an especially enchanting way that the universe is one. Even though Pythagoras may have been wrong in thinking that everything is numbers, and Kepler was probably wrong in his conjecture that there is a mind in the sun that watches and listens to the planets orbit, and Alexander is probably wrong that the universe is one gigantic vibrating string, all of them discovered patterns that repeat throughout the universe—in nature, in mathematics, and in the aesthetic domain. It is unfortunate that we often insist upon dividing domains of knowledge instead of cultivating the kind of mind that keeps the first great idea alive. That is the kind of mind that can revolutionize human thought.

# CHAPTER THREE

# The Mind Precedes the World: The Primacy of the Second Great Idea

## (THE RENAISSANCE TO THE 20$^{TH}$ CENTURY)

### *The Big Shift: Philosophy Confronts Empirical Science*

The idea that the world is a unity has survived every intellectual revolution in history. From that idea it follows that there must be a unity in knowledge. To say that there is unity in knowledge is much more interesting than to make the trivial point that knowledge in one domain cannot conflict with knowledge in another. It is to say that there are connections between one domain of knowledge and another. Knowledge of nature, of human beings, of morality, of mathematics, of God or Being beyond nature—all knowledge is connected because what it is knowledge *of* is connected. In the Middle Ages the grand unification of human knowledge drew together all the known sciences under the leadership of theology, which was called the queen of the sciences. But at the beginning of the period of history we now call the modern age, there was a dramatic change in the way people looked at how the domains of knowledge are connected, and that was because of two revolutions: the Reformation, and the Scientific Revolution. The Reformation brought about the demise of the centrality of theology. The Scientific Revolution brought about its replacement by science. Both required a response from philosophy.

The Protestant Reformation of the sixteenth century precipitated an enormous number of changes, not all of which were intended. Brad Gregory (2012) argues that the doctrinal conflict between Catholics and the Reformers unintentionally led to the intellectual marginalization of theology, which inadvertently aided the rise of science. Science produced a new method for studying nature, enormously enriching our understanding of the physical world, and it also produced a new interpretation of the nature that is studied. Nature as the object of the new science does not include consciousness and is a closed causal system that does not have room for interaction with a supernatural order or anything outside of it. The remarkable success of empirical science, combined with the remarkable failure of theology to give undisputed knowledge, led to the displacement of theology in the hierarchy of knowledge by empirical observation and reason, which appeared to be the only dependable faculties for getting knowledge of the natural world. By the seventeenth century the new astronomy of Copernicus and Galileo ensured the decline of religious authority and the version of the first great idea that had dominated European life for many centuries. Philosophy had to chart a path in a world in which everything was contested except science and mathematics.

Aquinas and most of the medieval Christian and Muslim philosophers thought of philosophy as the preamble to theology. Philosophy studies what can be known by natural reason; theology studies what revelation adds to what is known naturally. Both philosophy and theology tell us about God, the world, and ourselves. But with the fall of theology and the ascent of science, philosophy had to change. Descartes saw that clearly, and he proceeded to revolutionize philosophy by presenting a new method that would support empirical science and leave speculative metaphysics behind. He leaves no doubt about that at the beginning of his *Meditations:*

> Several years have now passed since I first realized how many were the false opinions that in my youth I took to be true, and thus how doubtful were all the things that I subsequently built upon these opinions. From the time I became aware of this, I realized that for once I had to raze everything in my life, down to the very bottom, so as to begin again from the first foundations, if I wanted to establish anything firm and lasting in the sciences. (*Med. 1*, A&C: 9)

Descartes was concerned for philosophy because it had not enjoyed the remarkable success of the new science, and he was concerned for science because science needed an epistemological foundation. In his *Discourse on Method*, whose full title is *Discourse on the Method of Rightly Conducting One's Reason and of Seeking Truth in the Sciences*, Descartes lamented the fact that even though philosophy had been cultivated for centuries by some of the most excellent minds, everything they wrote was in dispute, and "as to the other sciences, to the extent that they derived their principles from philosophy, I judged that one could not have built anything solid upon foundations having so little firmness" (*Discourse 1*, C:5). He then proceeded to describe what would make the foundations firm and introduced three treatises exemplifying his method: one on optics, one on geometry, and one on meteorology. Although he did not say so publicly, he intended his *Meditations* to be a new foundation for physics that would replace the old Aristotelian physics.[1]

Descartes is one of the primary persons in history responsible for the big shift from the dominance of the first great idea to the dominance of the second. His famous method of doubt leads to a single thing of which he can be certain: the existence of his own mind and its conscious states. His first two *Meditations* are among the most important and persuasive pieces of philosophy ever written. In a few pages Descartes made philosophy begin with epistemology (What can I know?) rather than metaphysics (What exists?). By the end of Meditation 6 he thought he had completed his project of building the foundation for science by giving a defense of the existence of an external world based on belief in the existence of his mind and the existence of God, the latter which he attempted to demonstrate in his brilliantly terse style twice—in Meditation 3 and in Meditation 5.

Descartes therefore reverses the traditional order of knowledge. He knows his own mind first, then God, then the world. Knowledge of the world rests upon knowledge of God and knowledge of God rests upon knowledge of his mind. All his knowledge derives from his grasp of the ideas in his mind. "I am certain that I can have no knowledge of what is outside me except by means of the ideas I have within me."[2] His defense of that statement led to hundreds of years of philosophy focused on the second great idea. The legacy of this order is so strong that some philosophers appear to be willing to give up the first idea entirely rather than to give up the primacy of the second.[3]

The second great idea was also basic for the other important strand of early modern philosophy, British empiricism of the eighteenth century. John Locke (2004, chaps. 12 and 23) proposed in his theory of ideas that we construct our ideas of objects in the world from simple ideas that we get from experience. The mind attempts to represent the world by putting together the perceptual pieces in the mind. Later empiricists have adopted variations of the same theory. I will comment not on how they differ from one another but on what they have in common, since it was so influential on the subsequent understanding of the epistemological underpinnings of empirical science. More than two hundred years later, Einstein wrote in a 1936 essay, "Physics and Reality": "Physics treats directly only of sense experiences and of the 'understanding' of their connection" (1950, 60). He goes on to describe two steps in the setting up of a real external world. The first is the formation of the concept of bodily objects of various kinds from complexes of sense impressions, and the second is our attribution to the concept of a bodily object a significance that is independent of the sense impressions that originally gave rise to it. He says that that is what we mean when we say the bodily object has "a real existence" (60). Of course, not all scientists share Einstein's metaphysical suppositions then or now. I mention it to show that Locke's theory of ideas not only influenced much subsequent philosophy; it penetrated the practice of science at the highest level into the twentieth century.

Varieties of empiricism continued to be influential throughout twentieth-century philosophy, especially in English-speaking countries, but the more fundamental idea that the mind grasps its contents first has been even more influential, and that idea derives from Descartes, who was no empiricist. As I mentioned in chapter 1, that idea is so widely accepted, it is virtually invisible. It expresses a view of the relation between mind and world in which the world is clearly separated from the mind, and the mind has to represent the world from its own contents and resources. In the seventeenth and eighteenth centuries there were debates about the issue of what resources the mind has in addition to the data of experience, with some philosophers maintaining that there are innate ideas and others denying it, but the view that the mind constructs a conception of the world out of its own materials was not in dispute, and even at the end of the twentieth century, it dominated theories of the mind that aimed at connecting with scientific methodology.

Despite the long history of the representational theory of the mind in either its Cartesian or its empiricist incarnation, it has had some challenges. Particularly important is the fact that both Descartes and Locke found that the theory required a distinction between primary and secondary qualities of objects. Descartes said that primary qualities are properties of objects independent of the mind—qualities such as motion, extension, solidity, and number. The ideas of primary qualities are like the properties in the object. In contrast, secondary qualities were said to be sensations in the mind—properties such as color, taste, sound, and smell, which are produced by the interaction between the observer and the object. The color or taste of an object does not exist in the object, but only in the mind of the observer.[4]

In Locke's version of the theory of ideas in his monumental *Essay*, the way simple ideas combine to form complex ideas can be compared to the way atoms or corpuscles combine to form physical objects. We cannot create simple ideas, we can only get them from experience, and we put them together to get more and more complex ideas. An idea is the immediate object of perception or thought; a "quality" of a substance is the power to produce an idea (2.8.8). Like Descartes, Locke distinguishes primary qualities from secondary qualities. Here is a well-known passage in which he describes the distinction:

The particular bulk, number, figure, and motion of the parts of fire or snow are really in them whether anyone's senses perceive them or no: and therefore they may be called *real qualities*, because they really exist in those bodies. But light, heat, whiteness, or coldness, are no more really in them than sickness or pain is in manna. Take away the sensation of them; let not the eyes see light, or colors, nor the ears hear sounds; let the palate not taste, nor the nose smell, and all colors, tastes, odors, and sounds, as they are such particular ideas, vanish and cease, and are reduced to their causes, i.e. bulk, figure, and motion of parts. (2.8.17, F: 84)

The idea that sound is a secondary quality reached the popular imagination in the familiar riddle: If a tree falls in a forest and no one is around to hear it, does it make a sound? The fact that people are puzzled by the question indicates that they at least entertain the possibility that the answer is no, and most people also realize that if the answer is no, that calls into question the status of many other qualities of objects. That is the intuition that underlies the notion of secondary qualities.

George Berkeley's famous attack on the distinction between primary and secondary qualities revealed how much Descartes's and Locke's attempts to explain the connection between the mind and an external world depended upon that distinction. Bishop Berkeley argued that the so-called primary qualities are just as perceptually relative as secondary qualities, and we have no more reason to think that the former really exist in bodies than do the latter. Everything Descartes and Locke had said about the relativity of color and sound to a perceiver could be said about solidity and motion. Moreover, he argued, it is senseless to think that an idea can be *like* a quality of an object as understood by Locke and all those philosophers who thought that ideas represent qualities of material objects. For instance, an idea of solidity cannot be "like" the property of solidity since no idea can be like a property of matter (Berkeley 1979, 41–42). His conclusion is that nothing exists but ideas in minds: consistent empiricism leads to idealism.

Berkeley was not the first to criticize realism about primary qualities. In the seventeenth century, Leibniz had argued that primary qualities do not provide a coherent conception of physical objects, and Pierre Bayle had argued that primary qualities are no more objective than secondary qualities.[5] But Berkeley's attack was the one with the most profound historical influence, including its influence on the skepticism of David Hume, who concluded that knowledge cannot go any further than the empirical study of ideas.[6] Berkeley was clever, and he understood the importance of calling attention to a weakness in the way philosophers described the physical world as discovered by science in comparison to the commonsense conception of physical objects. The distinction between primary and secondary qualities was intended to make the world of science closer to our experience, but Berkeley argued that it had the opposite effect. The commonsense view is that both primary and secondary qualities are real qualities of objects. Berkeley agreed with that and argued that since philosophical reflection forces us to conclude that both kinds of qualities are in the mind, it follows that the real object is in the mind. Idealism turns out to be on the side of common sense! At the conclusion of his *Three Dialogues*, Philonous (the voice of Berkeley) declares:

> My endeavors tend only to unite, and place in a clearer light, that truth which was before shared between the vulgar and the philosophers: the former being of opinion, that *those things they immediately perceive are the real things*; and the latter, that *the things immediately perceived are*

*ideas which exist only in the mind.* Which two notions put together, do in effect constitute the substance of what I advance. (Berkeley 1979, 94)

Notice how close Berkeley comes to collapsing the first great idea into the second.

One of the most important divisions between philosophers since Berkeley is on the issue of whether the primary/secondary quality distinction can be maintained. Even the most realist philosophers since Descartes have agreed that not all perceptible qualities of physical objects are really in the object, so the existence of secondary qualities was not in dispute. What was and continues to be in dispute is whether *any* of the perceptible qualities are in the object itself, or whether the so-called primary qualities are just as mind-dependent as the secondary qualities. In that debate Kant was on Berkeley's side, a critical move in the separation of mind from world:

> Long before Locke's time, but assuredly since him, it has been generally assumed and granted without detriment to the actual existence of external things, that many of their predicates may be said to belong not to the things in themselves, but to their appearances, and to have no proper existence outside our representation. Heat, color, and taste, for instance, are of this kind. Now, if I go farther, and for weighty reasons rank as mere appearances the remaining qualities of bodies also, which are called primary, such as extension, place, and in general space, with all that which belongs to it (impenetrability or materiality, shape, etc.)— no one in the least can adduce the reason of its being inadmissible. (*Prolegomena* § 13, remark 2) (1950, 36–37)

Here Kant seems to put all perceptible qualities of an object in the mind. However, he was quick to distinguish his view from that of Berkeley. In the immediately preceding passage, he writes:

> Idealism consists in the assertion that there are none but thinking beings, all other things which we think are perceived in intuition, being nothing but representations in the thinking beings, to which no object external to them in fact corresponds. I, on the contrary, say that things as objects of our senses existing outside us are given, but we know nothing of what they may be in themselves, knowing only their appearances, that is, the representations which they cause in us by affecting our senses. Consequently, I grant by all means that there are bodies without us, that is, things which, though quite unknown to us as to what they are in themselves, we yet know by the representations which their influence on our sensibility procures us. (1950, 36)

In the second edition of *Critique of Pure Reason*, Kant calls his position "transcendental idealism," which he distinguishes from what he calls "transcendental realism" (Descartes, Locke, et al.), a position that fails to distinguish the world of appearances from the world of things in themselves, and from "dogmatic idealism" (Berkeley), the position that maintains that all objects exist in minds (*CPR* A 369). The implication is that Kant intended his position to chart a path between realism and idealism.

Kant was up against a severe challenge. Hume's skepticism was not limited to qualities of objects in the external world. It extended to most of metaphysics and virtually all of theology, and it undermined natural science because skepticism about the external world led to the conclusion that there is no justification for the basic law of nature that all events have causes. Kant wanted to support science by showing that there can be *a priori* knowledge of universal truths about nature. But he also thought that he had demonstrated the illusions of speculative metaphysics by showing that it leads to contradictions.[7] His aim, then, was to produce a metaphysics that deserved to be called a science, one that was neither empirical science nor speculative metaphysics, but could show why scientific judgments and judgments of ordinary experience are justified.[8] The way to accomplish this, Kant thought, was to show that the judgments of space and time, cause and effect, substance, and number rely upon forms in the mind, not things in themselves. What saves science and knowledge in general is the separation of the world we can experience from the world of things as they are in themselves. The world of science is the former, not the latter. What preserves the first great idea for Kant is that he separates it into two ideas: the idea of the world as it is in itself, and the idea of the world as it can be grasped by human minds. It is not possible for the human mind to grasp the former, but it can grasp the latter, and that is good enough to give us knowledge.

The distinction between primary and secondary qualities was a critical step in the attempt to distinguish the contents of the mind from an external world once the second great idea took the form of the view that our grasp of our mind precedes our grasp of the world. Descartes and Locke thought that the world without minds would include primary but not secondary qualities. The way they made the distinction was attacked, but the idea of the distinction itself survived in large swaths of philosophy despite the attacks by Berkeley and Kant. The reason is that it held out an exciting promise. If the mind's contents begin with simple ideas of primary and secondary qualities and their combinations, and if the ideas of secondary qualities can be explained as caused by the primary qualities of material objects, then an account of primary qualities of objects can succeed in being both an account of the material world and an account of the human mind in that world.

That is obviously a tall order, but it was soon noticed that it fit well with a naturalistic metaphysics in which biology can be derived from physics and consciousness can be explained by evolutionary biology, a view that became increasingly prestigious after Darwin. Bernard Williams describes a way the project might go in his well-known 1978 book, *Descartes: The Project of Pure Enquiry*. Williams argues that if any of us has knowledge, there must be a coherent representation of the world as a whole that does not contain consciousness, and then there must be a more inclusive conception that explains how each of our minds is related to the material world and got its different representations. That would be what he calls "the absolute conception of reality" (229–230). When we accomplish that, he says, we will have completed the task of the early modern philosophers in distinguishing between primary and secondary qualities, where it is primary and not secondary qualities that characterize the material world as it really is (230). At the end of the book he says that it is philosophy that makes it clear why natural science can be absolute knowledge of how things are, while social science and ordinary perceptual experience cannot be. It is philosophy that tells us the place of science in giving us a conception of the world as a whole. Philosophy tells us that science provides the absolute conception (287).[9]

It is interesting to notice how seamlessly Williams connects the view that science can give us a satisfactory version of the first great idea with Descartes's and Locke's desire to understand the world through our minds. Our experience of the world is reduced to our experience of primary and secondary qualities. The former is objective; the latter is subjective. The former is primary; the latter is derived from the former. If empirical science can succeed in describing the former through physics, and can explain how the primary qualities give rise to beings with conscious awareness of themselves and the world in all the forms it has taken, and further, can explain the differences among the conscious states of those beings, then we would have a conception of the world that Williams thinks would be as complete a knowledge of the world as a whole as we can get.

There is, however, an important difference between primary qualities, as understood by Descartes and Locke, and the primary qualities of contemporary physics. The primary qualities of the seventeenth and eighteenth centuries were qualities perceivable by the unaided human mind and closely connected with the way ordinary people think of the world. As the eighteenth-century empiricists observed, ordinary people think of secondary qualities as part of the world also, but as long as the world without minds contains primary qualities, it looks like the world of experience is not too far removed from the world without minds. But the situation is quite different if the world without minds is the world discovered by contemporary physics, which bears no relation at all to the ordinary person's view of the world. There are physical particles without mass and there are particles without dimension. Solidity was one of the primary qualities identified by Descartes and Locke, but ordinary objects turn out to be mostly empty space. The difference between our subjective worlds and the objective world of physics has increased, yet think how little argument Williams needed to make his absolute conception based in physics persuasive to readers in 1978. In the ensuing decades, the idea that physics can give us a theory of everything has become so widely accepted that when it was attacked by Thomas Nagel in 2012, there was an enormous uproar from naturalists in response. From the point of view of the history of ideas, the story of how a way of investigating the natural world arising from the second great idea became the established expression of the first idea is fascinating. Equally fascinating is the resistance to it. I will return to the project of producing a view of everything out of the data of science in chapter 5.

Descartes's turn to the second great idea led to hundreds of years of philosophy that had numerous critical features that distinguish it from philosophy in the previous two millennia. The idea that our grasp of our mind precedes our grasp of the world led to the representational theory of the mind. It led to the objective/subjective distinction, and eventually to the idea that the many subjective worlds derive from the objective world, the world without consciousness. The separation of the world from the mind made it tempting to accept either skepticism or idealism. The option of embracing idealism was taken by Hegel and the German idealists, and although their strand of philosophy was quite different from Berkeley's idealism and Cartesian rationalism, they had the same goal of providing a philosophical basis for science. Schelling went so far as to attempt to give a scientific proof for idealism, and Hegel's project of putting together the philosophy of nature and the philosophy of spirit in what he called the *Realphilosophie* was meant to fold natural philosophy, cultural philosophy, and empirical science together into a common science.[10]

Ever since the Scientific Revolution, European philosophy has defined itself in relation to science, and since philosophy in the East never did so, there was a hardening of the difference between Philosophy East and Philosophy West. Traditions such as Native American philosophy and Islamic philosophy also do not define themselves in terms of a relation to science. Islam has never done that even though the precursors to modern science were advances made by medieval Muslims. An example is discoveries in perspective geometry that I will mention in the next section. Islam never lost prestige in its culture because of a Reformation, and it never had an "Enlighten-ment" in which the second great idea superseded the first. In cultures outside the Western world, empirical science never became the driver of the two great ideas, and the function of philosophy has been very different than it is in the West. It is useful to keep in mind that there are many areas of the world in which the relation between the two ideas is much more har-monious than it has been in Western history. Of course, we need to live out our own history, but when we face internal conflicts, alternative narratives can show us options we might not have considered. I will not pursue those narratives in this book, but occasionally, I will try to remind us that they exist.

## Art and the Rise of Subjectivity

The philosophy of the seventeenth and eighteenth centuries focused on the individual mind and used it to ground con-ceptions of the world believed to be more trustworthy than premodern conceptions. But for the most part, the philosophy of the era was missing one of the most important features of the rise of the second great idea: the idea of the uniqueness of each individual's subjective experience. The revolution in sub-jectivity first occurred in the arts, not in philosophy. Art and literature have the potential to express the individuality of the creator much more intensely than cultural forms that purport to be factual, and that is one of the ways in which the history of art and literature differs from the history of science or phi-losophy. Einstein reportedly remarked that if he had not for-mulated the theory of general relativity, someone else would have done so sooner or later, but if Beethoven had not written his C minor Symphony, it would never have been written by anyone.[11] He could have said the same thing about lesser art-works, although there is probably some level of art that is low enough that it does not express a singular personality. Tracing a pattern in needlepoint or telling a well-worn story might be examples.[12]

I think this means that art and literature are particularly well suited to express the second great idea unconstrained by the first. I have mentioned the Protestant Reformation, the social disintegration produced by the devastation of the Black Death, and the rise of modern science as historical forces that brought about the collapse of the first great idea and the rise of the second. Some people respond to catastrophic experiences like war and plague and the loss of trust in the authorities that had safeguarded their worldview by resorting to violence; others take up the pen; still others express themselves in art. For millennia, people used art and literature to depict a view of the world that was shared by everyone around them and which defined an entire civilization, but at some point, probably beginning in fifteenth-century Florence, art began to express what was inside the artist rather than what was outside. When it began to express the self, the self became the object of cultural awareness. In literature the novel became the primary form for the expression of the self, and I will discuss the novel as a distinctive creation of the modern era in the next section. In the rest of this section I will look at the turn in art and architecture.

As I mentioned in chapter 1, an important aid to the representation of the self in art was the discovery of perspective, which permitted the visual depiction of different points of view. Giotto was one of the first to experiment with linear perspective at the beginning of the fourteenth century, although he did not have a systematic method for achieving it. By the following century, discoveries by the Arabs in optics and perspective geometry were brought to Florence, and Brunelleschi used these discoveries to create a systematic theory of perspective in which receding parallel lines meet at a vanishing point. In a famous experiment, he painted an image of the Florence Baptistery that the viewer found indistinguishable from the real building.[13] The discovery of the formal features of perspective revolutionized painting and architecture. For the first time, artists could depict on a flat surface what people saw in three dimensions, and from whatever point of view the artist chose.

It has often been said that this discovery changed people's view of reality, but it is not obvious why it would do so. Here is a hypothesis. We try to represent what we see, but what we see and the way we think about it can be affected by other people's representations. We are more likely to be aware of perspective when perspective can be portrayed visually. In any case, the discovery of perspective geometry, together with the new science of Copernicus, eventually led to the idea that there is no privileged perspective. People began to think that now that we know that our planet is not at the center of the cosmos, there is no reason to think that our personal perspective has any more centrality than that of others. When pushed far enough, this line of thought led some people to the idea that there is no objective description of the world, no God's-eye viewpoint that trumps all the individual human points of view. Of course, the lack of an objective reality does not follow from the perspectival nature of human experience, but the collapse of the idea that we experience reality directly led to the contrast between subjectivity and objectivity, and that dichotomy became important for all aspects of human culture, including art.

The nineteenth-century art historian Jacob Burckhardt discovered (or invented) "the Renaissance" as a distinctive period of history, a name that quickly became commonplace, and his assessment of what made that era different is still standard. According to Burckhardt, the medieval worldview was overturned in the Renaissance and was replaced by a delight in Greek culture, in nature, and particularly in the beauty of the human body, all of which was experienced as liberating for the individual. Here is a particularly telling way that Burckhardt ([1860] 1954) describes it in his famous book:

> In the Middle Ages both sides of human consciousness— that which was turned within as that which was turned without—lay dreaming or half awake beneath a common veil. The veil was woven of faith, illusion, and childish prepossession, through which the world and human history were seen as clad in strange hues. Man was conscious of himself only as a member of a race, people, party, family, or corporation[14]—only through some general category. In Italy this veil first melted into air; an *objective* treatment and consideration of the State and of all the things of this world became possible. The *subjective* side at the same time asserted itself with corresponding emphasis; man became a spiritual *individual*, and recognized himself as such. (100 [emphasis in original])

There is more than one interesting thing to see in this quotation. One is that Burckhardt notices that the idea of subjectivity was accompanied by the idea of objectivity, a point that will come up many times in this book. But his real interest is in lauding fifteenth-century Italy in contrast to the medieval period. Leaving aside Burckhardt's bias against what he insisted on calling "the Dark Ages" (a label he applied to the entire period of history between late antiquity and fifteenth-century Italy), I interpret him as describing the move from the dominance of the medieval version of the first great idea to the rise of the second idea and a different form of the first. Whatever one thinks of Burckhardt's judgment on the Middle Ages, something important did happen to human consciousness beginning in fifteenth-century Italy, and it was first expressed in art. As art ceased to be a communal project that expressed a common worldview, it became the product of an individual talent, expressing a distinctive and original viewpoint. Artists cared about the fact that their works were the products of their individual minds, and it became much more common for artworks to be signed. The personality of the artist spoke through the work. That made originality an important value, whereas previously it would have been considered arrogant to think that one's own personality counted more than the centuries of tradition that defined a civilization. Originality emphasizes differences from one piece to another. The more original an artwork is, the more it expresses the individuality of the artist; and the more it expresses the individuality of the artist, the less it expresses the common viewpoint of the age. By the end of the sixteenth century, the Christian version of the first great idea no longer unified all the known arts and sciences, and art became solely an inner force. As Emile Mâle (1972) says, the thirteenth-century art of France gives full expression to a civilization, whereas the art of three or four hundred years later tells us very little of the thought of the day (398).

Originality and anti-tradition are still highly valued, perhaps now more than ever. Compare the originality and free-spiritedness of art glass by Dale Chihuly with the refined tradition of Venetian glass, in which the purpose of the artist is to perpetuate the tradition in its finest form, not to express an individual fancy. The same point could be made about the difference between jazz improvisation and classical music, or a pioneering chef like Alice Waters in the 1970s compared with a traditional French chef in a three-star Michelin restaurant. We retain both values as a society, and for many purposes there is room for both, but the values arise from different ideas about the mind's place in the universe. For millennia, originality was not a value, whereas perfecting an artistic tradition was. Creating works that will last for many generations was once important, but gradually became less so. If you create a work to last, you need to be confident that viewers in the future will experience what viewers experienced when it was created. If the artwork expresses your self or an original aesthetic that you do not expect to be permanent, you might not care whether it lasts or not.

Architectural styles have a long history, and the reasons for changes in style are social and technological as well as ideological and aesthetic. The second great idea in architecture could not reach a pinnacle of expression until the social and technological conditions were right, as they were in the late twentieth century when Frank Gehry designed the Guggenheim Museum. In the vignette at the end of chapter 1 I compared the Guggenheim with the Roman Pantheon as a visual contrast between the two great ideas. The Pantheon was built to sit in the center of an empire and glorify it; the Guggenheim was not intended to fit the surroundings, quite the contrary. Pythagorean symbolism is implanted in the Pantheon. The Gehry building quite consciously violates laws of form and symmetry, which made it difficult to execute because the laws of physics favor a building with straight vertical walls, flat surfaces, and no curvature or obtuse angles. The building gives maximum expression to the imagination of an individual person, but the fact that it was immediately popular suggests that people like to see how far the subjective world can be revealed within the confines of the physical laws of the objective world. Some fantasy buildings can be built.

Since the Renaissance there has been a profusion of art styles, many more than in the entire previous history of art, and even though the modern era has been frequently criticized, I doubt that anyone would deny that its art is captivating.[15] The styles changed in rapid succession, but they had something in common that distinguishes them from what went before. The creative surge that started six hundred years ago was driven by the rise of the idea of the self and confidence in its importance. I am not suggesting that the self is necessarily the object of the artist's expression; in fact, it usually is not. But what the discovery of the self did for art was to permit the imagination to express what the artist sees or feels without the constraints of a common view of reality. In chapter 2, I discussed the claim by Bakhtin that the modern novel was accompanied by a reorientation of consciousness. That reorientation also made possible an almost limitless number of artistic styles. That is because of two features of the self: it changes, and it is unique. Bakhtin emphasizes the former; I have stressed the latter. Both features of the self were revealed in art.

## The Novel

Bakhtin claims that the novel represented a revolution in human consciousness, but he does not give a date for its beginning. William Egginton (2016) argues that it happened more than thirty years before Descartes's *Meditations*, when Cervantes's *Don Quixote* was published to an explosive reception. This book is generally acknowledged as the first modern novel and one of the most important works of fiction ever written. When the Norwegian Nobel Institute, in 2002, polled one hundred leading fiction writers from fifty-four countries to name the single most important literary work in history, more than half chose *Don Quixote*. No other work came close.[16] To me this is amazing. I cannot imagine philosophers in scores of countries being asked to name the single most important work of philosophy ever written and coming to such extraordinary agreement. Cervantes obviously did something significant.

Egginton says he invented what we call fiction, and in doing so he helped to give birth to the modern world.

It is always fun to exaggerate, and it is doubtful that Cervantes should get full credit for inventing fiction, but he had an unmistakable impact on the way people see the world. What was different? Egginton says that Cervantes invented *characters,* and that required the creation of a new form of literature. What Egginton means by a character is an imaginary figure that seems just like a real person and is different from every other character. What makes each one unique is the uniqueness of their point of view, which the reader is able to inhabit by seeing the world through their eyes. Sancho Panza and Don Quixote have incompatible viewpoints, with the simple Sancho Panza playing the straight man to Don Quixote's outlandish fantasies of chivalry. Yet for all that, they love each other, and the reader empathizes with both of them. "[W]hen we engage with fiction we are both within and without the story we are reading or watching; we are simultaneously ourselves, rooted in our own particular view on the world, and someone else, maybe even someone very different from us, feeling how he or she inhabits a very different world from ours" (xix). What this teaches us, Egginton argues, is the ability to distinguish the real from the imaginary. It works because it is easier for us to make the distinction from the vantage point of an imaginary but possible world (165). We have no trouble distinguishing the real from the imaginary *within* the imaginary world of the novel because Don Quixote shows us what it is to fail in that world. That teaches us about ourselves because we cannot discover our own illusions without imagining ourselves otherwise (164). We have trouble realizing that we have a perspective until we imagine having a different one, and we recognize a perspective as illusory only when contrasted with a better one. Don Quixote is comical because the reader gets to have the better perspective on reality. We laugh, and the enormous number of people who read *Don Quixote* when the first part was released in 1605 found it hilarious.[17]

To laugh at Don Quixote is to acknowledge the difference between reality and imagination, a distinction that we find obvious even if we are not always very good at making it accurately. But the distinction was not always obvious. In mythopoeic thought according to the Frankforts (1946), ancient peoples treated everything that affected human life, including their dreams and imagination, as on a par with what we now like to call the real world, and the Frankforts credit the Greeks for being the first to distinguish the real from the imaginary, but Cervantes took another step with the idea of an objective reality that can be experienced differently by different people. He brilliantly cemented that difference in people's minds by making it funny.[18]

We are so used to the idea of objective reality that it can be surprising to realize that objective reality does not make sense except in contrast to subjective reality, a difference that did not become important until the rise of the second great idea. Egginton says that the first recorded use of the word "reality" in Spanish was two years after book 1 of *Don Quixote* was published. The word "reality" and its cognates entered the English language and other European languages starting in the middle of the sixteenth century, and were no doubt aided by the Scientific Revolution (172). If the Greeks invented the distinction between history and poetry, Cervantes showed us how we filter reality through our own minds, and he helped to make the second idea a great idea. That idea became truly great when it became possible to inhabit in our imagination someone else's interior space. The novel made possible the depiction of the uniqueness of individual perspectives. In this way the invention of the novel was like the invention of perspective in art.

What made the literary form of the novel better at depicting the uniqueness of individual consciousness than epic poetry or drama? Bakhtin (1981) says that the lofty epic hero has no deep interior life but appears as a completed image who represents the values of a whole culture. The novel is the opposite. It follows the character's consciousness. It is alive and unfinished, engaged with the time of the telling of the narrative, and able to penetrate the subjectivity of the characters and to rethink them. The creative urge for epic poetry comes from national memory. The creative urge for the novel comes from experience and knowledge that is continuously changing (15). In the novel, Bakhtin says,

[a]n individual cannot be completely incarnated into the flesh of existing sociohistorical categories. There is no mere form that would be able to incarnate once and forever all of his human possibilities and needs, no form in which he could exhaust himself down to the last word, like the tragic or epic hero; no form that he could fill to the very brim, and yet at the same time not splash over the brim. There is always an unrealized surplus of humanness. (37)

In the novel, there is a tension between the external and the internal man, something that does not appear in the Greek epic where everything is externalized. That tension allows the subjectivity of the individual to become an object of experimentation and representation (37). The novel has the critical quality of the present—its openness; we are in direct contact with a developing reality (39). We can empathize with the characters in a novel while they are going through their experiences, and we can follow their interior thoughts, choices, feelings, and actions as they see it as well as the way others see it, because we have an inside view as they are occurring.[19]

By the eighteenth and nineteenth centuries, the novel had become the most important kind of literature, and in the later nineteenth century, Arthur Schopenhauer (famed for being the "artist's philosopher") wrote about the novel:

> A novel will be of a high and noble order, the more it represents of inner, and the less it represents of outer, life; and the ratio between the two will supply a means of judging any novel, of whatever kind, from *Tristram Shandy* down to the crudest and most sensational tale of knight or robber. *Tristram Shandy* has, indeed, as good as no action at all; and there is not much in *La Nouvelle Heloïse* and *Wilhelm Meister*. Even *Don Quixote* has relatively little; and what there is, is very unimportant, and introduced merely for the sake of fun. And these four are the best of all existing novels. (Schopenhauer [1891] (2004), 57)

What a contrast with Aristotle! The difference is not just that Aristotle had not thought of the novel; he did not seem interested in a literary form like the one described by Schopenhauer. Aristotle praised "poetry" because it conveys the universal. Characters are interesting for what they portray about human types. Aristotle and Schopenhauer had completely different views on the form that literature should take because they had completely different visions of the relation between mind and world.

The ability to enter and follow someone else's subjective experience is importantly different from inhabiting one's own mind. We know that the first great idea is incomplete if it leaves out the grasp of our subjectivity, but both the two great ideas are incomplete if they leave out the subjectivity of other minds. Intersubjectivity is experienced in personal relations and is vividly expressed in fiction and in film, but it has not yet reached the cultural status that the modern period placed on one's own mind. Perhaps an investigation of intersubjectivity can help us overcome the great difficulty in understanding the connection between objectivity and subjectivity, one of the most intractable of philosophical problems since the modern era began. If it becomes a focal idea, that might give us an advance in civilization. I will return to that possibility in chapter 6.

## Autonomy and the Changing Ground of Morality

Systematic moral philosophy entered human history at about the same time as the systematic treatment of other forms of the first great idea. When that idea plummeted in status and the second idea rose to prominence, the foundation of morality was threatened. That was obvious to both the defenders of the supremacy of the second great idea and the traditionalists who never gave up the first. Morality needed to be invented on a completely different basis. The option of giving up morality itself was, of course, entertained from time to time, but rarely has that option been taken seriously for long. Morality—whatever it is—is important.

When the first great idea was supreme, morality meant living in harmony with the world. The universe was perceived as a unity with a rational structure that determined both physical and moral laws. Reason is a force we *obey* because reason is intrinsically authoritative. When the second great idea rose in importance, reason maintained its importance as the ground of authority, but it moved its location to the individual will. The premodern idea that the physical universe is mathematically structured was retained, but the Pythagorean idea that that structure is mirrored in the human soul and in society was given up. The ground of morality became individual autonomy rather than harmony with the universe.

The most important philosopher in the transition from premodern to modern moral philosophy was Immanuel Kant, and like philosophers in the previous era, his view of the relation between mind and world determined his view of morality. At the beginning of the *Critique of Pure Reason*, Kant speaks of the need for a new Copernican Revolution, one in which the categories of reality put the mind before the external world.[20] This paradigm shift was a clear call for the primacy of the second great idea, and it had a dramatic effect on the conceptualization of morality in the century leading up to Kant's work, masterfully described by J. B. Schneewind (1997) in his book, *The Invention of Autonomy*. Schneewind argues that the new foundation for morality was primarily produced by theists who thought it necessary to emphasize human moral capacities in a world of religious strife (3–9). Schneewind argues that the initial motivation to change the foundation of morality was not the rejection of the Christian worldview, but the recognition that the ground of morality must be something acceptable to everyone. It could no longer be taken for granted that morality comes from the place of a person in a world created and cared for by God and ordered by reason.

By the beginning of the eighteenth century, the primacy of the self was already taking root. Art and literature had already changed, and the influence of Descartes was spreading throughout European philosophy, so it is not surprising that the new foundation for morality was the self. According to the new idea, authority is rooted not in something external to the individual but in self-governance. Human flourishing, or the fulfillment of human nature, had to be given up as the end of the moral life once people stopped believing that there is anything morally important about common human nature, and it was replaced by an entirely different way of looking at morality and the proper constitution of civil society based on the authority of the self. The social contract is the form morality takes when it is ultimately based on the authority of individuals over themselves. Morality arises from contractual agreement among self-governing individuals, not from conformity to the moral order of the universe.

There is a two-sided explanation for the way the second great idea affected morality. The idea of the self was accompanied by the idea of subjectivity, but as I have already observed, subjectivity does not make sense without the idea of objectivity. The distinction between the objective and the subjective appeared with perspective in art and in Cervantes's novel before Descartes used the distinction to revolutionize philosophy. But in the hands of Descartes and his successors, the distinction hardened into a dichotomy between the world as seen from inside one's head and the world as it is without minds. Since modern science discovered features of the latter, objectivity became identified with the impersonal and the necessary. When applied to morality, it appeared that the only alternative to the subjectivity of morality is objectivity in the sense in which science is objective. It seemed to follow that morality had to be independent of any metaphysical framework or background conditions about human nature and human desires that do not have the status of necessity. Notice that if that is what is required for morality to be objective, Aristotle's morality based on virtue and human flourishing cannot deliver objectivity. But since Aristotle's idea is not subjective either, it does not fit either side of the modern dichotomy. That makes it difficult for many modern readers to understand ancient and medieval ethics, because we are so used to fitting everything into either the category of the world inside my mind— my subjective world—or the world independent of anybody's mind—the objective world.

The uncomfortable dichotomy of subjective and objective was vividly before the mind of Kant, who wanted morality to be in both categories. He grounded morality in the self, but he also wanted it to have the force of necessity, and he maintained that only the concept of obligation has the formal features of objective necessity. But once philosophers lost confidence in the objectivity of norms derived from substantive assumptions about human nature, obligation had to become procedural.[21] The connection between obligation and procedure was imbedded in the theoretical structure of the social contract, a form of theory designed to be both a moral theory justifying moral obligation in the will of the individual and a political theory grounding political authority in the consent of the governed. There is, then, a connection among three important aspects of the way morality was reconceptualized in the modern period that also changed political theory:

(1) Morality has the force of necessity.
(2) The basic moral concept is not flourishing or virtue, but obligation.
(3) Obligations come from the consciousness of the individual and get their authority from the individual whose agreement with others is the basis of civil society.

These changes meant that civil society is organized around the protection of individual rights rather than social harmony, and these protections impose obligations on others. All these changes in morality are connected with the rise of the second great idea and the dichotomy between the subjective and the objective that accompanied it. Maybe these changes seem too abstract to be of interest to the ordinary person trying to live a life in the twenty-first century, but I believe that they help explain confusion about passionately contested political issues, as I will argue in the next chapter.

The change in the way morality was understood in the early modern period was radical; nonetheless, something remained the same. I mentioned at the end of the preceding chapter that what is common to both the era dominated by the first idea and the era dominated by the second is the belief in the fundamental importance of reason. What changed was the locus of reason. According to the Greeks, reason permeates the structure of the universe, and according to the medieval philosophers, its primary locus is the mind of God. After the rise of the second great idea, the locus of reason was the individual human mind. So one of the major consequences of the rise of the second idea was a change in beliefs about reason and where it resides in the universe. Since reason was acknowledged to be the bearer of authority both before and after the rise of the second great idea, the shift in the locus of reason also shifted the locus of authority. The Greek and medieval idea that people are self-governing only to the extent that they share in the reason that rules the universe was replaced by the idea that the ultimate authority over people is themselves. Self-governance changed from one's share in the governing force of the universe to one's governance by one's own will. When that happened, it got a new name: "autonomy."

Kant attempted to combine the ancient idea that authority resides in reason with the modern idea that authority resides in the self by arguing that one's true self *is* one's rational will. But which is more basic? Is Kant's point that I should be governed by my rational will because it is *rational* or because it is *mine*?[22] If it is the former, reason remains the primary authority, and we need an explanation for why my reason should have a special status over me rather than reason in other persons. If it is the latter, there is no explanation for why it should matter that my will is rational rather than not. In fact, that is precisely the way the claim was eventually interpreted. By the nineteenth-century Romantic era, reason itself was under attack.

Kant may be primarily responsible for a Copernican shift from the centrality of the world to the centrality of one's mind in ethics as well as in metaphysics, but from the perspective of historical distance, we can see a slide from pre-Kantian ideas of authority to the post-Kantian idea that separated authority from one's reason. Each stage in the slide was not radical, but the bottom of the slope was drastically different from the top. In the long period before the rise of the second great idea, the dominant idea was that authority resides in reason, a force in the universe. At some point, probably with the appearance of divine command theory in the later Middle Ages, the grounding of authority became the rational *will*.[23] Kant then grounded authority over me in *my* rational will, and finally, in later philosophy, the ground of authority became my will, rational or otherwise. The sway of the second great idea probably began at the second step, but even at the third step, Kant wanted authority to be simultaneously grounded in universal reason and the individual rational will by arguing that universal reason is *attached* to my will. Kant is a pivotal figure in the confrontation of the two great ideas because he made a brilliant attempt to have it both ways, but the historical verdict is that the second idea won.

A good example of the primacy of the second great idea in contemporary Kantian moral thought is the theory of Christine Korsgaard. Korsgaard (2009, xi) directly addresses the question of the connection between reason and the self as the ground of authority and argues that the self's authority over itself does not derive from the authority of a rational will; rather, reason is authoritative because it is the rules that the self must set to govern itself. The self is a being with an executive function that must take control of itself because of the way self-consciousness operates. The rules of reason are the rules of a self-conscious being. Reason is not primary. What is primary is self-consciousness. In Korsgaard's theory, there is no doubt that the second great idea overcomes the first. It is a tribute to Kant's genius that his successors can go the other way, and I think that it is helpful to read Kant through the lens of the two great ideas because it reveals the influence of different intellectual temperaments on both textual interpretation and the kind of moral theory contemporary writers find appealing.

When the rise of the second great idea created the objective/subjective dichotomy, Kant wanted morality to be objective, but the idea that morality is subjective became influential as well, through the influence of David Hume. One of Hume's most famous legacies is his dichotomy between "is" and "ought." Hume argued that any sentence saying what *ought* to be the case is logically on a different level from sentences describing what *is* the case because what *is* must be either observed or derived by valid reasoning from what is observed, and no *ought* is in that category.[24] The is/ought dichotomy came to be closely associated with the broader fact/value dichotomy.[25] That produced the tendency to put everything to do with value in the realm of the subjective and all facts in the realm of the empirically observable. Hume says explicitly that he intends to apply the empirical method to an investigation of the mind, and the whole project of his *Treatise of Human Nature* is an investigation into the origin of our ideas. For instance, Hume's famous account of causation is an account of the origin of the *idea* of causation, not causation itself. Similarly, his account of morality in the third part of the *Treatise* is an account of the ideas of virtue and justice, not moral reality as it was previously understood. In shifting standard philosophical questions to an investigation of the mind, Hume was one of the preeminent philosophers of the second great idea. In doing so, he also solidified the subjective/objective distinction in a way that was influential for centuries: objectivity resides in method, in particular, the scientific method; subjectivity is the realm of human experience and ideas. Good and evil are not in the world, but in the human mind. When morality was interpreted as residing in the subjective realm, it lost the force of objective necessity. That idea continued in large swaths of Western culture up to the end of the twentieth century.[26]

The discovery of subjectivity changed moral philosophy, and it created a rift between the view that morality is objective and the view that it is subjective. In the premodern era morality was thought to be imbedded in the universe and the human mind is part of the universe. There was no issue of deciding whether morality is objective or subjective. Morality is about the flourishing life, which is living in conformity with nature, and during the Christian era it was believed that nature was created by God. There was no breach between an individual's morality and the morality of the larger society because the uniqueness of individuals had no moral implications. The philosophical shift begun by Descartes focused on the individual mind and began the separation of mind and world that was so significant for modern thought. In the first section of this chapter, I described the way that led to a change in the idea of nature. Nature is the objective world, and the objective world is the world examined by science. The assumption that science tells us what the objective world is like was among the most important reasons for Kant's attempt to give morality necessity and objectivity as modeled by science.

The awareness of subjectivity occurred first in art and literature, as I observed in the second and third sections above. The uniqueness of subjective viewpoints is obvious in the art of the period and in the rise of the modern novel. But with the modern assumption of a sharp division between subjectivity and objectivity, two competing views on the metaphysics of

morals arose. On the one hand, it was thought that if morality is objective, it must take the form of obligation centered
on self-governance, with Kant as the supreme example. On
the other hand, if morality is subjective, it is purely a natural phenomenon that can be studied empirically the way we
study the behavior of birds and animals in nature. This modern conflict was one of the results of the subjective/objective
dichotomy. The dichotomy goes deep. It is responsible for the
academic division between the sciences and the humanities. It
is responsible for the difficulty in grasping all of reality that we
will discuss in chapter 5. And it is responsible for the historical
change from the idea that morality is living in harmony with
the world to the idea of autonomy as the basis of both morality
and civil society. We are now dealing with the practical conflicts that produced.

## The Twentieth Century:
## The Attack on the Second Great Idea

The discovery of the unconscious by Sigmund Freud severely
undermined the confidence people had in their access to their
own minds. To be fair, philosophers and poets had known of
the unconscious long before Freud brought it into the field of
psychology—a fact that Freud acknowledged[27]—but his work
made the unconscious an object of scientific investigation and
clinical practice, giving Freudian psychology a prestige that
enabled it to rapidly gain popular attention in the years following World War I. One reason Freudian theory got so much
attention was its reputation for salaciousness, making it simultaneously fascinating and disgusting, a sure recipe for public
notoriety. Freud's method of psychoanalysis faced objections
then as well as now, but even its detractors admit that there
are depths of the self below the level of consciousness, and

there are ways to unearth some of those depths. There is much in our minds that is hidden, and much that we hide from ourselves.

Freudian psychology was one of the first major threats to the second great idea. It revealed not only that there are layers of the mind that are largely or even completely inaccessible to our consciousness but that we can be mistaken in what we consciously believe about deep features of ourselves, including our motives and desires. Perhaps worse, some of these features of our selves are more accessible to certain other persons than to ourselves. The threat was not only to the primacy of the second idea—which after all, is only an *idea*; it was perceived as a threat to the very existence of the self.

Ever since Kant, autonomy in the sense of self-governance has been the foundational idea in ethics. Control is our key value, whereas in previous eras it was virtue. It was shocking when Freudian psychology showed that the control we exercise over ourselves is much less than we thought. We are unaware of many of our impulses to action that explain behavior that is otherwise opaque to us. And in the decades since Freud, psychological studies have revealed even more ways in which we fail to control aspects of ourselves that we thought we could manage in reflective rational consciousness. The human person, whose incomparable value supposedly comes from rationality, turns out to be very irrational. Irrationality can often be understood; the problem is that it is so hard to manage. The self-governing self that was the centerpiece of Kantian ethics and political thought is a self covered in illusions and failures at doing what it really wants to do.

In the later decades of the twentieth century, the second great idea was attacked in a different way, with work on the social construction of the self and the effect of power relationships on self-identity. The work of Foucault was particularly important because of its influence on the understanding and self-understanding of marginal groups such as prisoners, the insane, and those whose sexuality is nonstandard. Foucault's idea is that the various modern fields of knowledge have an intimate association with the power structures of modern society. What Foucault called the "hermeneutic self" understands itself through self-interpretation, like the interpretation of a text. In the analysis of discourses, hierarchies of power can be uncovered and critiqued by analyzing the fields of knowledge that legitimate these hierarchies. Power structures permeate subjectivity because of the way subjects interpret themselves through discourses determined by powerful others. The fact that we interpret ourselves verbally and in front of others is an important feature of the connection between subjectivity and institutional power according to Foucault. He gives the emergence of the Christian practice of Confession as a particularly clear example.[28] Christians have a duty to know the truth about themselves, which comes from an examination of their conscience, and to tell it to an authoritative interpreter, a priest. The practice of talking to a therapist is a modern version of the same technique of knowing oneself through an interpretive discourse in which there are hierarchies of users of the discourse.

The social construction of identities is also a common theme in feminist philosophy and philosophy of race. One's subjectivity is constructed in part by discourses external to the mind and sometimes serving to maintain the power of someone else. Some writers have extended this argument to the social construction of biological categories. For instance, there are writers on race who have adopted a form of social constructivism or skepticism about the category of race,[29] and Judith Butler (1990) has given an influential argument that gender is a social construction.

Revealing the way discourse serves certain social groups at the expense of others is experienced as liberating to people when they realize that their self-concept has been manipulated to their detriment, and the political response can be explosive. Notice how this discovery undermines the second great idea even further. It means that an account of the social world has primacy over the self's knowledge of itself. Consequently, it is not clear that the mind's ability to grasp itself is any more dependable than the mind's ability to grasp the world.

By the end of the twentieth century, the second great idea was in almost as bad a shape as the first. Both ideas have continued to be attacked. Many people have lost the sense of the mind's transcendence that came from historically important versions of the first great idea in both the East and the West, and which I summarized at the end of chapter 2. Many people also have lost the sense that we know our own minds and therefore can be in charge of our lives. We are left with a great deal of skepticism about our ability to grasp either ourselves or the universe, and that is very bad for our ability to live lives that allow us to develop our human cognitive and social gifts to the fullest. But both ideas are in our intellectual and social history, and they are the backdrop of current political conflicts. I hope that attending to their history, as we have done in the last two chapters, can serve as an antidote to current confusions. Our practical confusions will be the topic of the next chapter, and our theoretical confusions will be addressed in the following chapter.

**A Vignette of the Extreme of Nonobjectivity: Malevich's *Black Square***

*Black Square* (1915) is an iconic painting by the Russian avant-garde artist Kazimir Malevich, the most radically abstract painting seen at that time. It depicts a black square on white with no visual textures and a perfectly symmetrical shape. Malevich had experimented for eighteen months in his studio with many nonobjective paintings, culminating in a series of paintings of which the *Black Square* is the most famous. It has often been

FIGURE 7. Malevich's *Black Square* (1915). Tretyakov Museum, Moscow.

called "the zero point of painting" in reference to Malevich's description of his own intention: "It is from zero, in zero, that the true movement of being begins." In his 1927 book, *The Non-objective World*, he wrote: "In the year 1913, trying desperately to free art from the dead weight of the real world, I took refuge in the form of the square." Malevich invented the label "suprematism" to refer to the superiority of the new form of artistic expression focused on "painting as such," without any reference to real life. The *Black Square* was a totally different art object than anybody had seen before, and it transformed the way artists think of themselves and the way people looked at art. It proved that the most ordinary shape can be revolutionary. It may have been the extreme of nonobjectivity, as Malevich intended, but it was also the extreme of nonsubjectivity. It is as far from the uniquely personal as from the objective world.

# CHAPTER FOUR

# The Moral Legacy: Autonomy vs. Harmony with the World

## *Persons and Selves*

I have offered a narrative of the confrontation of two great ideas in Western history: the idea that the human mind can grasp the world, and the idea that the human mind can grasp itself. These ideas are compatible and many non-Western cultures did not evolve in a way that created tension between them, so there is no reason to think that we have to choose one over the other, nor is it necessary for one to be superior to the other. But in the West a conflict arose after the discovery of subjectivity because of the specific form these ideas acquired. Before the Renaissance, when the first great idea dominated, it took the form of the idea that the grasp of the world precedes the grasp of one's mind. Starting in the Renaissance, the second great idea rose to dominance, and it took the form of the idea that the grasp of one's mind precedes the grasp of the world. These ideas do conflict, but it is important to distinguish the two great ideas from these not-so-great ideas that accompanied them. Our history has conflicting elements, and that may not be such a bad thing because the clash between them can drive conceptual growth. But growth is often preceded by confusion and ambivalence—in this case, ambivalence about the relationship between the mind and the world, and it has left us with two different conceptions of what human beings are.

Each of us is a person and each of us is a self. What we mean by a person is very different from what we mean by a self, yet the mystery is that a person *is* a self. The idea of a person comes from the first great idea, the idea of a self from the second. The history of the idea of a person gives persons a very different kind of value than the value of selves, and persons and selves are components of very different ways of grounding morality. It might seem that the two great ideas have only a distant and tenuous connection to our moral and political problems, but I believe that the difference between a person and a self is the link between the two great ideas and a host of moral problems and their political expressions.

A person is a being of a certain kind, existing in the social or natural or supernatural world. Persons are part of the equipment of the world. The fact that "person" is a label applied from the outside is obvious from its derivation from Roman law in which the word *"persona"* was a mark of a legal status, initially applying to members of a clan but eventually extended to all citizens of the state. The revolt of the plebeians (4th–3rd cent. BCE) resulted in the right of full citizenship to all free men, which meant that every free man was identified as persona, but persona was not coextensive with the human race. Women and slaves and foreigners were not recognized as persons. "Persona" was connected with *"dignitas,"* the respect due to citizens in virtue of their legal status, but respect was also owed to a person for military or political achievements, and Cicero (1887) was willing to say that what commands respect can be the excellence of virtue (*On Duties* 2.9), which characterizes the best man, the man of honor. Persona, then, was a social category recognized in law, giving the person dignitas. Dignity and personhood were connected, but being human was not enough for either one.

While the Western Roman empire was disintegrating in the fifth century, Pope Saint Leo the Great[1] proclaimed that all humans possess dignity and have it equally because all human beings are made in the image and likeness of God (1997, sermon 21). Pope Leo's recognition of the universality of dignity was decisive for moving the treatment of dignity into the domain of morality. Respect owed to a person for being a citizen or for their special accomplishments is one thing; respect owed to a person for being human is on an entirely different level. Dignity became a moral value, not just a designation of social or legal status, once it was attached to the natural category of humanity rather than to social categories. But Pope Leo did not leave behind the idea of dignity as rank or status because he also said that the fact that God became human raised the rank of humans in the created world. Dignity continued to be a status, but it was a status extended to the whole human race, making humans higher than other animals.

By the early sixth century, the definition of a person by Boethius became the locus classicus for debates about personhood for many centuries: A person is "an individual substance of a rational nature" (Boethius 1973, 85). This definition says nothing about human or divine natures, but it picks out a property that most philosophers since the ancient Greeks have thought distinguishes humans from other animals: rationality. Boethius divides the universe into God, angels, and humans in the category of persons at the top, and animals in the lower category of nonpersons.[2] All humans are persons, but there are persons who are not human. Notice that again, "person" was associated with high status, but the defining feature of personhood was a property thought to have supreme value.

The Boethian definition had some detractors, but it was defended by Aquinas (1922), who argued that *person* is a natural category: "'Person' signifies what is most perfect in all of nature, and that is rationality" (*ST* 1, q. 29, art. 3 corpus). In that sense it is appropriate to extend personhood to God, and Aquinas connected it with dignity:

> Although this name *person* may not belong to God as regards the origin of the term, nevertheless it excellently belongs to God in its objective meaning. For as famous men were represented in comedies and tragedies, the name *person* was given to signify those who held high dignity. Hence, those who held high rank in the Church came to be called *persons*. Thence by some the definition of *person* is given as *hypostasis* [substance] *distinct by reason of dignity*.[3] And because subsistence in a rational nature is of high dignity, therefore every individual of the rational nature is called a *person*. Now the dignity of the divine nature excels every other dignity; and thus the name *person* preeminently belongs to God. (*ST* 1, q. 29, art. 3, reply obj. 2 [italics in original])

Earlier in the same question, Aquinas specifies a certain aspect of rationality that eventually became one of the most important components of the rise of the second great idea— the idea that a rational being governs itself. Aquinas says:

> [I]n a more special and perfect way, the particular and the individual are found in the rational stances which have

dominion over their own actions; and which are not only made to act, like others; but which can act of themselves; for actions belong to singulars. Therefore, also the individuals of the rational nature have a special name even among other substances; and this name is *person*. (*ST* 1, q. 29, art. 1 corpus)

Two centuries after Aquinas there was a flowering of work on dignity that laid the groundwork for the idea of the self and the value of self-governance in the modern period. The Renaissance manifesto on dignity was Pico della Mirandola's *Oration on the Dignity of Man* (1486). For Pico, dignity lies in the human freedom to forge oneself in limitless ways. What makes this significant is that Pico does not focus dignity on rational nature and then connect rational nature with freedom, as we see in Aquinas; rather, he connects dignity directly with the power of free choice. His *Oration* is actually more of an ode to philosophy than an essay on dignity,[4] but it is justly famous for a particular delightful passage. Pico writes that after God created the world, but before he created humans, every niche on the Great Chain of Being, from the angel down to the worm, was occupied. God then decided to create a man and said:

> We have given you, Adam, no fixed seat or form of your own, no talent peculiar to you alone. This We have done so that whatever seat, whatever form, whatever talent you may judge desirable, these same may you have and possess according to your desire and judgment. Once defined, the nature of all other beings is constrained within the laws We have prescribed for them. But you, constrained by no limits, may determine your nature for yourself, according to your own free will, in whose hands We have placed you. We have set you at the centre of the world so that from

there you may more easily gaze upon whatever it contains. We have made you neither of heaven nor of earth, neither mortal nor immortal, so that you may, as the free and extraordinary shaper of yourself, fashion yourself in whatever form you prefer. It will be in your power to degenerate into the lower forms of life, which are brutish. Alternatively, you shall have the power, in accordance with the judgment of your soul, to be reborn into the higher orders, those that are divine. O supreme liberality of God the Father, and supreme and wonderful happiness of man whom I permitted to obtain what he desires and to be what he wills! (2012, 117)

When Pico focused dignity on free will, that was a subtle but decisive change from the focus on rationality. Rationality arguably comes in degrees and that was the basis for the idea that some people should govern over others, but free will in this period was thought to be a property that does not come in degrees. You either have it or you don't. When free will became the basis of human dignity, the equality of humans was assured. But free will was understood as a natural property. It was what was supposed to set humans apart from other animals. When individual humans grasped their own value and their status in the universe, it was through their grasp of the universe as a whole, as Pico says above, so even when the Renaissance writers glorified free will, it was assumed that free will was part of the grand design of the universe. Pico never leaves behind the idea of a human person as a being with a certain position in the hierarchy of created things. The value of a person—indeed, the very concept of a person—is a component of the first great idea.

The emphasis on free will laid the groundwork for a revolution in the idea of a person because reflection on free will requires us to focus on the consciousness of the free being and the conscious process of choosing. Free will initially was understood as the freedom to make choices in a world of rational law, but it eventually evolved into the idea that first and foremost, freedom is the power to govern oneself, and that was called "autonomy." The idea of autonomy was an effort to connect dignity with consciousness of a certain kind rather than with nature, and this idea helped to bring about the rise of the second great idea. But autonomy does not make sense without the idea of a conscious *self* that is both the governor and the object of governance. Once that idea got hold of the human imagination, it gave human culture in all its forms a vibrancy that it did not lose for many centuries. But the rise of the second idea was accompanied by the decline of the first, and when the first great idea declined, the idea of a person as a being with high standing in the universe declined with it, and people lost their sense of importance in a world in which human beings are just another animal—probably the smartest, but definitely not the nicest.

The idea of a self appeared with the rise of the second great idea. Presumably, a self is just a person from the inside viewpoint, but that is more easily said than explained. A self is a being that is conscious of itself. Its power of self-consciousness cannot be identical to its power of grasping the world since we can imagine creatures who have one power and not the other. Self-consciousness is the awareness of something incommensurate with what we are aware of when we exercise the power of grasping the universe. When I grasp myself, I am aware of grasping something that is a completely different kind of thing than anything that is a component of my idea of the world. When I think of the world, I think of objects with qualitative properties that are connected in a unified structure. That includes human minds, each of which can be fit into the map of the world because of its likeness to other minds. But unlike the furniture of the universe, a self is unique in a very strong sense. Not only does it happen to differ from every other self and every other thing; it must differ for it to be a self. I do not know how to defend that claim, but I think that belief in the uniqueness of the self is very widely shared. My own consciousness is something no one else can have, and of course, the same thing applies to you. The idea that what makes you *you* is at least partly your differences from rather than your similarities to other human beings led to the conviction that there is something valuable in the differences between one self and another.

In the preceding chapter, I observed that the modern conception of the self arguably can be traced back to *Don Quixote* and the beginning of the modern novel. The concept of the self in philosophy took longer to develop. I have mentioned the importance of Pico della Mirandola for the subtle shift from rationality as the defining property of persons to free will, an important move in the historical development of the idea of self-governance as the ground of human dignity. But there is no evidence that Pico had a conception of the self in the sense I am talking about. The idea of the self in philosophy probably started with responses to Descartes's view of the *I*, notably critiques of the *I* as a substance given by Locke, Hume, and Kant. But subjectivity probably did not become a fundamental category of philosophical attention until the generation after Kant in the work of Fichte,[5] who thought that an account of subjectivity was necessary to solve the problem that Kant lacked a unitary account of the self. However, I do not see in Fichte the idea of the uniqueness of the subjectivity of each self.[6] For the origin of the idea of the uniqueness of consciousness, Charles Taylor (1991, 28–29) argues that Kant's student, Johann Herder, proposed that each of us has a unique way of being human, although Herder does not connect personal unique-ness with subjectivity. By the twentieth century, the prominent theologian Hans Urs von Balthasar (1986) identified dignity with the irreplaceability of the person, not with their human nature as such (18), and a focus on the uniqueness of persons appears in the personalist movement of the first half of the twentieth century, particularly in the writings of Karol Wojtyla (Pope Saint John Paul II) (2008), who explicitly connected the uniqueness of persons with subjectivity. So we can see a grad-ual move in modern philosophy from the Cartesian ego to the idea of subjectivity, to the idea that each human is unique, and finally to the connection between uniqueness and subjectiv-ity and the claim that that is the ground for the irreplaceable value of each person. Each person is irreplaceably valuable because each person is also a self.

The value of the person is the value of rationality. The value of the self is the value of subjectivity. Each is valuable in a dif-ferent way. Rationality has historically been interpreted as valuable because it is the property possessed by the highest beings in existence. Subjectivity is valuable because it is what makes each self irreplaceable. If human beings are both per-sons and selves, each of us has two different kinds of value. One is high value, a value that makes persons (whether human or not) more valuable in the world as a whole than nonpersons. That value has been called dignity. The value of irreplaceability is completely different. It is not the value of being a member of a class of beings that are higher than others because of a share-able property. It is the value of being unique, of being one of a kind. That value also has been called dignity.

It needs to be admitted that being irreplaceable does not by itself make something valuable. Lots of things are irreplace-able that are not very good. An original work of art might be bad art even though it is irreplaceable. Many artifacts are thrown away because of defects even though there is nothing else exactly like them. There are also unique features of humans that are trivial, such as the form of our irises and our fingerprints. If a human is killed, we would not bemoan the fact that a unique iris was lost to the world. The dignity of irreplaceability requires not only that we are unique but that we are valuable in the respect in which we are unique.

That leaves us with a puzzle about human dignity. If dignity is a combination of two distinct kinds of value, how are we to understand the way they come together in a human being?[7] I suggest that we start by saying that it is partly constitutive of human nature to have rationality, and that grounds our infinite or at least superior value. A being with this value is a person. That gives us a kind of dignity that is clearly shareable and has nothing to do with uniqueness. If there are rational natures that are not human, then there can be nonhuman persons and they have this value.

In contrast, irreplaceable value is grounded in our subjectivity, which makes each of us necessarily distinct from every other person. If you die, something of irreplaceable value is lost, but because you are also a rational being and infinitely valuable, the loss of you is not like the loss of a bad work of art. I propose, then, that you have infinite value because you are a person, and you have irreplaceable value because you are a self.

In Zagzebski (2016a), I offered a hypothesis that ties together the two values inherent in dignity with the idea that rationality is a power with infinitely many variations, each of which has only one possible instantiation. Each individual human person has a supremely valuable power that is actualized in an irreplaceable way. To get this to make sense, rationality needs to be an unusual property in the way it is related to its instances. Generally, for any property—say, the property of being a specific shade of blue, each instance of blue is the same as every other in so far as it is an instance of that shade of blue. I propose that rationality is not like that. It is a property that can only attach to the consciousness of beings whose consciousness is unique. If rationality entails uniqueness, each instance of it differs from every other, and the differences are intrinsically connected with rationality.

But how is that possible? My answer is that dignity in both senses pertains to the human capacity for self-reflective consciousness. Ever since ancient Greece, that power has been called rationality because it is the power to control our consciousness through the rational element, or what Plato called the rational part of the soul. Traditionally that was identified with the faculty of reason, exercised in the process we call reasoning, which has nothing to do with individuality and is the same in everyone who exercises it. But surely rationality is not limited to the reasoning process, and I think that we can avoid confusion if we attend to the purpose of human reasoning. We reason in the course of managing our conscious states. In some cases, we want those states to fit their objects. We want our beliefs to be true, our memories accurate, our perceptions veridical. In other cases, we want the objects to fit our states. We want the world to fit our desires and our values, and we manage our conscious states to direct our future actions according to a narrative partly of our choice. Rationality is the power to manage our consciousness in this way. It is not limited to the ability to see that one proposition logically follows from another. The formal process of logical inference from one set of propositions to another is the same in everyone who uses it, but there are differences between persons in the way they manage their psychic states.[8] At some point in the development of the second great idea, people began to think that two rational persons need not be identical insofar as they are rational. They may make different choices and have different beliefs, and the differences are equal in rationality. We almost always acknowledge that other people must make up their own minds about their lives, and we do that because we acknowledge that there may be more than one rational way to go, but that does not mean that their path of self-direction is random. When we defer to others in the management of their own conscious lives, we recognize that there is something in their consciousness about which they are the expert. It is rational, but it may differ from one's own rationality.

My hypothesis explains why a self should govern itself. Self-governance cannot be justified on the grounds that a self is a rational being. Rationality alone does not explain why a self should be governed by itself rather than by other rational beings, a problem I raised in my discussion of Kant in the last chapter. My proposal is that a self must govern itself because it is unique. No other being could accomplish the same thing. It is subjectivity that confers uniqueness on the self, and the uniqueness of subjectivity is necessary to make self-governance a defensible value. But if the uniqueness of subjectivity is no different than the uniqueness of our irises, it would be trivial and there would be no reason to think that self-governance is important. Our subjectivity is valuable because of the way it is connected with the value of rationality. Rational beings govern themselves, as Aquinas said in the quotation above, and I am suggesting that individuals govern themselves differently because of their unique subjectivity.

When the first great idea took the form of the idea that the world precedes the mind, the human being was conceptualized as a person; the defining property of a person was rationality, and the fundamental value was harmony with the rationally governed world. When the second great idea took the form of the idea that the mind precedes the world, the human being was conceptualized as a self; the defining property of the self was subjectivity, and the fundamental value became autonomy or self-governance, a value that sits uneasily with the recognition of the person's place in the world as a whole. Kant made a valiant attempt to identify the rational will with the autonomous will, as we discussed in chapter 3, but the understanding of autonomy in subsequent history exacerbated the tension between the two values and eventually led to the perception of irresolvable conflict. It is significant that a person *is* a self and that the two great ideas are not in conflict. We sometimes pay attention to only one side of ourselves—the side that is like everyone else and gives us the dignity of being a person, or the side that is unlike everyone else and gives us the dignity of being a self. It is understandable that we feel a tension, but we would not want to ignore a big part of what we are. If it is possible to combine the two great ideas, it must be possible to combine the value of the person and the value of the self.

## Autonomy and Rights

The first great idea gave human beings a sense of power in the best sense of power because it meant that humans have responsibility to or for the world they grasp. Grasping the universe generated responsibility because the first great idea never made humans passive spectators. Instead, the first idea amounted to this: "Here is the universe and this is your part in it." In the theistic version, it included God telling humans to play their role. In the Greek version, both the human and non-human parts of nature were governed by reason. In the Hindu version, human beings are responsible for nature because they are dependent on nature. The idea that humans are responsible for the rest of nature appears in many cultures. When we grasp a world with creatures who are unable to grasp their part in the world, that gives us a sense of responsibility to care for them. That awareness has increased in the last few generations with the growth of environmentalism, but we see it in a very different but still powerful way in the book of Genesis. After God creates Adam and Eve, we read: "God blessed them, and God said to them, 'Be fruitful and multiply, and fill the earth and subdue it; and have dominion over the fish of the sea and over the birds of the air and over every living creature that moves upon the earth'" (Gen. 1:28). Here human beings are told that they are responsible to God for the care of all living creatures. The responsibility is hierarchical; humans have the responsibility of monarchs over their subjects. That kind of responsibility clearly differs from the kind that we have when we see how our place in the biological world is interwoven with the place of other creatures, and that comes from the demise of the idea that humans have a special status in the universe. But in both cases, there is a sense of responsibility that arises from the human grasp of the world as a whole.[9] If we grasp higher beings in the universe whose authority we can recognize, that gives us a sense of duty *to* such a being or beings to fulfill our responsibilities in the world. The first great idea made human beings aware of the duties that come with status. Beings with duties are beings with dignity. As I argued in the preceding section, the human place in the universe is the ground of dignity in one of the senses of dignity. It is the dignity of persons.

Ever since the second great idea became dominant, the focus of human dignity has shifted from the dignity that accompanies our place in the universe to the dignity that inheres in the power of self-governance, something to which each self has a natural right. A right is protective of the self. It is a claim against others. Rights impose duties on other persons because the requirements they impose are mandatory. The shift in the

foundation of morality that occurred with the rise of autonomy in the Enlightenment made the idea of an individual right
the focus of moral discourse. Morality became both stronger
in force and narrower in scope. The violation of a right is a
serious violation of justice, requiring the intervention of the
law, unlike acts that are wrong because they violate classical
virtues like kindness, compassion, loyalty, temperance, courage, truthfulness, and practical wisdom. Vices that Aquinas
called capital sins, like pride and greed, also do not pertain
to anybody's rights, at least not in their original formulations.
The virtues are the qualities that persons need in order to live
harmoniously in well-functioning communities; they are not
public demands. Unsurprisingly, virtues and vices faded from
theoretical ethics at the same time as ethics began to focus on
rights. We entered an era focused on the demands of the self
rather than the well-being of persons.

Basic human rights are moral rights. Examples commonly
given in the literature on rights include the right to life, freedom of speech and religion, and protection from enslavement
or torture—rights that exist independently of whether they
are found in the laws of a particular country, and that are so
important that they ought to be protected by law. If they are
not protected by law, there is something wrong with the law.
Other rights are given by the laws of a certain place and can
justifiably vary from place to place. The right to absentee vot-
ing is an example. The connection between a right and the law
tied moral and political theory together from the Enlighten-
ment through at least the end of the twentieth century,[10] and
there was less and less distinction between public morality and
the law.

The historical origin of the idea of a right is contentious.
It did not become dominant until the modern period, but the
idea of basic human rights is arguably implicit in medieval

natural law theory. In Catholic social thought, Jacques Maritain (1943) defended the idea of human rights by reference to the objective standards of the natural law, an impressive effort to incorporate the moral insight of the importance of rights with a worldview grounded in the first great idea. Maritain's contribution to the drafting of the Universal Declaration of Human Rights in 1948 demonstrated one of the ways in which modern moral thought need not be interpreted as conflicting with premodern moral theory, and the fact that the document was adopted by the United Nations General Assembly without a single dissenting vote underscored the fact that the language of rights can be accepted by people from many different cultures with many different worldviews, and certainly not all of them were dominated in their thinking by the second great idea.

Whether or not the moral framework of natural law can ground a theory of human rights, the story of the adoption of the concept of a right is more closely associated with the rejection of natural law and its replacement by social contract theory and a very different idea of the place of a human being in the universe.[11] Thomas Hobbes was a pivotal figure in the move from the first to the second great idea in political theory. Hobbes gave up the idea that a person's place in the universe gives them dignity, and maintained that human beings have no value apart from a social contract. Hobbes (1994) makes that explicit: "The value or worth of a man, is as of all other things, his price, that is to say, so much as he would be given for the use of his power; and therefore is not absolute, but a thing dependent on the need and judgment of another. . . . The public worth of a man, which is the value set on him by the commonwealth, is that which men commonly call DIGNITY" (*Leviathan* 1.10.16–18). Hobbes follows up four chapters later with his famous redefinition of a natural law: "A Law of

Nature (*lex naturalis*) is a precept or general rule, found out by reason, by which a man is forbidden to do that which is destructive of his life or taketh away the means of preserving the same, and to omit that by which he thinketh it may be best preserved" (*Leviathan* 1.14.2).

From the idea of natural law as a right or liberty to pre-serve oneself, Hobbes deduces the rational need to lay down part of one's natural right and to form a social contract under the authority of a sovereign. In John Locke's version of the social contract, the scope of natural rights was expanded to the rights of life, liberty, and property, and that eventually made social contract theory the leading theory of political legitimacy. Locke's well-known influence on the foundational principles of the American Republic continues in contemporary debates about the relationships among government, religion, and the individual.

Since the focus on rights tends to narrow the scope of morality, sometimes the only duties recognized in moral and political discourse are the duties that are the complement of rights. I have a duty to respect your rights, and you have a duty to respect mine. Acts that are vicious but not a violation of a right have faded into the domain of the private sphere where it is commonly believed that religion dwells. Public moral dis-cussion is about the law, and the law is about rights. That leads to the idea that any part of morality that does not involve a violation of a law is one's personal business. However, there are many kinds of acts that harm the community but do not fit well into the category of rights, either because they are less serious than the violation of a human right, or because there is no set of individual victims. I have mentioned acts against virtues such as kindness, compassion, courage, and trust-worthiness as examples of the former. Acts that harm our common physical environment or jeopardize the fairness of the economy are examples of the latter. Structural inequities would also be in that category.

When public discourse is conducted almost entirely in the language of rights, it threatens the ability of democracies to function well because rights cannot be balanced the way we can balance priorities grounded in commonly accepted values. The point of a right is that it is the sort of thing that does not need to be balanced because it is an immunity. It is meant to protect the morally fundamental category of the self. People know that, and then use rights language when they move into adversarial mode and wish to make claims against others rather than to request that a certain value be more highly promoted in the public sphere. For this reason, rights language raises the stakes for both sides in a policy debate. It creates a dialectical situation in which one side claims a right and the other side denies it. There is very little, if any, room for compromise or a softening of positions because the language of rights is inherently combative. But claiming a right gives a person a rhetorical advantage because it puts the other side on the defensive, and that is one of the reasons the use of rights language has exploded in recent decades. Strong language gets attention; it also can produce pushback, making compromise harder.

The reduction of all of morality to rights has meant that the scope of rights claims has expanded over time to include anything that could be put into the category of treating people and animals well, while retaining the strong force of an obligation and its correlative right. Originally the scope of human rights was limited to a few of the most important rights, such as Locke's list of rights to life, liberty, and property, but over time, the range of rights claimed by their proponents kept increasing. Recently, the scope of rights claims has expanded to include such things as the right to information held by public authorities, the right to marry a person of the same sex, the right to be addressed by one's preferred pronoun, the right to keep one's movements and one's passwords secret, and the right to die, not to mention the rights of animals.[12]

A good example of the way that rights language has affected a public policy issue is abortion. Before the 1960s, laws against abortion protected fetal life, but generally without explicit mention of a fetus's right to life. The laws expressed a set of values, but it would not have been natural to express those values in the language of rights, which are demands. Rather, abortion was perceived as antithetical to a way of looking at the world and the place of parents and children in the world that made parental responsibilities vital. When this view weakened in the 1960s, there was a move to liberalize abortion laws in a number of states in the United States. Daniel K. Williams (2016) argues in his detailed book on the early history of the American pro-life movement that the movement was originally led by New Deal Democrats who saw the abortion issue as a civil rights matter in which they were defending the inalienable right to life of a defenseless minority—the unborn fetus. The other side called themselves "pro-choice," focusing on protecting a woman's autonomy in making decisions that directly affect her body. From the beginning, then, the abortion debate took the form of a claim to a right and a denial of the claim. Significantly, the labeling eventually changed when the "pro-choice" side took the offensive, becoming advocates for "abortion rights." The pro-choice movement went from a stand of "Leave the decision to the woman since the fetus's rights are not being violated if she has an abortion," to "A woman has a right to an abortion." The point of the pro-choice stance was that *she* is not blameworthy if she has an abortion. The point of the abortion rights stance is that it is blameworthy for *somebody else* not to give her the means to have an abortion, and the logic of that claim led within a few decades to the demand for public funding for abortions.[13]

The impassioned, adversarial nature of rights language makes it more difficult for people to come to agreement about abortion. People who find abortion morally problematic may hesitate to say that a fetus has an inviolable right to life, and people who believe that abortion should sometimes be permitted are often hesitant to talk about a woman's abortion rights. But there is widespread agreement that the human fetus is valuable, and that the mother's life with her plan for her future is also valuable. Both lives also have value to other persons. Public focus on these values is difficult because the values are complex and do not reduce to slogans, but discussion of them can lower the heat of the arguments about abortion and more closely express the thinking of the many people who have never been sold on the idea that morality reduces to a set of rights.[14] Even after the four-hundred-year ascendance of the idea of autonomy and the restructuring of morality into a competition of the moral claims of selves, the idea that one's identity and its value is partly determined by one's proper place in the community—and, in fact, in the universe—still drives the moral thinking of many people.

Another example of the way the language of rights can distort a moral issue and make agreement more difficult is the current conflict over racist or degrading speech. When virtue is ignored, there is nothing to do in public debate except fight over rights. The virtue of civility had almost no public presence until recently. Without it, there is just the right of free speech. Civility is a virtue that governs the expression of respect for the dignity of other persons in speech and behavior. Civility is a virtue, and incivility is a vice. Incivility detracts from the flourishing of both the uncivil person and others in the community. From the virtue perspective, to observe that someone has a "right" to be nasty, offensive, or racist is beside the point. We do not want to live in a community of uncivil people, and we are harming ourselves if we are uncivil. But when the virtue of civility is not part of public consciousness, there is nothing to debate except the clash between the right to free speech and the right not to be offended. People have noticed this problem and civility is now getting attention, although it has sometimes been politicized, which does not help resolve the conflict. More promising is the approach of Amy Olberding (2019) who draws from early Chinese philosophers in treating civility as fundamental to our social nature and linked to the respect that all humans deserve even in, and perhaps especially in, the midst of social turmoil. There are other virtues that are not politically divisive and which ought to be common ground for persons of all political viewpoints: compassion, generosity, tolerance, trustworthiness, honesty, sympathy, open-mindedness. These virtues are critical for a well-functioning society, but they are not enforceable in law. Their importance lies in their potential for increasing social harmony and getting agreement.

Alasdair MacIntyre (1991) objects to the rhetoric of rights in a way that is relevant to the rise of the second great idea. He observes that the concept of a right is grounded in the idea of an autonomous individual apart from a teleological conception of a human being in a social reality, and he says that the idea of universal rights implies a kind of individualism that ignores traditions and the communities that give a person an identity.[15] I think there is something right in MacIntyre's position. I agree that the idea of a right presupposes the intrinsic value of an autonomous individual, and I have suggested that that was a consequence of the collapse of the first great idea in Western thought. Human beings lost faith in their ability to grasp their place in nature and a social order to which they were responsible, and which gave them a vision of the good life to which they could aspire. The first great idea had given them a sense of duty to other human beings and to their communities and ultimately to God. When that was lost, what was left was each person's independently determined view of the good for herself and her right to pursue it.

Although MacIntyre has a point, I think that we must acknowledge that the widespread recognition of human rights gave individuals protections that they did not have before the rise of the second great idea. When the good of an individual is subsumed under the good of the community, certain individuals suffer an attack on their ability to govern their lives. Even worse, the history of totalitarianism in the twentieth century reveals what can happen when the so-called good of the community turns out to be the delusions of a charismatic monster. I doubt that we would want to live in a world in which rights such as those listed in the Universal Declaration were not recognized, but we think *that* because the second great idea has a prominent place in our thinking. Before it did, many of those rights were consciously and flagrantly violated. The problem as I see it, then, is not the rise of the second great idea, but the collapse of the first.

The second great idea led to the demise of virtue, but it is also responsible for the modern recognition of the worth of the disabled, and MacIntyre has written persuasively about that in *Dependent Rational Animals* (1999). Because of the second great idea, we see the value in each individual person's subjectivity, whether or not that person has to the fullest the properties that we value in humans as a species. An individual person might not make any contributions to civic life, and when evaluated from the point of view of the good of the community, could be seen as replaceable by someone who has normal human abilities. From the standpoint of the world as a whole, the disabled can seem superfluous. If there is any doubt about that, it is enough to consider the history of the treatment of persons with intellectual, physical, or psychiatric disabilities. It is only in recent history that there has been a recognition of them as full persons with dignity. I am not suggesting that a moral framework arising from the second great idea is the only theoretical defense of the rights of the disabled. L'Arche communities in which disabled persons live in small homelike communities with volunteers are examples of the recognition of the dignity of the mentally disabled on Christian grounds rather than on anything explicitly based on the second great idea. That is another example of the fact that a moral framework based on the first great idea and one based on the second need not conflict.

The idea of virtue disappeared when morality changed with the rise of autonomy and the focus on rights. But virtue has made a comeback in philosophical ethics and epistemology, and it is beginning to spread to the general culture. In the last few decades many books have been written about virtue and the individual virtues, including books for a general readership, and more recently virtue has become a subject for work in psychology and education theory.[16] I have already mentioned that the virtue of civility, ignored for generations, is reappearing in public discourse, if not in practice, and there have also been a number of initiatives and public engagement on the virtue of humility.[17] Character education has been popular for a generation and has become increasingly sophisticated and rigorous in assessment.[18] The explosion of studies on intellectual virtue has also led to the development of curricular materials on intellectual virtues and the teaching of intellectual virtue in schools.[19]

In summary, rights language became dominant because the rise of the second great idea was accompanied by the rise of the idea of autonomy. The recognition of human rights is one of the most important advances ever achieved in human civilization, but the language of rights is now ubiquitous. Both sides of almost every public policy dispute use the rhetoric of rights because it is stronger, but it heightens emotion and makes consensus more difficult. The language of rights has expanded to include most of what a sizable number of us believe is included in a well-functioning society. Everything is a demand made by somebody against the rest of society. That makes the need to resolve disagreement harder at the same time as the need is greater.

## The Two Great Ideas and Political Conflicts

The two great ideas form part of the deep conceptual background of clashes of moral perspective in the public domain. People frequently refer to autonomy in the sense of self-governance to support positions on a wide range of issues from abortion to environmental ethics to gun ownership to economic policies to the right to say what one wants, and I have argued that the centrality of autonomy is connected with the second great idea and the focus on the self. But that does not mean that the rejection of arguments from autonomy have a direct connection with a worldview grounded in the first great idea. The history of that idea is much longer and more geographically extensive than the history of the second great idea. In American society it has many more forms than does the second idea, and it appears in the moral positions of Christians from several continents, in different forms in the views of immigrants from Islamic and Buddhist and Hindu countries, and in still other forms in the views of Native Americans. There are also secular forms that have the worldview of the Christian Middle Ages in their historical background and retain the moral ideal of "love they neighbor," but without God.

I have summarized the moral point of view of the legacy of the first great idea as harmony with the world. Granted, not many moral issues have anything to do with parts of the world far removed from our own, although I will mention shortly an imaginary example of a moral issue in which the entire physical universe is involved. Still, the many moral frameworks behind the opposition to the centrality of autonomy have something in common. They all value harmony with something larger than oneself over the value of autonomy. From the earliest times when people began to live together in cities, large groups of people learned to act together as one. For most of human history this was primarily accomplished by force, but Western theism gave people the sense that we are all united under God's law. When morality became secularized in the modern period, the morality of the first great idea evolved into the value of social harmony or harmony with the natural environment rather than harmony with the universe as a whole. With whom do we identify? It can be a religious or racial or ethnic group, a gender, a nation, all living creatures on earth, and in fiction, the human race against imaginary extraterrestrial invaders. Moral issues arising from these identities are among the most powerful issues of our time, and they force us to examine how narrowly we define the self and how the self is related to personhood as a category that all humans share. I have proposed that a necessary condition for the value of self-governance is the uniqueness of individual subjectivity, but self-governance would not be valuable were it not for its connection with rationality, a property that we have in common. Each of us is both a person and a self, so there should not be a conflict between our rationality and our subjectivity, harmony and autonomy, virtues and rights. But there is lots of conflict in the rhetoric deriving from these values.

A revealing example of the interplay between the two great ideas in the public domain is environmental ethics. For most of the history of the West, morality was thought to involve only the relationship of human beings to each other or to God. Until the 1960s or 1970s there was little attention to the moral relationship of human beings to the nonhuman parts of nature, although the idea had been around for at least a century.[20] In any case, the idea that it is morally wrong to pollute or destroy parts of the natural environment or to consume large quantities of the earth's resources is relatively new in the history of ethics, at least in the West. An interesting question is whether the argument that these things are wrong rests solely on the claim that they harm future human beings, or instead that nature itself has intrinsic value. A famous thought experiment to test that value is the "last-man argument."[21] We imagine that all human beings are dead except one man who is about to breathe his last. The last man alive decides that since humans are about to go extinct, he might as well destroy every living thing on earth—every plant, every animal, every organism of any kind. Imagine that he has the technology to accomplish that and proceeds to do so. Has he done anything wrong? If human beings are the only things that matter morally, he has not. But that does not seem right, and Sylvan and many others conclude that nature must have value independent of human interests, and it is a value that ought to be respected.

An early environmental concern was population growth, sometimes focused on its effect on human lives and sometimes focused on its effect on nature as a whole. There was the worry that the population could outstrip the capacity of the earth to support ecological systems, and there was also the worry that population growth would lead to widespread famine. The latter has a much stronger grip on the moral imagination than the effect on the nonhuman environment, and we see the same thing with moral concerns about climate change. Climate change has an effect on the planet apart from human life, but what has made global climate change a crisis is its projected effect on humans. Either way, it is imperative that we get consensus, but so far that has not happened. What is hard to deny, however, is that a morality centered on individual autonomy is not up to the task.[22] Rights language also seems insufficient to guide debate. To speak of the rights of future generations, much less the rights of nature, is a stretch, but to those who believe that morality reduces to a set of rights, there is no other option. It appears to me that the response to climate change is an example of the need to frame some moral issues by reference to virtues and responsibilities rather than to rights.[23]

One of the most interesting examples of the first great idea in modern discourse is the deep ecology movement, developed in the 1970s by the Norwegian philosopher Arne Naess. Naess (1973) argued that people should conceptualize themselves and the world in relational terms, so that caring for nature is an extension of caring for themselves. Deep ecology was not just the communitarian idea of relatedness to a group of other humans with which we live our everyday lives; it was an expansion of the idea of human identity to include all of nature. It was an explicit rejection of an ethical outlook derived from the second great idea, and it came as close to a reintroduction of the first great idea as we have seen in many decades, perhaps centuries. The relational view of human identity may not strike most contemporary readers as remarkable because it has now become familiar, but it was dramatic and inspirational a half century ago.

Concern for ecological wholes is a modern version of the first great idea. It is obviously less ambitious than the first great idea's reach to the whole of reality, and it usually extends no farther than a concern for planet earth, which is already much farther than our moral imaginations usually reach, but we might consider what the reaction would be if we found out that our actions were destroying life on other planets. We could even postulate an extreme variation of the "last-man argument" in which the last human on earth had the capacity to destroy the entire physical universe. If we hesitate to rule out such an action, we must think that it is at least possible that we have a responsibility to keep the universe in existence. Caring for creation usually means caring for a very small part of creation, but the logic of doing so might commit us to caring for as much of creation as it is within our power to affect. Our power already reaches farther than we can collectively manage, so it is undoubtedly a good thing that it does not reach beyond the earth, but reflecting upon what it would mean if we did have that power reveals something about how we think of morality and its implications for public policy.

The politics of climate change is an example of an issue where the "liberal" position is one of rejection of the second great idea and comes close to the moral viewpoint of the first, and the "conservative" position is one that embraces the second great idea. But on other issues the difference between the perspective of the second great idea and one more closely associated with the first does not line up with the liberal/conservative division in the same way. In the last section we looked at the issues of abortion and civility in speech. The pro-life, anti-abortion position is connected with a moral viewpoint grounded in the first great idea and the pro-abortion-rights position is closely connected with autonomy and the second great idea, but the pro-life position is almost always considered conservative and the pro-abortion-rights position liberal. In contrast, the value of protecting demeaning and uncivil speech is generally associated with conservatives and the political Right, but it is based on autonomy and the second great idea, whereas the criticism of such speech as undermining respect for persons is usually associated with a liberal or left-leaning stance.

The conservative position on gun rights is also based on autonomy, including (in some quarters) concern for the autonomy of the individual against the government. Advocates of gun control argue that the harmful effect of guns on the community outweighs the autonomy of gun owners to choose their own means of defense or recreation. Gun control advocacy does not have any direct connection to the first great idea, but it clearly puts social harmony and peace ahead of the autonomy of gun owners.

I am writing this while there is a public debate going on about the best response to the COVID-19 pandemic. The individual right to free movement did not receive much attention in civic discourse until it was threatened by a virus that significantly endangers public health and safety, leading to a situation in which the autonomy of the individual, which grounds the right to move freely, clashes with the communal need to prevent the spread of the virus. It appears that the objections to shutdown orders on the grounds of individual liberty are coming mostly from the political Right, whereas the strongest defenders of the restrictive measures are coming from the political Left.

In contrast, the value of autonomy in the choice of sexual partnerships, including marriage, is generally interpreted as liberal, and the rejection of autonomy as a sufficient defense for gay marriage is usually treated as conservative. The right to self-governance in any matters that do not directly harm other persons is a central tenet of political liberalism, and ever since the widespread availability of contraceptives separated sex from childbearing, liberals have treated sexual and romantic relationships as no concern to anybody except those involved in the relationship.

The politics of group identity is particularly interesting because it goes both ways politically and reveals the evolution of the idea of the self in the later twentieth century.

Francis Fukuyama (2018) argues that what underlies identity politics is a sense of dignity in which people demand
respect as members of subgroups of society rather than as
human beings, groups whose status has been overlooked
or denigrated.[24] If Fukuyama is right, Blacks, Hispanics,
women, immigrants, members of the LGBTQ community,
and others have turned political attention to a sense of dignity that is not the same as the dignity we have as human
persons, the first sense of dignity, but it is not quite the second sense of dignity either. It is not the dignity that inheres
in one's uniqueness, although it is the dignity of identity.
One of the most interesting aspects of the way the idea of the
self has developed in recent decades is that the self is often
defined in part by features that are not unique to us alone,
but which are not found in the majority of the human population either.[25] Respect is due to each of us not only because
we have the superior value that accompanies being human,
and not only because each of us is irreplaceable as a unique
self, but because we have features that we value as part of
ourselves but which are ignored and sometimes disparaged
by others. There is a lot of space between being a member of
the community of humans and being a member of a community of one. Religious identity, ethnic identity, gender identity, and national identity are all examples of group identities
that have psychological and emotional power. Few of us feel
any emotional power in being a member of the only known
rational species, and as important as it is to be a unique self,
we need the identification with others who share some of
our most valued features, particularly if those features are
not valued by many others.

Some of the group identities I have mentioned are associated with left-wing politics, although national identity is not.
For many people national identity means downgrading the

importance of identity arising from race or gender, as well as downgrading the importance of the dignity of our common humanity. There are also group identities that have the same kind of psychological basis as gender, race, and ethnic identities but are right-wing in political orientation. Recently, lower-income white workers and residents of rural communities have felt that cultural change has left their identities behind, and they are producing another kind of identity politics. The issue of our identity group or groups has different answers depending upon how we each think the self is related to the world. We may all prize our common rationality, but our rationality is usually not under attack. People often feel that aspects of their subjectivity are either ignored or disparaged. But whatever one thinks of the way identities are used in politics, it is hard to deny that linking with people who share these aspects of one's subjectivity and urging appreciation for them from those who do not share them is required by the second form of dignity I discussed in the first section— the dignity of the self.

I suggest, then, that the difference between the conservative and liberal sides of public policy issues does not line up with positions on the importance of autonomy and its roots in the second great idea. The second great idea on abortion is liberal, whereas the second great idea on the environment is conservative. The second great idea on gun rights is conservative. The second great idea on gay marriage is liberal. The second great idea on the protection of offensive speech is conservative. The second great idea on the response to COVID-19 is conservative. Identity politics is usually liberal and is closer to the second great idea in the sense of dignity it champions, but the idea of national identity and anti-immigration is conservative, yet it also glorifies group identity. I think that it would help us a lot if we had clarity in identifying the values underlying the disagreements on these issues because they have much deeper roots than the ordinary political divisions imply.

James Davison Hunter (1991) brought the term "culture wars" into the common vocabulary thirty years ago. Hunter explored the virulently opposing sides on social issues, tracing the passion of these divisions to a clash of different moral frameworks. Hunter called the two polarized groups "the orthodox" and "the progressive." In the decades since Hunter wrote that book, the differences have become even more intense. People are increasingly alienated from people on the other side. Both sides manipulate the political process for their own ends. Their deepest loyalty is to something they perceive as more important than political and cultural institutions and even more important than the rule of law: morality is on their side.

But how should we label the sides? The terms "progressive" and "orthodox" are helpful in identifying a set of moral/political positions, but they do not tell us what is supposed to justify each position over the opposing side. If you know someone is "progressive," you can make a good guess at what they believe about a range of issues, and similarly if you are told they are "orthodox." But if you are on one side and they are on the other, you will want to find the place in their conceptual framework at which they begin to diverge from yours. That place might make them close to you on other issues. If the value of autonomy is that place, you might be able to figure out why it leads you to agree about a certain issue before you move to the issue about which you disagree. The same point applies to the value of harmony with the social or natural world.

A problem with calling one side "progressive" is that what counts as progressive is continuously changing. Sometimes the change that is called progressive moves in the direction of the first great idea (e.g., climate change, civility); sometimes it changes in the direction of the second (e.g., sexual morality, racial identity). Sometimes the "progressive" person is opposed to a social change (e.g., the proliferation of guns, the rise of nationalism). The terms "progressive" and "orthodox" are still useful and people often recognize themselves as falling under one of those labels; my concern is that those labels are not helpful in calling attention to the source of the differences in perspective that form the background of what appears to be irresolvable moral and political disputes. It is helpful when people can identify the value they find foundational in supporting their position as autonomy, or alternatively, something like social harmony or community with God or nature. That permits us to focus on the source of these values and their respective justifications. It is one of the theses of this book that underlying the deep conflict in moral frameworks is a difference in perspective on the relative importance of one's own mind versus the world. Although the two great ideas do not conflict, the idea that the world precedes the mind and the idea that the mind precedes the world do conflict, and we have seen a history of that conflict. But it is doubtful that very many people embrace one view over the other wholeheartedly, and so almost all of us relate to both the value of harmony and the value of autonomy. For that reason, it is very unlikely that our disputes cannot be resolved. I will return to that problem in chapter 6.

The first great idea focuses the mind on the world as a whole. A human being is a person, defined by its place in the universe and grounded in the property of rationality. The dominant moral value is harmony with the world, a world governed by reason. In order to achieve harmony, individuals need the virtues. The second great idea focuses the mind on the mind. A human being is a self, defined by its property of subjectivity. The dominant moral value is autonomy in the sense of self-governance. Moral discourse focuses on rights rather than virtues. Duties are the complement of rights, not the responsibilities of individuals to the whole.

I have argued that these different ways of conceptualizing mind and world affect a host of practical problems, but few of us think exclusively one way rather than the other. That is because the history of *both* ideas is in us, whether we consciously study that history or not. I proposed that when we disagree about significant moral issues, we can backtrack to find the values that underlie the disagreement, and hopefully, we do not always have to backtrack as far as the values of harmony or autonomy to find commonality. But sometimes we might need to backtrack even further than harmony and autonomy, and when we do so, I think we will find the two great ideas. When we do that, we will need to admit that we have not done a very good job of putting the ideas together.

---

### A Vignette of the Utopian Self: Ralph Waldo Emerson

Ralph Waldo Emerson opens his riveting essay "Self-Reliance" (1982) with the words *"Ne te quaesiveris extra,"* a peculiarly constructed line from a satire by Persius, which can be translated "Do not seek yourself outside yourself," or "Do not seek for things (answers, opinions) outside yourself" (which you will notice is not quite the same thing). Emerson uses it to great effect in his stirring call to trust yourself. Do not look without; look within you for whatever it is that you seek—your ideas, views, values. The self-sufficient person is closest to God because self-existence is the attribute of the Supreme Cause, and the degree to which self-existence enters into the human soul, or any lower form, is the degree to which that form

"Standing on the bare ground, — my head bathed by the blithe air, & uplifted into infinite space, — all mean egotism vanishes. I become a transparent Eyeball."

Nature, p. 13.

FIGURE 8. Emerson originated the idea of a transparent eyeball that is absorbent rather than reflective. He proposed it as a tool for a person to become one with nature. Christopher Pearse Cranch illustrations of the New Philosophy (MS Am 1506), Houghton Library, Harvard University.

is good. Although Emerson does not mention Plato, he seems to accept the Platonic view that reality and goodness coincide. The more something is real, the more it is good (191).

Emerson announces that the secret fact of the world is that the soul *becomes*, and that fact forever degrades the past and makes tradition useless (190). Morality unfolds within the self, not from the so-called wisdom of past ages. Each soul expresses a unique divine idea. It follows that to be true to yourself, you must be a nonconformist. Society is in a conspiracy to make us imitate others, but we must have the courage to resist. "Imitation is suicide," Emerson proclaims, but "God will not have his work made manifest by cowards" (176).

The mystery is that what you find within you is the divine light of the world. "When we discern justice, when we discern truth, we do nothing of ourselves, but allow a passage to its beams" (187). The law is in our own person: "The relations of the soul to the divine spirit are so pure that it is profane to seek to interpose helps. It must be that when God speaketh he should communicate, not one thing, but all things; should fill the world with his voice; should scatter forth light, nature, time, souls, from the centre of the present thought; and new date and new create the whole" (188). In Emerson's view, then, there is within your self a direct opening to the original miracle of creation.

To Emerson, the spirit within *is* the spirit without. It is the force from which all things have their common origin (187). Trust the second great idea, and you get the first for free.

# CHAPTER FIVE

# Can We Grasp All of Reality?

## Can the Eye See Itself?

Someday people like us will know much more than we do about who and what we are, and how each of our unique minds fits into the whole of the universe we inhabit. It may take hundreds of years for us to make noticeable progress, but the progress will be ours—yours and mine, because it will be done by human beings who know the history of human thought about these questions, and that includes whatever progress we are making now.

We may not know much about the mind, but we know that it exists, or to speak more cautiously, we are aware, and we are *aware of being aware*. We call whatever it is that is aware the mind. We are also aware that we are aware *of* something that is not the thing that is aware, and we call it the world. The idea that a human mind can grasp the whole world is a natural extension of the idea that a human mind can grasp part of the world, and the idea that a human mind can grasp itself is a natural extension of the idea that the mind is aware of itself being aware.[1] The two great ideas are different ideas, but they arise out of natural powers of the same mind.

Iain McGilchrist (2009) has told the history of Western culture in terms of the different functions of the left and right hemispheres of the brain, and he argues that the dominance of the left over the right hemisphere in certain eras of history, including our own, has left us with an enormous problem because the left hemisphere makes a poor master. The left hemisphere is detail-oriented, divides and analyzes, and is the source of language. The right hemisphere is oriented towards the whole, has a more immediate relationship with the physical environment and our own bodies, and is the source of music and nonverbal communication. According to McGilchrist, both hemispheres give us knowledge, but they operate in different ways. I think that the fact that some of what we grasp cannot be expressed in language is an important insight, connected with the way we grasp and express subjectivity. I do not know whether McGilchrist is correct in his thesis, but I think that his point about the neglect of the right hemisphere in the contemporary West is related to the neglect of subjectivity. It is possible, then, that the tension between our grasp of subjectivity and our grasp of the objective world has a biological basis. In any case, we have not done a very impressive job of connecting them in our conceptions of reality as a whole. The way we think of the objective world almost always dominates.

I said at the beginning of this book that I do not assume that the two greatest ideas are true, but they express deep aspirations of the human spirit, and neither one of them has ever disappeared. We have already seen some of the limitations on the two great ideas. Subjectivity is a problem for the first great idea because an idea is not an idea of the whole of reality if it leaves out subjectivity. The first great idea drives us to try to combine the subjective and objective worlds, and I will discuss two general approaches to doing so in the next two sections. We have also seen limitations on the idea that the mind can grasp all of itself. If it cannot, that is also a problem for the first great idea because any way in which we cannot grasp all of our own mind is also a way in which we cannot grasp all of reality since our mind is part of reality. Some limitations on the ability of the mind to grasp itself might be solvable, but in this section, I want to address a problem that suggests that the mind cannot grasp all of itself in principle. Since antiquity this problem has appealed to the imagination by its expression in a particularly vivid question: "Can the eye see itself?"

It is possible that when the mind turns inward, there is no boundary. Perhaps it can engage in a continuous movement of introspection, going deeper and deeper and never reaching its innermost place. If that is what happens when the mind grasps itself, there is no inner boundary, but the mind never grasps all of itself because it can always go farther.

Another possibility is that when the mind delves more and more deeply into itself, it encounters something farthest from itself—God, or the ground of the universe. An example of this idea appears in Augustine's *Confessions*, where he addresses God in the course of an extended reflection on the power of his memory:

What am I to do now, O my true Life, my God? I shall mount beyond this my power of memory, I shall mount beyond it, to come to You, O lovely Light. What have You to say to me? In my ascent by the mind to You who abide above me, I shall mount up beyond that power of mine called memory, longing to attain to touch You at the point where that contact is possible and to cleave to You at the point where it is possible to cleave. (10.17)

Augustine seems to be suggesting that his mind is in a sense open on the inside. There is no bounded core. If he is right about that, something outside can be bridged from inside the mind, not only on its outer perceptual surface. But it is very difficult to conceptualize a mind without a bounded core because it is tempting to think of the mind on the model of a three-dimensional physical object like a sphere, where the center of the object is farthest from what is outside the object. But many profound thinkers say that that is not what happens. They say that when they try to remove the contents of the mind there is still something there, something that unites them with the external world more intimately than when they are united through the operation of the senses. That sounds like the mind has a hole in the middle through which it can enter something outside of it, like a donut. Or there might be no boundary, no difference between the inside and the outside, like a Klein bottle. That suggests a model of something with more than three dimensions. But it is unlikely that it has dimensions at all, so our models fail.

There is another kind of limit on the mind's grasp of itself that may be unbridgeable if there is always a difference between the thing that is grasping and the thing that is grasped, and that is the limit I want to discuss in this section. When we introspect, what is doing the introspection? What is it Augustine is using when he penetrates his memory and beyond? Augustine says: "I cannot totally grasp all that I am. Thus the mind is not large enough to contain itself; but where can that part of it be which it does not contain? Is it outside itself and not within: How can it not contain itself: [How can there be any of itself that is not *in* itself?]" (*Confessions* 10.8). This passage suggests that something is always hidden from the mind, as Wittgenstein implies when he asserts: "The eye cannot see itself" (*Tractatus* 5.633). Is part of the mind blocked from our grasp because part of it is always doing the grasping?[2]

We are not forced to that conclusion. To see why not, let us look again at the line, "The eye cannot see itself." Wittgenstein was not the first to think of this question. Plato uses it in *First Alcibiades*.[3] In that dialogue Socrates gets Alcibiades to agree that the eye cannot see itself directly, but it sees itself when it is reflected in the eye of another, and he argues that the eye sees itself best when it is reflected in what it resembles, in particular, in the place in the other's eye that generates what is most excellent in the eye, namely sight. Similarly, he says, if a soul is to know itself, it must look at another soul and especially at that part of a soul where the excellence of a soul—wisdom, is generated. That part of the soul resembles God, and "anyone who looks at it and knows everything divine, God and understanding, would also most know himself" (132E–133c). So the soul knows itself best by knowing what generates its most excellent property, something it best grasps by seeing it in another soul. Think how far that is from the modern idea that there is something in your soul that distinguishes it from other souls and makes it essentially your individual soul.

Augustine also addresses the idea that the eye cannot see itself, but with a different conclusion:

> Why, then, when it knows other minds, does it not know itself, since *nothing can possibly be more present to itself than itself*? But if, as other eyes are more known to the eyes of the body, than those eyes are to themselves; then let it not seek itself, because it never will find itself. For eyes can never see themselves except in looking-glasses; and it cannot be supposed in any way that anything of that kind can be applied also to the contemplation of incorporeal

things, so that the mind should know itself, as it were, in a looking-glass. (*De Trinitate* 10.3.5 [italics added])

What is true of the eye is not true of the mind, according to Augustine, because the mind does not know itself the way it knows corporeal objects, through images. The mind knows itself by being continuously present to itself. Why, then, does it need to seek itself?

The answer is that it associates itself with the images of corporeal things that it loves, and it cannot separate itself from those images. That means that when it is bidden to become acquainted with itself, it should seek itself within by withdrawing from itself the images that have been added.

> Therefore let the mind become acquainted with itself, and not seek itself as if it were absent; but fix upon itself the act of [voluntary] attention, by which it was wandering among other things, and let it think of itself. So it will see that at no time did it ever not love itself, at no time did it ever not know itself; but by loving another thing together with itself it has confounded itself with it, and in some sense has grown one with it. And so, while it embraces diverse things, as though they were one, it has come to think those things to be one which are diverse. (*De Trinitate* 10.8.11)

Augustine does not refer to the subject/object distinction that became so important in the modern period, but he implies something close to that distinction in his solution to the puzzle of how we can be told "Know thyself" when we already know the self. Awareness of oneself as the subject of experience is different from the awareness of anything as an object, including oneself. Returning to the passage I quoted from the *Confessions*, Augustine says that the mind cannot "contain itself," and asks himself, "Is it outside itself and not within? How can it not contain itself? How can there be any of itself that is not in itself?" (*Confessions* 10.8) The answer lies in rejecting the idea that awareness is always *of* an object. Augustine says repeatedly that nothing is more present to the mind than itself (e.g., *De Trinitate* 10.3.5), but that is not the same as saying that the mind contains itself as it would contain an object of perception or thought. The soul is not like the eye. It does not need to see itself the way our eye sees another eye and can only see itself in a reflection. The soul is aware of being the seer but not as an object seen. The presence of the *I* in awareness is something we always carry with us, and that is why Augustine insists that nothing is more present to the mind than itself. It is when we "wander among other things" that the *I* gets covered up by objects.

It was another thirteen hundred years before the post-Kantian philosopher J. G. Fichte presented arguments that support Augustine's position, but as far as I can tell, without mentioning Augustine. Fichte made self-consciousness the focus of a systematic account of subjectivity, the first philosopher in Western history to do so. He argued that unless we possessed an immediate acquaintance with ourselves, we would never know that when we turn our attention to ourselves (or part of ourselves) in reflection, what we are aware of is *our own self* rather than an external object (see Henrich 1982, 21). Furthermore, unless the self were always acquainted with itself, there would be no explanation for what would motivate the self to turn to itself in self-reflection. There would have to be some awareness of a self in order to know that there is something there to look at and where to look (20).[4]

These two points are simple but profoundly important, in my opinion. They support Augustine's claim that the mind is always present to itself, and they do so by revealing a problem in thinking of awareness as essentially divided between a subject and an object. Dieter Henrich (1982) says that the idea of a look that sees itself fascinated Fichte until the end of his life. He thought of it as the foundational problem of philosophy and kept trying to express it in increasingly clear terms. Henrich says he found evidence for that in a manuscript that was probably written in the summer of 1812. In it, Fichte writes: "August 18. Holidays. In a dream a task shone forth quite brightly to me. Seeing is an eye seeing itself." Fichte goes on to say that the relationship of the self to itself is knowledge that is manifest to itself, and it can be used to explain everything else except its own existence (33).

I will return to the idea that self-consciousness can be used to explain our grasp of everything else, but for my purposes here I want to say that I find the conclusion that the self has an awareness of itself as subject convincing, but many philosophers side with David Hume who argued in the eighteenth century that when he inspected his mind, he found no impression of a self.[5] He found impressions of sense like the impression of red, and impressions of reflection like the impression of sadness, as well as their copies in ideas, but no impression of a self underlying them, and since there is no idea without a preceding impression, no idea of a self either. The self is a string of mental states. To use the eye metaphor again, for Hume there is no eye because the eye cannot be perceived, and we have no grounds for believing that anything exists that cannot be perceived.

Hume's claim is based on introspective experience, and we might use guided experience to test Hume's claim. There are popular techniques of mindfulness meditation in which the meditator practices becoming aware of her mental states as an observer, not as the bearer of the states. In one variation you begin by observing your sensations of breathing, which is easy; then observing sounds, also easy; then observing your thoughts passing by as if they are clouds in the sky. Observing thoughts, we are gently told, is not controlling them, just letting them be and noticing them as they pass by and fade away. In my experience this is hard because thoughts, even when spontaneous, immediately become the object of reflective control. Even harder is observing one's pain. The exercise gets us to practice noticing the separation of the observing self from the mental states *of* the self, a technique that presumably only works if the observing self *is* separate from the experiential mental states, contrary to Hume. But more advanced meditators say that as meditation progresses, the self disappears. Contemporary mindfulness meditation arises from Buddhism and is an example in the popular culture of the influence of Asian thought on Western views of the mind.[6] I have no opinion on the Buddhist experience of no-self, but it is fair to say that the more we can relate the wisdom of Eastern thought to Western philosophy and empirical science in an investigation of the mind, the better will be our prospects for understanding our minds. The issue of what we experience when we go deep into our minds is at the heart of the relation between the two great ideas. That experience shapes the ideas and can change them.

The mind that grasps the world is the same as the mind that grasps itself. If the mind is like an eye, it is an eye turned on itself as well as outside itself, and we have noticed some problems with the analogy. Tibetan Buddhism uses a different analogy for the relation between the mind and itself. The Yogacara concept of *svasamvedana* (reflexive awareness) is compared to a lamp in a dark room that illuminates itself while it is illuminating objects in the room. We might pursue this analogy further. When the lamp illuminates itself, the difference between the lamp and the objects in the room is clear. But what is the lamp other than the power to shed light?

We can imagine a lamp that changes itself by adding features to itself as it lights up the room. The core of the lamp is the source of its power of illumination, and I think that Augustine is right that that is always illuminated when it illuminates anything else. But as Augustine says in the passage above, the images the mind illuminates distort the mind's image of itself, hiding the core of the mind where there are no images. We often talk about a self-image or self-concept that changes over time. The benign interpretation of that phenomenon is that we get to create a self by accruing images to the core of our illumination. Perhaps the self is just what we make it to be, as Sartre insisted in the mid-twentieth century. But surely Augustine is right that there are many ways the self can hide, damage, or distort itself in this process. And there are many ways in which the self can be distorted by external forces, one of the most important themes of twentieth-century thought. Augustine's assessment of the mind's power to grasp itself was ultimately optimistic, but that power has been under attack for at least a century, and those attacks are immediately before our minds. The ascent of the second great idea in the Renaissance was experienced as empowering. Unsurprisingly, its descent has been experienced as enfeebling. The challenge posed by whether the eye can see itself is only one skirmish in the attack on the second great idea. The deeper challenge is to combine the eye's power to see itself with the eye's power to see the world.

## Reality from the Inside Out

The division between the objective and subjective worlds solidified in the modern period, and that made the task of grasping the whole world harder. Before the discovery of the self, leaving out the self in conceptions of the world as a whole was unintentional. After the self was discovered, the self was left out of many conceptions of the world by design. That was not the only response, and in the strand of philosophy coming out of nineteenth-century idealism and twentieth-century phenomenology, the subjective/objective division was resisted and subjectivity was given a central place, as it was in the work of Fichte. In this section I want to look at the response in analytic philosophy, where the dominant reaction to the rise of the second great idea was to create a greater separation between self and world, producing a dichotomy between the subjective and the objective. Subjectivity is missing from most versions of the first idea since the beginning of the early modern period because of the view that the world of objects is primary. Subjectivity was left out on purpose. That made it hard to resist the temptation to divide our minds and to divide our domains of discourse into the hard sciences and the arts and humanities. Anything that has to do with subjectivity was assigned to the arts and humanities, and those fields that originated with the first great idea but were receptive to subjectivity, like philosophy and theology, were forced to choose sides.

In the next two sections I will make the common assumption that the world as a whole is divided between the objective world—the world without subjectivity in it, and our own unique subjectivity. If we start with that division, how could we then try to combine the two into a view of reality as a whole? I can think of two general ways we might go about constructing such a view. One way would be to start with a conception of the objective world and then attempt to add our subjectivity to it. The starting conception could be ancient or modern or something completely new.[7] But it would have to be a conception of the entire objective world. We might think of this approach as building a conception of reality from the outside in.

An alternative approach would be to build up a conception of the world from the inside out. Start with the contents of one's own mind and use the power of that mind to gradually construct a conception of the objective world, and then a larger conception of the whole that includes both one's own mind and the objective world in it. In other words, try to build the idea of the one universe by starting with one's own subjective consciousness.

The outside-in approach would attempt to insert the self as subject into a previous conception of the world that contains minds, including one's own mind, as objects. That approach would be an attempt to *add* one's unique subjectivity to an objective conception of the world in a sequence. The inside-out approach, in contrast, would work by *subtracting* what is unique in one's consciousness from a conception of the world arising from the contents of one's mind (presumably with other people), and then attempting to relate them to each other. Since subjectivity is an entirely different order of reality than the objective world, the challenge for the outside-in approach is to smuggle a different kind of reality into an objective conception. The inside-out approach has the same problem in reverse. It seems as if it would take a magic trick to get an objective order of reality out of the subjective states of one's mind and relate them to each other. How can we get objectivity out of subjectivity?

Let us begin with the inside-out approach. We are driven to form an inside-out view of the world because we know that the world is not the world as we view it from inside our heads, and we know that from within our own heads. The task would be to start from a basis in our own subjectivity, and then attempt to construct out of it a conception of all of reality, objective as well as subjective. Can we stretch our mind and keep stretching it until we get to the social world, then the natural world, and then put them together in the totality of what exists?

To address this question, we need to say more about the difference between subjectivity and the objective world. The difference between the subjective and the objective is not the same as the difference between the mental and the physical, and it is not the same as the difference between what is inside the self and what is outside the self. We know that it is not the same as the difference between the mental and the physical because Berkeley's idealism does not solve the problem of putting subjectivity and objectivity together. Berkeley elegantly argued that a number of philosophical problems are solved if nothing exists but ideas in minds. The mystery of how a mind can grasp an external object made of alien stuff—matter— is solved if grasping the world is grasping ideas. There is no matter. Nothing exists independent of minds. Ordinary objects like chairs and stars are bundles of ideas, and God is an infinite spirit who causes these ideas in us. So grasping our mind is grasping a chunk of the world. By moving the external world into minds, it would seem that Berkeley made the problem of putting the two great ideas together easier, but actually he did not because subjectivity is not the same thing as mental stuff. The problem of the relation between the subjective and the objective is not a problem about what mind and world are made out of, but of the way to combine the unique perspective of a subject with the one universe we inhabit.

The difference between the subjective and the objective also is not the same as the difference between what is inside our mind and what is outside of it. We can treat our own mental states as objects and the mental states of others as subjects. Self-reflection is the former; intersubjectivity is the latter. The objective is what is subject-independent. There are objective features of our mental states and subjective features of the mental states of others. The problem in constructing a view of the objective world starting from one's own mind is to get to something subject-independent by starting with what is subject-dependent.

If objectivity is the point at which uniqueness disappears, the only way to figure out where that point is is with other people. Bernard Williams sees this point immediately in the book I mentioned in chapter 3. Williams proposes an inside-out approach to obtaining what he calls "the absolute conception of reality," a project he traces back to Descartes, and which continues in the construction of the scientific representation of the world. He endorses the view (from Charles Peirce) that the objective material world would be the point of convergence of a community of inquirers relating the contents of their minds to each other's. By comparing our consciousness with the consciousness of others, such a community would be able to create a representation of the world without consciousness, then the conception could be extended to include consciousness, and extended again to relate the various points of view of conscious individuals comprehensibly to each other and to the world without consciousness. When that is done, Williams says, we would have the absolute conception of reality (2005, 229–230), and that would be a version of the first great idea.

The inside-out project of attaining a comprehensive conception of the world need not make science central, but the project described by Williams does. It is one in which natural science is the driver of the first great idea, the principal competitor to theism and Buddhism in the contemporary world of ideas. Naturalism in its simplest version is the doctrine of physicalism, the belief that nothing exists but physical entities, where what is meant by physical entities are the entities posited by physics.[8] There are no nonphysical beings. Individual human consciousness is composed of repeatable features of consciousness. Consciousness reduces to living matter and living matter reduces to nonliving matter. All human culture, including the practices of morality, religion, art, literature, philosophy, and indeed science comprises an enormous number of combinations of the basic elements of the physical world as they have developed over billions of years. Where do we find a creation of music, a feeling of reverence, an act of love? We find it in the physical world and the interactions of its parts. We may call something by a nonphysical name and our concepts for entities in the world may be mental concepts, but they still refer to physical entities and their properties.[9]

Part of the explanation for the attraction of the physicalist version of the first great idea is the magnificent progress of empirical science since the seventeenth century in describing and permitting us to manipulate the physical world. Physics rapidly expanded to encompass chemistry, biology, and at least part of psychology. Physics has seemed to swallow up all the other empirical sciences while it has permitted the development of technologies of mind-boggling scope, affecting almost every aspect of our practical lives. There have been some obstacles to reducing biology to physics (e.g., Harre 2006), and there have also been objections to reducing psychology to biology (e.g., Hardcastle 1999), but the plan is elegantly simple and has a lot of support in spite of obstacles.

Why would we think that what is discoverable by the empirical methods of physics exhausts reality? To say so is not an empirical statement; it is not a deliverance of physics, but of metaphysics. Another piece of the explanation was mentioned in chapter 3. It is the belief that physics is a closed causal system. Anything outside the world of physics does not interact in any way with what is inside the physical world as physics describes it. But that is not enough to get the worldview of physicalism either. What is really driving the view is the desire for a unified grasp of all of reality and the belief, or at least hope, that at last it is within our reach. Physics indisputably unifies a vast portion of the real world, so if physics is a closed causal system, and there is something outside of it, our knowledge of reality is not unified. Or to put the point more carefully, reality is not unified around the phenomena of physics and its laws, although it could be unified from another direction. The first great idea is not a scientific idea, but science is capable of expressing it.

The major competitor for the status of primary expression of the first great idea in the West is theism, and it is unsurprising that theism declined in intellectual culture at the same time as science rose in prestige. In the opinion of many, theistic philosophers have not succeeded in providing a unified metaphysical picture that folds the deliverances of science into theism. Few people believe that theism is incompatible with science, but the more serious challenge is that the result of combining theism with empirical science gives us a divided view of reality.[10] The reason is that physics does not *need* theism to explain physical phenomena, so if theism is added to a comprehensive picture of reality that includes empirical science, the result is a picture that seems to have two disconnected realms of existence: the realm of physical reality, on one side, and the realm of consciousness, intention, value, and God, on the other.

It is interesting to note, though, that the picture is not divided because of theism, but because of the way modern philosophy redefined mind and nature. In ancient Greek and medieval philosophy, mind was a part of nature and mind included consciousness. Descartes wanted to separate what empirical science studies from what it does not, so he removed mind from nature and made nature a mechanistic object following scientific laws, while mind became identified with the conscious substance. The division between mind and nature created the problem of explaining how mind is connected to the body and the physical world of which the body is a part. If everything that exists is connected, mind and matter must be united, but modern science and modern philosophy divided them, and then created the problem of how to reunify them.

In the twentieth century, the story of the attempt to unify consciousness and physical reality took a fascinating turn. The new empirical science needed an epistemological justification, and Descartes, Locke, and the idealists eagerly provided it. Descartes's reliance on the existence of God as a link between his certainty about his conscious states and his justification for belief in the external world was not popular among scientists and philosophers who wanted to leave God out of it, but the empiricism of Locke was historically important, and Berkeley's empiricist idealism was influential as late as the 1930s to 1950s in the logical positivists' idea that the physical world is a construction out of sense data. The bolster to modern science given by modern philosophy was grounded in the second great idea, according to which we construct our idea of the physical world out of perceptions in the mind. But at some point in the later twentieth century, the scientific worldview switched from one arising from the primacy of the contents of the mind to one in which the mind became secondary to the product of empirical investigation.[11] Once the product of empirical science took over the status of a theory of everything, the problem of explaining the existence of consciousness in the closed causal system of physics meant that the conscious mind became a puzzle. Daniel Dennett's (1991) reaction is to kick it away. There is no mind in the sense of mind that is expressed in the second great idea. In a curious historical twist, the rise of the second great idea supported the advancement of science, but once science reached the point where some philosophers realized it could be used to explain all of reality provided that consciousness does not exist, at least one philosopher concluded that consciousness does not exist.[12] Of course, not all adherents of naturalism agree with Dennett, but then we are back to the problem that the existence of consciousness needs to be explained in a worldview in which everything that exists is either reducible to physical phenomena or, in more moderate versions, anchored and explained by such phenomena.

It is worth pausing for a moment to review the global context of the puzzle of consciousness and to look at how differently many non-Western cultures understand the place of mind in nature, and how differently they understand the function of empirical observation in their epistemologies. The divorce of consciousness from nature made by Descartes and continuing into contemporary thought in the West is unusual in world history. The idea that the story of all of reality makes something without consciousness basic and consciousness derivative from it is even rarer. For instance, in Native American cultures consciousness pervades nature at its core. Bruce Wilshire (2000, 17) argues that it is difficult to know how to even comment on Native articulations of the natural world since they completely lack the division of the physical from the psychical that Western thought takes for granted. In the Native American understanding of the world, there are thoughts and feelings in the world from its origin. There is a whole invisible realm of being that is constantly changing. There is a form of evolution, but it is not evolution from inert matter to consciousness. Rather, it is a constant unfolding of incipient forces in nature. The idea of causal laws independent of conscious choice is missing, and the objects of observation are completely different than in the West. We see the same lack of separation of physical nature and natural or supernatural consciousness in traditional religions in Asia and Africa.[13]

The contrast with non-Western viewpoints reveals the way that the modern view of nature and scientific empiricism are codependent. For the contemporary Westerner, nature is defined as whatever it is that science investigates, so the metaphysics of nature and the epistemology of science are mutually reinforcing. But that leads to the pressing need to explain where consciousness comes from. In the early modern period, the attempt to add consciousness to nature took the form of the connection between primary and secondary qualities, as we saw in chapter 3. In the later twentieth century it took the form of contemporary physicalism in which all human culture can be explained by our evolutionary origin, which is in turn explained by the origin of life in a universe of physical particles.

Many people have argued that consciousness can never be reduced to purely physical phenomena because consciousness is an entirely different kind of reality than the physical. The desire to accept the reduction arises from the idea that all of reality must be explainable by a single story linking together everything that exists. It can be argued that if only one kind of thing exists, then it is mind, not matter, because we are more certain of the existence of our own conscious minds than of the existence of a world of physical objects. That is why idealism was always easier to defend in post-Cartesian philosophy dominated by the second great idea.

At present, idealism is not treated as seriously as naturalism and theism in a battle for preeminence in expressing the first great idea. In that battle, the arguments have turned to how we can ground the ordinary facts of our conscious experience. That would include the facts that we think, we feel, we remember, we have beliefs, we act. It includes the fact that many of our beliefs are true and that many of our perceptions and memories are accurate. We take for granted that there is a world outside our minds and that we are in touch with it. Even if the ordinary facts do not go as far as the two great ideas, we think at least that much. We all use the concepts of a belief, an act, a memory, a perception, a feeling, and a world. Hans-Georg Gadamer (1981, 12) maintains that it is the task of philosophy to bring these ordinary concepts to the reflective level, and it is philosophy that is concerned with the whole. If so, our question is this: What metaphysical framework best explains these ordinary facts of our experience?

Alvin Plantinga (1993, chap. 12; 2011) has argued that the reduction of consciousness to physical phenomena with evolution cannot explain facts like these. In particular, he argues that the probability that our belief-forming faculties reliably produce truth on the hypothesis of naturalism is either low or inscrutable. Natural selection rewards adaptive behavior and penalizes maladaptive behavior, but it does not care what you believe. According to naturalism in the popular form of physicalism, a belief as a component of a physical system would be something like an event in the nervous system, presumably including a certain number of neurons firing at a particular rate and intensity, and related in a certain way to each other and to other structures in the body—sense organs, muscles, et cetera—and changing over time in response to other events in the body. These neuronal events cause movements in the organism, and in that sense a belief would cause the behavior that is the material of evolution. But a belief is experienced by the believer as having content—for example, *There is a storm coming*, or *Naturalism is a good theory*. However, under the assumption of naturalism, it is difficult to see how a belief can have any causal influence on our behavior by virtue of its content. The content is irrelevant to the neurophysiological properties of the belief, and so the content of a belief has no effect on behavior. But it is the content that has truth value.

Plantinga says, "The neurophysiological properties seem to have swept the field when it comes to the causation of behavior; there seems to be no way in which content can get its foot in the door. But, of course, it is having the *content* it does that determines the truth or falsehood of a belief; a belief is true just if the proposition which constitutes its content is true. Under this scenario, therefore, the content of a belief would be *invisible* to evolution" (Plantinga 2000, 234).

Plantinga's conclusion is that we have no reason to think that on the hypothesis of naturalism, our beliefs are reliably true. Naturalism is inconsistent with the ordinary facts that Gadamer says a theory should bring to the reflective level. The consequence is that it undermines itself. The naturalist's own theory tells her that since naturalism predicts that the processes that produced her beliefs, including the belief in naturalism, are unrelated to the truth of the belief, she has no reason to believe the theory.[14] Either the belief is likely false, or the probability of its truth cannot be determined. Either way, the assumption of naturalism should undermine confidence in its truth.[15]

Plantinga's argument can be extended. If naturalism undermines confidence that our beliefs accurately represent the world outside of us, it undermines every psychic state that purports to relate our consciousness to the world. On the hypothesis of naturalism, there is no reason to think that the content of any psychic state puts us in touch with external reality. Just as we would have no basis for thinking that our beliefs are reliably true on that hypothesis since the content of a belief has no evolutionary bite, we would have no basis for thinking that our memories are accurate or our perceptual states are veridical. The theory predicts that the neurological correlates of those states generate fitness-enhancing behavior in the long run, but they predict nothing about the conscious content of our perceptual and memory states. The experiential content of seeing blue, or seeing a square shape, or hearing a roaring sound, or calling to mind a past idea, or recalling an image of a friend—nothing about the content of any of these experiences has any effect on evolutionary processes, and the same point applies to any conscious experience whatsoever, including the experience of making observations in controlled experiments. Only the neural correlates do so. According to naturalism, consciousness is superfluous. Dennett implicitly recognizes that when he denies that it exists.

I think that what this dispute reveals is deep disagreement about the reality and importance of subjective consciousness. The resistance to naturalism expressed by Plantinga puts fundamental importance on the content of conscious states, whereas the naturalistic perspective puts fundamental importance on the exciting prospect of getting a complete conception of the world out of the data of physics. The battle is between two different ways of expressing the first great idea.

We do not know yet whether the inside-out approach to forming a conception of the world can succeed. In one way the task has become easier; and in another way, harder. It looks easier as we get more and more evidence of the connection between the physical world and human consciousness, but as physics progresses, the objective world has become even more detached from human subjective experience. The distinction between primary and secondary qualities drove a wedge between the mind and the world in the seventeenth century, but since Descartes and Locke maintained that our ideas of primary qualities are like the qualities in the objects, their view partly connected our experience to the world. But as empirical science progressed, human experience became more detached from the world as revealed by physics. Physics has taught us that the qualities originally identified as primary—motion, solidity, spatial shape—are nothing like qualities of the objects in the external world, and since the advent of quantum physics, theories of the physical world are fundamentally constituted in mathematical terms. The world is nothing like the world we experience, even in its most basic properties. Our experience is an accidental feature of that world as it evolved over millions of years. In that respect, the project of explaining subjectivity in a naturalistic conception of reality has become harder.

## Reality from the Outside In

Instead of attempting to form a conception of reality by starting from inside our heads, we could try the reverse approach. Can we start with a conception of the total objective world and add our subjectivity to it? We know that we are not the only beings in the universe with subjectivity, but our own subjectivity has been given central importance for hundreds of years. A necessary condition for including the subjectivity of every conscious being in a total conception of the universe is the capacity to include our own. If that cannot be done, the task of forming a total conception of the universe is hopeless.

When we devise conceptions of the world as a whole, we strip it down to the bare bones to make it comprehensible. The bare bones could be the fundamental particles of physics, or Leibniz's monads, or Plato's Forms impressed on the physical world, or Pythagoras's numbers. They could be the Tao, or Spinoza's substance, or creation out of a divine mind. They could be Aristotle's combination of matter and form. The simplest version of the first great idea is always the idea of the bare bones. We start with the simple and make it more complex, but never so complex that we cannot maintain our grasp of the whole.

The problem is that if subjectivity is missing from the bare-bones view of the objective world, it is still missing when flesh is put on the bones and the conception becomes more complex. We can always put more objects into our conceptions, adding greater and greater detail, and when we do so we reveal the amazing human ability to see patterns and to imbed phenomena of every kind into those patterns. But patterns are the world with subjectivity stripped out of it. That is, in fact, the *point* of seeing and reproducing patterns. The Pythagoreans with their magnificent numerical relations raised the urge to see patterns to the highest level ever achieved. Pythagoreanism is wonderful because it is so elegantly simple. But simplicity is a virtue only so long as it includes directions for inserting the complex phenomena of the world into the simple framework.

To illustrate this point, I find it useful to think of a conception of the world on the analogy of an ordinary map of a city neighborhood. The map displays the pattern of the streets and landmarks—the bare bones of the neighborhood. But if the map is good, it is designed in such a way that the viewer can figure out where items left off the map fit onto it. You see that this building is not on the map, but you can tell where it would be placed if the map had more detail. The same thing applies to all the other buildings, smaller streets and alleys, signs, trees, light posts. The map succeeds at depicting a portion of the objective world that can be expanded to include more and more objects.[16] But it intentionally leaves something out—the *experience* of that portion of the world. It leaves out what you feel when you walk around the neighborhood. It leaves out the fragrance of the delphiniums in the sidewalk flower stall, the sound of the traffic going by, the feel of the breeze on your skin. But these may be the reasons why you are taking the walk in the first place. Life is subjectivity, but we grasp an objective world.

Let me repeat that there would be nothing wrong with leaving subjectivity off the map of the world so long as we can see where it would fit on the map. We can figure out where our house would appear on the map if it included more features, and if the map is digitized, it often allows us to zoom in and reveal more and more objects—the house, the yard and trees around it, the driveway and sidewalk. But no matter how hard we look, no matter how much we enlarge our map of the world, we never find subjectivity. We never get the fragrance of flowers or the feeling of the breeze by zooming into the map. That makes it very hard to see how the outside-in approach to putting subjectivity into a previous objective conception can succeed.

This brings us back to the problem discussed in the first section of this chapter, the idea that the grasping mind is threatening to both the two great ideas. When the mind grasps the universe, the idea of the grasping mind is not *in* that idea of the universe. Likewise, the idea of the grasping mind is not in the idea of the mind that is the object of the grasp. The commonsense answer to the question "Can the eye see itself?" is no, but as we have seen, Augustine's reaction was to reject the analogy between the mind and the eye. The mind is always present to itself, he says, but not as an object. An object is separated from the subject, but the mind is never separated from itself, although he said that it can be clouded over with the accumulation of images.

The separation of the subject from the objective conception of reality gives us an important condition for the truth of the two great ideas. Both ideas are doomed if their truth requires getting what we like to call a "view" of reality. The problem with a view is that it is always from a different position than that which it is a view *of.* The viewer is not in the view except distorted into a nonviewer.[17] That makes it a challenge to see how any outside-in approach to getting a conception of all reality can get off the ground. The same point applies to a conception of the self. So long as a conception is an object in the self, the self is never in it. It cannot include the whole self in it. In particular, it cannot include the self's forming of that conception.

A related problem, and a vexation to philosophers since antiquity, is that the mind's attempt to be aware of all of itself seems to lead to an infinite regress. Imagine that you have a conception of your mind. Call it conception A. The idea of your forming conception A cannot be *in* conception A, but you can form another conception that includes both conception A and the idea of your forming conception A. Call that conception B. The idea of your forming conception B cannot be in conception B, but you can form a conception C that includes both conception B and the idea of your forming conception B. This process goes on to an infinite series of conceptions, and since the sequence can never be completed, it seems to follow that the process of forming a conception of your whole mind can never be completed. That is not a happy result for the second great idea. It is not a happy result for the first great idea either, because the same regress threatens when the mind attempts to form a conception of all of reality. Under the assumption that a "view" or a "conception" separates subject from object, no view or conception can succeed at including the subject. The conclusion seems to be that either the two great ideas are false, or else their truth does not require the possibility of forming a conception in which all of reality is contained *in* the conception.

This is a general problem for any theory of mind that interprets consciousness as having a dual aspect—subject and object; in particular, the representational theory of mind. The regress arises out of the representational theory of the mind together with the idea that the subject of consciousness is *something*, a part of reality. In the first section we looked at Augustine's idea that self-consciousness must be nonrepresentational and the reemergence of that idea in the work of Fichte, who made the systematic account of subjectivity as nonrepresentational self-awareness the key to an entire metaphysics.[18] The nonrepresentational view continued into the twentieth century, and we see it in Sartre, who declared: "[T]here is no infinite regress here, since a consciousness has no need at all of a reflecting [higher-order] consciousness in order to be conscious of itself. It simply does not posit itself as an object" (1960, 45).

Aristotle did not use a representational theory, and he avoided the regress. Since the mind is only the capacity to receive forms, the act of perceiving or grasping is identical to what the mind perceives or grasps (*De Anima* 425b26–30). The regress does not even start on Aristotle's view.[19] That is why Aristotle was able to say that the mind is in a way all existing things, a position discussed in chapter 2. One conclusion we could draw from this line of thought is that a condition for the truth of the two great ideas is that the representational theory of the mind is false. In this respect Aristotle's looks better than most modern philosophies because his view avoids the problems with the subject/object dichotomy, and it also permits us to pursue the idea that grasping is union.

What should we say about the regress and related puzzles? One response is just to say "So what?" Maybe the regress means that the mind can never grasp itself in its entirety, and therefore the mind cannot grasp all of reality in its totality, but perhaps it can come close enough to satisfy us. If the only problem with the representational theory of mind is that the act of grasping is left out of the object of the grasp, that might be something we can live with. It means that there is always something we cannot grasp even though we know that it exists. That might strike us as a fascinating philosophical fact, not a problem in need of a solution.

In any case, I am not convinced that the outside-in approach is hopeless even if we retain the subject/object distinction and the representational theory of mind. What we need is a way to add ourselves as subjects into an objective conception of reality—not minds in general, but our own unique minds. That is a requirement for any conception that leaves out subjectivity, so it is as much a requirement for Aristotle and Aquinas as for Locke and Descartes. If the subjectivity of the grasping mind is something over and above a human mind as objectively described, the subject needs to be added to a conception of objective reality. Minds as objects have always been included in versions of the first great idea from antiquity to the present. What we want is a way to put the mind as a subject into the same conception as one that includes that same mind as an object. We need a bridge between ourselves as subjects and ourselves as objects in a conception of all reality.

I would like to propose a temporally extended conception as a way to handle the problem of combining the subject with an objective conception of the world. Earlier I mentioned Fichte's argument that because you possess an immediate acquaintance with yourself, you know that when you turn your attention to yourself (or part of yourself) in reflection, what you are aware of is *yourself* rather than something else. When you recall an incident that occurred yesterday, for example, you know immediately that it is your memory, not the memory of someone else. Of course, you can make mistakes in your memory, but the mistakes are not about the bearer of the memory. Any time that you think about a past experience, belief, or feeling, you know that you are reflecting on something that existed in your own mind, and that is significant for this reason. When you turn your mental states into objects of reflection, you are aware that they are *the same states* you had as a subject. Since you can always "turn around," so to speak, and reflect about your subjective mental states as objects—and know that that is what you are doing, two important things follow: (1) you must always be aware of yourself as the subject of your experiences, and (2) you can turn your subjective experience into an object of thought if you want to. It is easy for us to turn a subjective state into an object. We do it all the time.

This does not yet tell us that when we turn our subjective state into an object, we can easily insert it into a previous objective conception of the world, but we have gotten past the most critical stumbling block to adding subjectivity to objectivity, which is how I know that the person I express as "I" and the objective person Linda Zagzebski are the same thing. This is the same problem we encountered in chapter 4 on the identity of the self and the person. My proposal above is intended to answer that question by linking a particular state of the *I* to an objective description of that state through memory. If we think that our subjectivity is attached to a certain place in the objective world—a certain objective being, we need a way to link them together in our own consciousness. I believe that Fichte's point can be used to help solve the problem of inserting our subjectivity into an objective conception of the world. The key is that we can think of a certain conscious state as an object and recognize it as the same one we previously experienced as a subject. We could not do that unless we are always aware of ourselves as the subject of an experience, as Augustine and Fichte maintained, and can then turn it into an object by reflecting on it. If we can do that, there is nothing in principle preventing us from continuing the task of putting that object into its place in a larger conception—a map, of objects.

Awareness of ourselves as subject and awareness of ourselves as object are two different things. We can express the self as subject and refer to the self as object, and they are importantly different. Whenever we say "I," we *express* the self, although we invite others to refer to it when they report what we have said. If I say, "I saw Jim yesterday," what I say will typically be reported by others as "She said that she saw Jim yesterday." My first-person pronoun is converted into a third-person pronoun. Our conventions have to permit a switch from the use of the grammatical "I" to the third-person "he" or "she," but the switch from my report as a subject to someone else's report of me as an object changes what I say, although they are about the same event.[20] I can also turn my experience of seeing into an object of reflection myself. I can think about it and comment about it or assess it, as when I say, "When I saw Jim yesterday, I forgot to tell him about the meeting." In this sentence I turn my previous subjective experience of seeing Jim into an object and treat it objectively as other people can. I can say that my previous state was mistaken or accurate or silly or funny or worth remembering. The mind moves in reflection from itself as subject to itself as object in order to govern itself.

We are able to identify the self that is the subject of experience with a person in an objective conception of the world because we have already learned the objective conception of ourselves and our place in the world. We have already learned a language of description and evaluation, and we apply that language to ourselves as well as to other persons, but we also know what it is like to be the person to whom those descriptions apply. And what it is like to be the person who falls under some set of descriptions is much fuller and richer than can be captured by any description, however precise, because a person is a self who experiences something unique.

We can use the idea that in reflection the mind moves from the self as subject to the person as object in order to put our subjectivity into an objective conception of the world. We cannot do it in one conscious moment, but we can do it in a sequence. I would like to propose a way to attach the subject to an objective conception in three steps.

Begin by forming your total objective conception of reality. Let's call that conception "TOC." Choose the version of TOC that you think is the best we have to date: a premodern view like that of Aristotle or Aquinas, a modern view like that of Descartes or Locke, a contemporary naturalistic view, or some other. There is no need to assume that the objective world is the physical world, although that is not ruled out. Aristotle's idea that the world is composed of matter and form is objective. Berkeley's idealist view of the world is objective. There are no restrictions except that it be total and leave out nothing but subjectivity.

None of us is acquainted with all the details of the world, of course, but that does not prevent us from forming a total conception because we know where each new object we encounter fits into our TOC. A TOC is total, not because it is inclusive of every object, but because every object has a place in it, and as we acquire knowledge of more objects, we know where to place them in a TOC. We will need to assume the best-case scenario in which your TOC includes the existence of minds as objects in the world and an objective description of their ability to form conceptions. It also has to include a conception of specific mental states as objects. To return to the analogy with a digital map, when we enlarge the map, we see enough detail to include individual mental states as those states would be objectively described. Conception TOC must include an objective conception of consciousness and an objective conception of your own consciousness, and you must be able to recognize it as such.

Second, turn your state of awareness of having a TOC into an object by reflecting on it. When you reflect upon your awareness of having a conception of the world, you turn your previous subjective state into an object just as you do when you reflect back on your previous mental state of seeing your friend Jim. You grasp the self that was the subject of your previous conception now as an object, and once it is an object, it can be imbedded in your conception TOC, just as you can integrate any object of your experience into that conception. When you turn your *awareness* of having conception TOC into an object of reflection, let us call it "OA." You now have conception TOC and conception OA, both of which are objective.

The third step is to fit conception OA into TOC, thereby giving TOC more detail. You do this all the time with other objects you encounter. You encounter trees, animals and humans, stars and sky, objects in a laboratory. When you observe a particular animal or tree or star and form a conception of it, you are capable of fitting that conception into your conception TOC, since TOC includes a conception of animals and trees and stars and (in the ideal case we are imagining) a description of particular differences among animals and trees and stars. You can add a conception of an individual animal to your conception TOC, and when you do so, you are giving TOC more detail, thereby making it more inclusive. Other people can have their conception TOC and add your conception of an individual animal. When you communicate that conception to them, they understand how to place the conception of that animal into their own TOC, and you will have helped them make their TOC more inclusive.

The same point applies to your body and to your mind. Other people can grasp TOC and OA. They can see your mind and its states as objects just as they see your body and its states as objects. When you think of your body as an object, you have no trouble taking what you know about human bodies and seeing your body as a particular one, one recognizable by others. In the same way, once you form a conception of your mind as an object, you can take your objective conception of minds in the world and see your mind as a particular one recognizable by others, and capable of being inserted into a total objective conception.

The key is that in reflection I see that my mind as an object is the same mind I experienced as a subject moments before.

The self as subject differs from the person as object in that the latter is a publicly accessible object and the former is not, but I grasp the identity of the self as subject and the same self as object through memory. The distinction between the subjective self and objective person arises from the nature of reflective consciousness and the self's ability to reflect upon itself in the same way that it can reflect upon external objects.[21]

It is your awareness of the identity of the subject of the previous conception and an object in the expanded conception that permits you to say that putting the conceptions together gives you a complete view of reality. It is a moving view of reality. There is a temporal gap between your awareness of your mental state as a subject and your awareness of it as an object. I describe it as "outside-in" because it starts with an objective conception of the whole and puts the subjective experience of having that objective conception into it. The mind has the power to do that because of its ability to reflect. Memory bridges the self as subject and as object.[22] We recognize ourselves as the object of our own reflection, so even though we cannot form a single representation of all of reality at a single moment, I am proposing that in principle we can do so in a sequence when a series of mental acts are combined.

The process I have described is a step in combining the two great ideas, provided that neither is the idea that the mind can grasp reality or itself *all at once*. But many conceptions are temporally extended in the mind, and the fact that a conception has temporal components does not prevent it from being a single conception. For instance, we can form a conception of causation by moving from the mental state of conceiving of a cause to the mental state of conceiving of an effect, linked together by whatever we call the causal relation. The grasp of complex conceptions is often temporally extended whether or not the object itself is spread out in time—the conception of a university, the conception of yesterday's football game, the conception of the banking system. Almost every conception of a complex object is grasped by our mind in a moving manner. The object need not move, but the mind moves in grasping it. Similarly, a temporally extended conception of all of reality could move from one mental state to another in memory, linked together by an awareness of the identity of the subject in the first mental state and an object in the second. If this works, memory would permit us to put our subjectivity into an objective view of the world.

The procedure I am describing depends upon the trustworthiness of our awareness of a current mental state and the memory of a very recently past mental state. These states are generally thought to be epistemically secure. My argument does not depend upon the trustworthiness of introspection and memory in general. The process I am describing requires only an awareness of a conception as it is occurring and the ability to recall it a moment later. Forming a TOC is, of course, exceedingly complicated, and we face enormous difficulties in doing so. We need a TOC with enough detail to include the objective person that I and others take myself to be, and I must be able to recognize it as the same thing I experience subjectively. The TOC must be capable of expansion to include the objective details of each mental state I have, and I must be able to recognize my mental state objectively described as identical to the subjective state I just had.[23] No one has accomplished that so far. The major burden is on the creation of the objective conception, not the task of adding one's own subjectivity to it. But under the assumption that we have a total objective conception and that there is an awareness of the self as subject, there is a way to insert the second into the first.

Let us return to the regress problem. That problem is that it appears that we cannot form a total conception of reality including our own state of having that conception in one conception. My solution to that problem is that a single conception need not be one that we grasp in a single moment. It can be a moving conception. Given the way we experience the world temporally, our conception of the world is already moving. We have a map of the world in our minds that is continuously expanding in detail as we encounter more and more objects and have more and more mental states. Of course, we are free to change our TOC at any time, and we may have to do so if we find that we cannot insert our mental state as object into the total conception we have. But I propose that the project of inserting our subjectivity into a total objective conception is solvable in principle.

But we still face a serious problem. Even if this approach succeeds at creating a conception of the world in which our own subjectivity is added to an objective conception, we are not finished. Obviously enough, one's own mind is not the only mind in the universe. Subjectivity is multiple, and the conception of the world as a whole needs to include multiple subjectivities. Even a bare-bones conception of the world must have a place for both your own mind and the conscious minds of every other being who possesses subjective consciousness, and there needs to be an explanation for those differences. Since a description of someone's subjective consciousness as an object misses what is distinctive about subjectivity, we need to add that person's consciousness as a subject to our total conception. Intersubjectivity is missing from both of the approaches to forming a total conception of reality I have investigated in this chapter. To form a conception of all reality, we need to explore intersubjectivity. In the next and final chapter, I will look at the critical need for a science of intersubjectivity, and the possibility that it might permit the idea of intersubjectivity to become a third great idea.

## A Vignette of the Person and the Self: "Borges and I"

It is a mystery how a person and a self can be the same thing if subjectivity is an entirely different order of reality than the objective world. Which one is more real? Which one is more important? Which one gets the last word? Jorge Luis Borges wrote a one-page piece of short fiction about this problem. I will quote the sentences at the beginning and the end of the work:

> It's Borges, the other one, that things happen to. I walk through Buenos Aires and I pause—mechanically now, perhaps—to gaze at the arch of an entryway and its inner door; news of Borges reaches me by mail, or I see his name on a list of academics or in some biographical dictionary. My taste runs to hourglasses, maps, eighteenth-century typefaces, etymologies, the taste of coffee, and the prose of Robert Louis Stevenson; Borges shares those preferences, but in a vain sort of way that turns them into the accoutrements of an actor. . . . I shall endure in Borges, not in myself (if, indeed, I am anybody at all), but I recognize myself less in his books than in many others', or in the tedious strumming of a guitar. Years ago I tried to free myself from him, and I moved on from the mythologies of the slums and outskirts of the city to games with time and infinity, but those games belong to Borges now, and I shall have to think up other things. So my life is a point-counterpoint, a kind of fugue, and a falling away—and everything ends up being lost to me, and everything falls into oblivion, or into the hands of the other man.
>
> I am not sure which one of us it is that's writing this page. (Borges 1998, 324)

Borges says: *I* am much more than Borges. It is lamentable that what I do keeps getting taken over by the person,

FIGURE 9. Borges and the self-portrait he drew after going blind. Emily Temple/Literary Hub.

Borges, the one with a place in the objective world. What I am either evaporates with each passing moment or endures in the person whom others can grasp but who feels nothing. I am the one who lives and dies, and if I am important, so is the entire subjective world—*you*, which also is an *I*, an *I* that moves around from self to self. We are all attached to an objective person, and when we interact with each other, we face the same problem of the difference between the self and the person, the *you* and the *he/she/they*. When we talk to someone, to whom are we talking? The *you* or the person with a certain name? Maybe Borges could have written another short work called "Gonzales and you."

This work of Borges is classified as fiction. Why isn't it imaginative philosophy? Possibly the answer is that it expresses the personality of Borges, and we might think, as Hegel remarked, that personality does not enter into the content of philosophy.* But I think we have seen many examples that indicate that Hegel is mistaken—including, perhaps, this book.

*Hegel makes this remark at the beginning of his *Lectures on the History of Philosophy* (Hegel 2020, 1). He says that that is one of the reasons why the history of philosophy differs from political history.

# CHAPTER SIX

# The Future:
# A Third Greatest Idea

## *Intersubjectivity*

The two great ideas express magnificent powers of the human mind, and they have been connected to enormous changes in human culture for almost three millennia. When the second great idea rose to supremacy, it created the modern world, and it permitted each mind to think of itself as a self with an inside world. But the idea that each self is unique could not have come from the second idea alone. It must have taken another idea to reveal the differences between the subjective world of one self and that of another. The idea is so important, it deserves to be the third greatest idea: *the human mind can grasp another mind.*

What is it like to be another person? Could we ever find out? People sometimes reveal themselves to us in intimate exchanges, and we think that we can grasp what it is like to have lived some portion of their lives and to have their attitudes, beliefs, feelings, hopes, values. We see how all the elements of their consciousness fit together in a coherent narrative. That is not to say that we always grasp others as well as we think, and even in the best case in which our consciousness matches someone else's very well, we are never really imagining what it is like to be that person because we never forget who we are, even in our most vivid imagining of their experience. When I imagine a feeling I do not currently have myself—say, being immersed in the depths of grief, I always remain one step removed from the grief since I am experiencing grief in imagination, and I always know that that is what it is. My own *I* is always behind my grasp of the other person for me, but not for her.

Is it possible to forget who I am for a while and think I am someone else? Could I get so absorbed in a movie that while watching it I think that I am the character? Probably not, but we would not want to go that far anyway since we want to expand our subjective reach, not substitute one limited subjective world for another. In any case, understanding another's point of view does not require a loss of one's own subjectivity. Sometimes we can see a path from our own past self to the self another person has become, even if we judge him immoral or irrational. It is common for us to call someone who differs from us too much in political or moral viewpoint "crazy," but when I call someone crazy, I am just attempting to excuse myself from making the effort to see why their view does in fact make sense in the context of a chain of experiences and reflections they have had. Almost everybody makes sense, even people who arouse our indignation. Moral indignation may be a great motivator for action, but it is a poor motivator for understanding the object of the indignation.

Intersubjective knowledge, or second-person knowledge, has not received anywhere near the degree of attention of first-person and third-person knowledge for most of the eras of Western history. Knowledge of one's own subjectivity and knowledge of the objective world have dominated, but in chapter 5 I argued that knowing one another's minds would fill an enormous theoretical gap in understanding the world. Even more urgently, there is a practical need for intersubjectivity because it may be our only hope for mitigating rancor in personal and political disagreements. Other subjectivities take up a huge amount of metaphysical space. We know that, but we prefer to think about our own subjectivity and the objective world, the part of the world that is the same for everybody. Perhaps we think that is easier.

The subjectivity of other conscious beings permeates the world outside our minds, and perhaps more revealing, the subjectivity of others permeates our own. The language in which we express our minds is the product of other minds. We have learned many of our emotions from other people. We have learned how to reflect upon our minds from other people. Since both of the two great ideas depend upon our ability to reflect, both ideas depend upon other minds. Once we notice that, we will naturally be led to investigate the idea that minds grasp minds besides their own.

It is even possible that we *cannot* grasp our own mind apart from other minds. In a famous argument, Wittgenstein claimed that it is incoherent to have a private language, one that refers to private mental states and is understandable only to the person who originated it.[1] That argument has the implication that language is essentially social, and arguably it implies that our access to our minds is social. If that is right, it would be impossible for the second great idea to be supreme; the third idea would be at least as fundamental. Since we have already seen what human culture looked like when the first great idea was the fundamental one, and what it looked like when the second great idea had that honor, what should we say about the third idea and whether it can rise to the level of the other two?

I have noted that the ideas of subjectivity and objectivity are contrastive. The objective world is not the whole world; it is the world with subjectivity stripped out of it. It is the public world—the world that human minds share, or in a more extreme version, the world unaffected by minds of any kind. On either interpretation, the objective world is contrasted with the many subjective worlds, or the worlds experienced by individual minds, each of which has a unique first-person perspective. I have said that the objective/subjective distinction differs from the distinction between physical stuff and mental stuff; Berkeley's idea that everything is mental stuff is a theory of the objective world. It also differs from the distinction between the world outside my mind and the world inside my mind; I can treat states in my mind as objects and states of other minds as subjects. Furthermore, the objective/subjective distinction must be distinguished from the difference between reality and appearance. The objective/subjective distinction is modern; the reality/appearance distinction goes back to the origin of philosophy. Subjectivity is not a mistake about the objective world. It is an entirely different order of reality than objective reality, but it is reality, not appearance or illusion or error. The subjective world is not an illusion about the objective world, although we can sometimes mistake the former for the latter, as Don Quixote does in a particularly humorous way. In chapter 3 we looked at Egginton's argument that Cervantes helped to invent the modern world with the idea of an objective reality that can be experienced differently by different people. He made us sympathize with Don Quixote's subjective world and his radical mistake in identifying it with the objective. It is significant that Don Quixote, for all his humorous lovability, is wrong. Mistakes like that have made it common to think of subjectivity as less real than objectivity. But there is a big difference between thinking that a wash bowl is a magical helmet, as Don Quixote does in a famous scene (Cervantes 2003, 390), and expressing one's own way of looking at a bowl of fruit in a still life painting, as many painters have done. All subjective worlds are real, and one of the most important things Cervantes did in *Don Quixote* was to give us a vivid and entertaining experience of the subjectivity of others. That leads to a question we have come up against repeatedly in this book: How is each subjective world connected to every other and to the objective world? In other words, how are all of them components of one universe?

A standard topic in introductory philosophy courses for decades was the so-called "problem of other minds," which takes the form of the question: "How can I know that other human beings have minds with consciousness similar to mine?" Notice that this problem takes for granted that the second great idea is fundamental. Our grasp of our own mind precedes our grasp of everything else. Our only access to other minds is through the same mechanisms that give us access to the physical world. Just as we put together the perceptual pieces in our minds to represent a world outside of us, we put together the same perceptual pieces to represent other minds. But if that is the case, it is a problem to attribute consciousness to certain objects that we call other humans and other conscious animals. With this approach, it is no wonder that other minds are opaque and we have to infer their consciousness by analogy with ourselves, but that is only the case if our philosophical method leaves us no choice. In contrast, when the first great idea dominated, people thought that their grasp of both their own mind and the minds of others was primarily through their grasp of the world as a whole, a world that contains minds. The discovery of subjectivity changed that.

It brought one's own mind to the forefront of philosophical awareness, and it simultaneously pushed other minds into the background. At the beginning of the modern period the minds of others got even less attention than in the premodern period when all minds were on a par. But the discovery of subjectivity means that both one's own subjectivity and the subjectivity of others need to be accounted for in a comprehensive conception of reality. The attempt to grasp other minds the way we grasp the objective world is problematic, but there are other options. What I am calling the third great idea might not be as great as the second, but we did not get the idea from the second, nor did we get it from the first.

Once the distinction between subjectivity and objectivity became ingrained in our conceptual framework, it left us with the task of attempting to relate them to each other, and it appeared that we had to choose between a view of reality rooted in our own limited subjectivity and a view of reality rooted in no subjectivity at all. In the preceding chapter we looked at problems in getting a view of the whole of reality out of either approach. Each approach has its own problems, but the most serious one is that both approaches ignore intersubjectivity; an enormous part of reality is left out.

An investigation of intersubjectivity was not begun in earnest in Western philosophy until early-twentieth-century phenomenology. By the mid-twentieth century, feminist philosophers were among the first to focus on the importance of empathy, one of the main forms of intersubjectivity.[2] The grasp of other people's standpoints became a theme in popular culture as well as in philosophy, and the conscious valuing of intersubjectivity is now everywhere. The communication of subjectivity has become an object of study in neuroscience with the exciting discovery of mirror neurons.[3] In psychology, there has been considerable research on the effects of empathy, both on the empathizer and on the target person.[4] Intersubjectivity is attempted by the news media in conveying points of view on public policy issues, and it is produced in varying degrees in our most common forms of entertainment—movies, television, and novels.[5] The development of empathy has become a goal in education (Mirra, 2018; Baehr, 2016), and it has been studied as an aid to the functioning of democracy (Morrell, 2010). Thousands of years before intersubjectivity became a critical topic for scientific and philosophical work, practices of deep meditation in Buddhism led people to the experience of dissolving the boundaries of self and others, and these practices are making their way into Western neuroscience (Varela et al., 2016). The paths into intersubjectivity have exploded and are starting to become interconnected.

There is evidence that our ability to grasp another mind is not derivative from our ability to grasp physical objects, nor is it derivative from our ability to grasp our own mind. Of course, everything we grasp is through the exercise of our own minds, but that does not mean that we grasp other minds through the grasp of our own. That depends upon how the imagination functions. In imagination we put ourselves into the mind of another person all the time. In empathy, we imaginatively project ourselves into the feelings of someone else, taking on those feelings as if we were in their place. We might not always do it very well, but we clearly succeed up to a point. I have read that in hunting cultures, trackers can learn to get inside the mind of the animal they are tracking, acquiring in imagination what the animal was thinking and feeling when it left its tracks, and if they can do so they are more likely to succeed in the hunt.[6] Most of us are not trackers, but we are used to doing the same thing with other humans. We can project ourselves into their train of thoughts, their beliefs, what they value and disvalue, their decisions, and their plans, as well as their emotions, sensations, and moods. I mentioned that we do this when we watch movies or read novels, and we do it in personal conversation. Even philosophers like me, whose time spent on abstract thought is well above average, nonetheless spend many hours of the day in interpersonal communication and other activities that are intended to grasp the subjectivity of others. We are all well practiced in intersubjectivity.

Some of the earliest work on intersubjectivity comes from phenomenology. Edmund Husserl was one of the most important philosophers of the first half of the twentieth century, primarily due to his many contributions to the study of consciousness and his novel way of connecting consciousness with the outside world. I have argued that the discovery of subjectivity split the first great idea into two. The world as a whole had to become the objective world plus the world of my subjectivity. But it must have been obvious that subjectivity is not limited to one's own mind. There is also the subjectivity of every other being who has subjective states. That split the first great idea again. The world as a whole, then, appears to have three parts: the objective world, my own subjective world, and every other subjective world. To grasp all of reality is to grasp all three parts. Generally, philosophers have not given equal attention to all three parts, but Husserl was one of the few who did. He made intersubjective experience fundamental to both our constitution of ourselves as subjects and our constitution of the objective world. This is an intriguing idea for an investigation of the way the third idea connects with the other two.

On the one side, Husserl maintained that consciousness of self and consciousness of others are inseparable. They are linked together in his phenomenological analysis of the body in its two-sidedness.[7] I have an interior experience of my body, but it also has an exterior public face that I can experience at the same time as my interior experience in the phenomenon of double-sensation. For instance, when my hand touches my other hand, my body is simultaneously touched and touching.[8] I experience myself as both subject and object. It is interesting to reflect about the difference between the experience of touching and the experience of being touched, and whether we could tell the difference without sight. Sight is the primary sense bridging our experience of ourselves from the inside with the outside for most philosophers in history, so it is interesting that Husserl focuses on touch.[9] The interplay between the interior and the exterior of my body allows me to recognize other embodied subjects and is a link between my awareness of my own subjectivity and intersubjectivity. Merleau-Ponty goes further, claiming that subjectivity is essentially embodied, which means that we experience ourselves as neither pure subject nor pure object, but the self's experience of subjectivity contains an anticipation of the other (Zahavi 2005, 159). I am aware of my subjectivity as having a side open to the world, and the access that others have to me allows me to access them.

Husserl and Merleau-Ponty are arguing that my subjectivity is not an exclusive first-person phenomenon limited to myself. The possibility of intersubjectivity is included in the experience of self. I recognize others as embodied subjects because I experience myself as an embodied subject with a public face. We live in a common world permeated with intersubjectivity. To say so is to ask modern philosophers to rethink the way we learned to separate self from everything that is not the self, going back to Descartes. It also forces us to rethink what it means for one self to encounter another self and its moral implications. Does one autonomous self encounter another autonomous self? It is hard to answer that without understanding how one subjective world is related to another.

According to Husserl, Merleau-Ponty, and later Heidegger, empathy is not the primary encounter with another's subjectivity (Zahavi 2005, 165). Prior to an individual empathic interaction, intersubjectivity is already present as co-subjectivity (167). Subjectivity for each of us is the experience of a shared world. For the most part we do not need to make a special effort to grasp the experience of others. We understand it well enough. According to Heidegger, it is only when our shared experience breaks down that we need to exercise empathy (165), a point worth remembering when we think about the place of empathy in democratic deliberation and the attempt to use it to ease clashes between perspectives that result in anger and hostility. For the most part our experiences are very similar. We inhabit a common world that we have learned to interpret together. I think this approach deserves more attention because if it is right, finding commonality should be possible even when it is hidden by layers of hostility arising from political discord.

On the one side, Husserl and Merleau-Ponty argue that intersubjectivity is intertwined with the experience of one's own subjectivity. On the other side, they argue that intersubjectivity is the basis for our understanding of objectivity. Husserl (1967) criticizes the common view that the world studied by the natural sciences is prior to, and independent of, the human cultural world (*Ideas* 2, sec. 9). He argues that, in fact, the world of scientific investigation is a cultural achievement carried out by people with a historically specific and socially acquired attitude arising after the Scientific Revolution—a concept of nature as mathematically formalized and more basic than the cultural world. He believes that it is the reverse—the cultural world is the more basic one. I observed in chapter 3 that the idea of nature changed with the rise of the second great idea, but Husserl's claim is stronger. He argues in *Cartesian Meditations* (1960) that the intersubjective world is more basic than the objective world in that we would not have the *concept* of an objective world without intersubjective experience (4th meditation).[10] The key idea is that in order to grasp the concept of objectivity I must be aware of multiple perspectives, and I cannot recognize that without interacting with others and seeing through their eyes. Husserl seems to be suggesting that what I hypothesize as the third great idea is as basic as the second great idea and as basic as the idea of an objective world.

Compare the optimistic interpretation of intersubjectivity by Husserl and Merleau-Ponty with Jean-Paul Sartre's perspective in a famous passage called "The Look" from *Being and Nothingness*. Sartre describes a situation of being in a park, presumably alone. When I am in a park, I see trees, grass, benches, walkways. All this space is centered on me. Unreflective consciousness according to Sartre is not consciousness of a world of objects. Objects only appear in reflective consciousness as they relate to me, the subject. My reflective consciousness organizes the world around me, the subject. My ego is not a thing; it is a way of seeing a world of objects. But suppose, now, that I see a man in the park and realize that he is a man, not just an object like the bench. And he looks at me! Suddenly I see myself as an object to the man. I realize that since I create a world of objects with my gaze, he creates a world with his gaze, and in his world, he is the subject and I am an object. But when I imagine what he sees, I cannot simultaneously perceive the world as before. Sartre says we cannot both perceive as a subject and imagine what the other sees at the same time (1993, 97). By looking at me the man steals my world from me, and I realize that (94). In doing so, he alters my relation to myself because in his gaze there is a world in which I am not a subject, and so I am not free. The look threatens me with annihilation as an object-creating subject.

Sartre says I can respond to the look with shame, or I can assert myself by looking back and threatening him the same

way. All interpersonal relationships take this form of asser-
tion/counter-assertion. We can never escape the bondage of the
other's gaze, although we invent many strategies in the attempt
to do so. Ultimately, as Foucault later noted, the other's look
becomes internalized. The implications for mechanisms of
power in relationships is obvious, particularly in the relationship
between men and women. Sartre's longtime companion, Simone de Beauvoir, argues in her important book, *The Second Sex*
(2009), that the idea of *woman* is socially constructed as man's
other, which denies the value of women as subjects apart from
the perspective of men. Beauvoir is widely regarded as the source
of the idea behind "The Look," but her own account of subjectivity and its relation to the other is importantly different because it
does not include Sartre's postulate of the original solitariness of
the self, nor does it include the idea that the encounter of one self
with another is inherently a conflict. In Sartre, the dominance of
the second great idea is obvious; not so in Beauvoir.

In recent philosophy there have been a number of pro-
posals rejecting the traditional "me first" view of the mind.
According to what is called "theory theory," for example, we
attribute mental states equally to ourselves and to others by
means of a tacitly held theory of mind. We grasp concepts for
mental states through our possession of the theory, which is
neutral regarding first-person and third-person ascriptions of
those states (Carruthers 1996). It has also been proposed that
the capacity to understand the mental states of others comes
first, and self-consciousness emerges as a self-directed form
of mind reading (Carruthers 2011; Carruthers, Fletcher, and
Ritchie 2012). I do not have an opinion about this theory of
mind, but I think that research of this kind is bringing the connection between the second and third ideas closer together,
and that is one of the ways in which the third idea is becoming
more important.

FIGURE 10. Jean-Paul Sartre and Simone de Beauvoir. STF/AFP via
Getty Images.

In chapter 5 I proposed an idea for inserting one's own
subjectivity into a previous conception of total objective reality. The heart of the idea is that we know how to turn one of
our subjective states into an object in reflection. The state of
*having* a total objective conception is a subjective state, and
since we can reflect upon that state in the next moment, we
can turn it into an object. Can we do something like that with
the subjective states of other people? Clearly, we do not experience their states directly as subjects and then turn them
onto objects in reflection, but if we can experience their states
through intersubjective experience, then as long as we can
reflect upon those states, we can, in principle, fit those states
as objects into a total objective conception. It should be no
harder to turn our grasp of other people's subjective states
into objects than to do the same thing with our own. In fact,
it might be easier if other people's subjective states are already

in between subjects and objects for us—something in between Sartre and Husserl. It should also be easier if the "theory theorists" are right that we attribute mental states to both ourselves and others by means of a theory that is neutral about the possessor of the mental state.

I do not know whether we can link the world of subjects and the world of objects in the way I have suggested, but I think that the work of phenomenologists in bringing the intersection of these worlds to our attention deserves careful study more than a century after the publication of the first volume of Husserl's *Ideas*.[11] Husserl must be right that our constitution of the features of the objective world needs to be done with other people, whether or not he is right that the existence of such a world comes through awareness of other minds. Our awareness of our self as a self is also interwoven with our awareness of other selves as both subjects and objects, and although the subject/object dichotomy is very deep in Western thought, we have seen many places in which the division has been challenged. I have insisted throughout this book that subjectivity is a different kind of reality than objective reality, the world with subjectivity removed, but that does not mean that there is no such thing as the whole of reality unified in a way that a mind can grasp. We just have not yet figured out how to do it.

What speculation can we make about the future trajectory of the idea of intersubjectivity? The psychology work is recent. The cognitive science work is recent. Studies connecting phenomenology and the sciences is very recent. There is a need for work relating the sciences, philosophy, and ordinary experience with the knowledge we gain from literature and film, the most advanced media for achieving the transfer of subjectivity civilization has ever produced. A great actor both interprets the subjectivity of the character he or she is playing and expresses it to the audience. Acting can make the subjectivity of a single imagined character reach millions of people. Although it goes only one way, people love to talk about movies with others, and their interpretation of a character's subjectivity is often easier to express than their own subjectivity because it is less emotionally threatening. All of that is data for our common exploration of intersubjectivity, combining fields that often have not had much to do with each other—science, philosophy, psychology, film, and literature. If we can find the places at which the work in these fields overlap, we might be able to start constructing a conception of intersubjectivity itself. In an essay on science and philosophy that I mentioned in chapter 5, Gadamer (1981, 12ff.) argues that we need a language that connects our common experience with the language of science. I believe that we also need a language that connects common experience and science with the languages of the arts, including music, which is often said to be a universal lingua franca. We have no such language, and so we live with a disjointed view of reality. Gadamer says that it is the business of philosophy to devise a language of the whole, and if he is right, philosophers have a very demanding job.

## "I," "You," and Disagreement

Propositions containing "I" cannot be reduced to any set of propositions about oneself in the third person. That is one of the implications of the fact that subjectivity differs in kind from the objective world. For the same reason, propositions containing the word "you" do not reduce to third-person propositions either. If the subjectivity of one person cannot be expressed by a description of the objective world, neither can subjectivity between persons.[12] If I address you, the reader, as "you," I am doing something different than stating what I want to state in the third person, and I am aware that that is what I am doing. We use the word "you" on purpose. Of course, in many cases I do not know you, and so I cannot be appealing to anything unique about you, but there is still a difference between addressing you as another self and stating something about the way I think the world is in the impersonal way we call "the third person."

In other work I distinguish what I call "third-person reasons" for belief from "first-person reasons" (Zagzebski 2012, chap. 11). Third-person reasons are those that can be laid out on the table for anybody to consider. They do not express or appeal to anyone's subjectivity, although they can include propositional facts *about* a person's subjectivity (e.g., "She is feeling uncomfortable being in that place") and facts about her memories and values. Everyone can take them into account through ordinary discourse. In contrast, what I call first-person reasons are the items of people's subjectivity that operate to give them beliefs. They include personal experiences and memories (not facts *about* the experiences and memories), as well as ideas and emotions that have developed over their lifetime, and their current beliefs.[13] People respond to third-person reasons, assuming they are rational, but we each have our own first-person reasons and our own way of putting those reasons together with the reasons that can be laid out for everybody. We are sometimes surprised when others are unmoved by the third-person reasons we give them for moral or political positions, but we should not be surprised because many of their first-person reasons differ from our own. We cannot understand another person without grasping their first-person viewpoint.

In political debate, the attempt to rely on the exchange of third-person reasons to resolve disagreement has not worked. That is one of the problems with the view of deliberative democracy resting on the concept of public reason, deriving from Rawls

(1996, 1999) and Gutmann and Thompson (1996). According to Gutmann and Thompson, citizens must "publicly appeal to reasons that are shared or could be shared, by their fellow citizens, and if they take into account these same kinds of reasons presented by similarly motivated citizens, then they are engaged in a process that by its nature aims at a justifiable resolution of disagreement" (25). This is a plain statement that public deliberation should involve the exchange of third-person reasons alone. I will not comment on whether it *should* work because it clearly has not. Even worse, there is a problem of the motive to engage in public reason in the first place. Studies have indicated that people will not try to rationally debate important issues if they believe that the other side will not do so as well, and they are quick to attribute suspicious motives to citizens with opposing positions.[14] Public reason is an ideal that depends upon trust, and trust is an intersubjective condition for successful debate. When there is a healthy degree of trust among people in a society, it is usually not noticed, but when it sinks lower than a level that permits the proper exchange of third-person reasons, it is crucial to focus on the subjective connections among citizens.

Studies on empathy have been getting attention as a remedy for political polarization. For example, Michael Morrell (2010) cites studies, including some of his own, that support the conclusion that citizens need to engage in the process of empathy if democratic deliberation is to work properly (126ff.). This work has not gone on long enough to give us confidence of the efficacy of empathy and the ways to encourage it;[15] there is not even agreement on what empathy is.[16] But it is heartening to see that intersubjectivity is being noticed as an object of study for our urgent practical problems.

Robert Talisse (2019) argues for the sufficiency of a less demanding form of intersubjectivity than emotional empathy—what he calls "civic friendship." An important cause of political polarization is the phenomenon of physical, social, and political *sorting* (80–88). A large body of research indicates that during the past several decades in the United States, there has been a steady pattern of spatial segregation in which demographically similar people occupy the same social and physical spaces. This leads to belief polarization because when like-minded people engage in discussions of a politically charged topic, their beliefs become both more alike and more extreme. For example, people initially favoring affirmative action become more strongly in favor of it while those opposed intensify their opposition.[17] Given the geographic sorting phenomenon in which people associate mostly with like-minded others, belief polarization leads to political polarization in which the distance between the views of people in different geographical areas increases, trends that are reinforced in social media use and network news.[18] People do not even hear viewpoints very different from their own, and then they are shocked when they find out how many people voted the other way, as happened during the 2020 presidential election. Talisse believes that because the environment of political discussion inflames civic enmity and exacerbates polarization, democracy is undermining itself (151–152).

To break the dynamic and encourage what he calls civic friendship, Talisse proposes that citizens join nonpolitical groups, which I surmise would include amateur sports teams or exercise groups, charitable organizations, book clubs, cooking classes, gardening clubs, bands or orchestras, hobby clubs, and similar groups that attract people with different political viewpoints (163). We talk to people about their lives and gradually learn their personal history and the experiences that shaped them from their own viewpoints. Nonthreatening, sympathetic, intersubjective exchanges come first. Reasonable debate about divisive issues only comes after basic trust is established. If Heidegger is right that most of our experiences are similar, this should be possible.[19]

The crisis of trust reveals the importance of understanding intersubjectivity. We will need to grasp each other's first-person reasons for beliefs and attitudes if we want to have a harmonious society. Wanting a harmonious society is not a rejection of autonomy and the importance of the uniqueness of each self. Quite the opposite. It is giving the greatest attention and respect to all viewpoints and the differences among the subjective worlds from which these beliefs arise. Respect for the selfhood of others means going to the trouble to see the world from their point of view.

I would like to propose that in addition to first-person and third-person reasons, there are also second-person reasons for belief, reasons each of us can propose to someone as *you*. These reasons are not the same as third-person reasons that are intended to apply to anybody, nor are they the same as first-person reasons, reasons a person has for her own beliefs. They are the reasons *I* propose to *you* or *you* propose to *me*. When I address you as "you" and offer you a reason for a belief, I am not offering a reason I would mention to anybody at random, nor am I giving you my own first-person reasons for a belief. I am attempting to appreciate your first-person reasons and offering a reason for you to consider. To address each other as "you," we do not necessarily need much interaction with each other. We might even have no interaction, as when I address you, the reader, because we do not have to know anything more than that somebody is a unique self to know that intersubjective interaction is possible and that we also have many things in common. We can offer reasons for beliefs to each other as partners in many joint ventures, some of which involve only the two partners in conversation, but one of which is the attempt to find the truth about some matter.

The successful exchange of second-person reasons requires a degree of trust that need only extend far enough to apply to the domain within which the reasons are offered. The more emotionally sensitive the area of discussion, the more trust is needed. If you are talking to a friend about her marital woes, a very high degree of trust is necessary. One must tread carefully because giving second-person reasons easily approaches giving advice, a project obviously fraught with danger. But if you are only talking to your plumber about your choice of a water filter system, not much more than ordinary trust between strangers is required. I think that the trust needed for democratic deliberation today is in serious trouble. The political process cannot function without basic trust in common sources of facts, which presumably requires only a low degree of trust. The process also requires enough sympathy with all participants in the democratic process that an exchange of first-person and second-person reasons for positions on contentious issues is possible. That requires a higher degree of trust. Unfortunately, the trust level in American society has reached such a low point that there is no longer even trust in a common body of facts. Not only are many people unable to grasp or even attempt to grasp the first-person reasons possessed by people on the other side of a political debate, many are not even able to engage in the exchange of third-person facts. If I think the facts you give me are *your* facts, and I don't trust you, I will say they are not facts.

In chapter 4 I suggested that the values of autonomy versus harmony lie beneath a range of deep moral and political disagreements. These values express different ways of looking at our human identity—as a person who is fulfilled by relationship to the world or some important part of it, or as a self whose singular identity needs to be protected from intrusions from without. The values can clash, but most of us have both values simultaneously. We are a combination of values. There are many different approaches to putting them together, and although small differences can add up to big differences, we have a great deal in common. I agree with Heidegger that for the most part, we are co-subjects in a shared world, and it is only a small part of our experience that drives us apart and for which we need to exercise empathy. Empathy is important, but it is not the whole of intersubjective experience. We mostly experience a shared world, and it should be possible to cultivate the emotions of shared experiences as an antidote to the poisonous emotions that divide us.

Political polarization gets a great deal of attention, but it is only one symptom of the gap in our understanding of the relationship between one mind and another. It is striking to see how little we know about intersubjectivity compared with what we know about the objective world and our own minds. I have mentioned some of the few ways in which intersubjectivity is becoming the subject of rigorous investigation, and what little we know of it is promising for both theoretical and practical reasons. An advantage of looking at the long history of reflection on minds and world is that the gaps in our understanding become conspicuous, and that can show us where to devote our resources. The vignette at the end of chapter 2 highlighted Kepler's ability to see in a flash the relationship between planetary motion and musical ratios, an insight that would not have been possible unless there is a unity of physical laws. Subjectivity is no doubt unified also, although probably not in the form of general laws. Nobody has yet discovered what unifies it, certainly not on the same level as Kepler at the end of the sixteenth century or Pythagoras 2,200 years earlier. Perhaps we will be lucky and such a discovery is in our future.

## *The God's-Eye View: What Is the Whole of Reality?*

The passion for reaching our minds outward as far as we can led to the first great idea, but the passion for knowledge has almost always been interpreted as the desire for what we now call objective knowledge. Aristotle opens the *Metaphysics* with the famous line, "All men by nature desire to know." He goes on to say that an indication of this is the delight we take in our senses, particularly the sense of sight. "The reason is that this, most of all the senses, makes us know and brings to light many differences between things." The senses give us knowledge of particulars, Aristotle says, but they do not give us wisdom. Wisdom is knowledge of first causes and principles, a goal that has been acclaimed for thousands of years, and justifiably so. But notice that Aristotle says nothing about the desire to know other people, even though the minds of other people are the most important part of the world outside our own mind. The passion to reach farther and farther outward gave us the first great idea. The passion to reach farther and farther inward led to the second great idea. I do not know if the passion to penetrate the minds of others is equal to these other passions, but I would like to conclude this book by reflecting on what it would take to make that idea a pivotal one in human history.

We have already seen at least two important reasons why the possibility of intersubjectivity *should* be a third great idea. It fills an obvious gap between our grasp of our own subjectivity and our grasp of the world without subjectivity, and it also has the potential to help us overcome our many interpersonal and political conflicts. I have mentioned some of the ways in which intersubjectivity is currently being examined, but there is no single practice emerging that has the features that would move our grasp of the subjectivity of others to the level of our grasp of the objective world, and so far it has not produced cultural products as important as the other two ideas. An exception is the modern novel and film, perhaps another instance in which art rather than philosophy is the cultural leader of an idea. But there is nothing yet that advances our grasp of the third idea in a systematic way.

If the third idea is to become one of the greatest ideas in history, I think that we will need a revolution in subjectivity on the scale of the Scientific Revolution. The new science I am imagining would examine the subjective world in a way that is comparable to what philosophers and scientists have done at length for the objective world. What made modern science revolutionary for human understanding was that it became a practice in which large numbers of people cooperate, permitting the advancement of knowledge on a vast scale, and with a method to determine when it succeeds and when it does not. It led to the establishment of many individual natural sciences, each of which has produced important work during the last four hundred years—chemistry, biology, geology, astronomy, and physics, not to mention cross-fields such as biochemistry and astrophysics. It also led to technological innovation, including the invention of tools to aid experimentation, as well as technologies that have greatly improved human life.

As wonderful as these accomplishments are, the scientific method requires the separation of the objective world from the multitude of subjective worlds, and its tremendous success has been limited to the former. That suggests to me that we need to develop an analogous systematic cooperative practice in which we advance knowledge of subjectivity in all its forms and with the development of new methods that permit us to determine the difference between success and failure. Such a

revolution would hopefully produce new branches of knowledge and academic fields as vast in scope as the numerous
natural sciences and fields of engineering that did not exist
prior to the seventeenth century. If I may push the comparison even further, perhaps it would even be possible to develop
something like technologies of subjectivity with the capacity to
solve practical problems in the subjective realm.

In chapter 2 I observed that the dates of intellectual revolutions tend to get pushed backwards as historical research
progresses. Antecedents to the Scientific Revolution appear in
the Middle Ages; the Renaissance seems to have begun earlier
than Burckhardt noticed; modern philosophy began in the
century before Descartes. We notice the precursors to revolutions in retrospect. Nobody in the Middle Ages would have
said, "I think a scientific revolution is coming." Similarly, we
might be experiencing the precursors to a revolution in the
study of subjectivity, but it will not be noticed until the revolution is well underway. However, we do know that intellectual
revolutions are always preceded by tentative steps, and I do
not think it is out of line to notice that there are tentative steps
in the study of intersubjectivity.

The Scientific Revolution eventually gave us a map of the
physical universe, but it was preceded by pieces of the map.
Likewise, the science of subjectivity would have to give us a
map of subjectivity in all its forms, but it will be preceded by
pieces of the map of subjectivity. There are probably laws of
subjectivity, but they could not be laws in the same sense as
laws of nature since the point of a natural law is generality,
and generality is precisely what subjectivity lacks. But there
*are* predictable ways in which the consciousness of one person changes when encountering the consciousness of another,
and in the respects in which it is unpredictable, we can predict
when it will be unpredictable. We have plenty of disconnected

evidence of the impact of one person's subjectivity on that of another, but we want to grasp subjectivity itself as a feature of the universe. I suspect that the power of one person's subjectivity when encountering the subjectivity of another produces powers that no one mind can have. Intersubjectivity is a creative force in the universe, but to understand it and direct it in the future, we will need to discover what makes intersubjectivity create new powers, such as the power of democracy or the power of collective emotion. We know the latter has too often produced collective hatred beyond the sum of individual hates, but if a collective emotion can be negative, it can presumably be positive. We need to discover what makes intersubjectivity lead in one direction rather than another, why it sometimes succeeds and sometimes fails, whether and how it can lead to the emergence of new entities. We need a map of the intersubjective universe. In chapter 3 I mentioned the importance of dreams in mythopoeic thought, and in chapter 2 I remarked that while mythopoeic thinking had a disadvantage in understanding impersonal nature, we have the opposite problem. We may have gone no further than mythopoeic thinkers in grasping the personal. Progress will probably have to include the profound study of dreams and imagination.[20]

The interpenetration of one subjectivity and another expands the subjectivity of both minds, but since the human mind is finite, we realize, or at least suspect, that we are never going to go very far in intersubjectivity. Even so, we can go far enough to see what the aim would be. The ideal would be the subjective counterpart of the so-called God's-eye viewpoint of the world, a term often used to refer to a total objective conception of reality. In the latter sense it is a term used by atheists as well as by theists because the viewpoint of a being who sees everything is the goal of inquiry, whether or not there is such a being. What I am proposing here is the subjective counterpart of such a view. It would be the subjective perspective of a mind who can grasp all the subjective perspectives of every conscious being, including itself. In previous work I have called this property "omnisubjectivity." What I mean by omnisubjectivity is the perfect grasp of every conscious state of every conscious being who ever lived or ever will live from the first-person perspective of that being. It includes the grasp of the subjective states of every creature that has subjective states, including any animals or other nonhumans that have subjectivity. If there is a being who can grasp everything that exists, that being must not only have knowledge of all objective facts but must also be omnisubjective, and so I argue that the God of Christian theism must be omnisubjective (Zagzebski 2008b; 2013; 2016b). Omnisubjectivity would be the ultimate goal of inquiry in the science I am envisaging. Of course, we are not going to reach the ultimate goal of inquiry, whether it is understood as the total objective world in all details, or the total subjective world in all details, or both together, but unattainability has never been a reason to stop moving towards an ultimate goal.

We have already seen innumerable problems in explaining the origin of subjectivity by reference to the objective universe. Perhaps we should delay the project of getting a comprehensive conception of the universe until our grasp of subjectivity has made noticeable progress. We might then try the reverse process—explaining the objective world by reference to subjectivity. It is revealing that the origin stories of almost all religions describe the physical universe as coming out of a mind. I take that to mean that in all these cultures, subjectivity precedes physical nature. If we assume that the subjectivity of a being with a mind comes first, the source of human subjectivity and the source of the physical world would be the same thing. In principle, that would have the potential to give us a unified conception of reality that includes both the subjective and the objective parts of the universe. The ultimate goal of inquiry would still be the God's-eye perspective of the world, but the God's-eye perspective would be one in which subjectivity is the ground.

Several times in this book I have mentioned Hinduism, Neo-Platonism, and Thomistic theology as examples of the first idea in its strongest form: the idea that the human mind can unite with the universe. It is revealing that people often experience intersubjectivity as a form of union with another person, so when the object of the grasp is subjectivity, the idea that grasping is union is natural. If the objective world can be grasped through the grasp of the subjectivity of the being who grasps everything, the possibility of union with the universe is an extension of the goal of intersubjectivity. Many mystics have said that they have experienced union with the being who experiences all of reality, and Aquinas believed that the reward of the faithful in heaven is a vision of God in whose essence all things are grasped. The Beatific Vision does not make us omniscient, but curiously, Thomas says that the saints in heaven are aware of the prayers of the faithful on earth, so in heaven they grasp what is going on in the minds of many people on earth as well as others in heaven. Aquinas's explanation is that the saints must be aware of anything that perfects their happiness.[21] Heaven is a state of happiness in which there is a communion of souls who have both intersubjective and objective knowledge through their vision of God. That view is the closest I have ever heard to an idea that would make the goal of the first great idea attainable.

The two greatest ideas have invigorated human civilization since the dawn of history, and we would not want to see either one of them fade away. The second idea took over the place of supremacy only a few hundred years ago, and the third idea is becoming more prominent in our common consciousness. But as important as the second and third ideas are, they have never superseded the first. In fact, it is because of the first great idea that we are driven to find a way to combine our grasp of our mind and our grasp of other minds with our grasp of reality without minds. We are painfully aware of how hard it is to get a conception of all of reality that does justice to everything we know exists, but the urge to get such a conception has survived every attack in human history. The second and third ideas make the first idea harder because we know that any attempt at expressing the first idea fails unless it includes the idea of the subjectivity of every being with subjectivity. To grasp the whole of reality, we must grasp the subjectivity of all minds. That means that the second and third ideas must be included in the first.

For thousands of years, human beings have tried to form a conception of everything that exists. They have tried it in many ways, but not all possible ways. They have often forgotten to include subjectivity, or they left it out on purpose. They sometimes privileged the self, and sometimes they privileged nature or God or reason. In this book I have canvassed some of the major ways a conception of all of reality has been attempted, and I have explored a few ideas to help us get closer to such a conception. Everywhere the story has gone, we have been confronted with missing pieces of reality, and that tells us that we have failed. We have always tried and will continue to try to put the pieces together to form the whole, and we will not stop until we have succeeded. That is why my story leads to an unmistakable conclusion: the greatest idea of all is the first.

## A Vignette of Dante and Beatrice in Paradise

In *Paradiso*, the final part of *The Divine Comedy*, Dante ascends the spheres of heaven guided by the spirit of Beatrice, the woman he loved in life. He has been on a long journey through hell and purgatory, an exile from his city of Florence, torn by political divisions and violence. His art is a response to grief and the pain of being an outcast, feelings as real to us as they were in the fourteenth century. Beatrice guides Dante by her wisdom and the beauty of the light of God reflected in her eyes. Dante is

FIGURE 11. "Apotheosis of Dante Alighieri in Florence: the Love that moves the sun and the other stars." Work created on the occasion of the 700th anniversary of the death of Dante (1321–2021). Giovanni Guida, via Wikimedia Commons.

transfixed by the rays, but Beatrice tells him that her eyes do not hold Paradise (canto 18.21). He must go farther and farther, and she gives him the strength to move upwards. As he gets closer to the final vision, he sees what Beatrice sees in heaven, in a series of visions in which the whole structure of the universe is bound together in a single light. As he approaches the final vision, he sees a human form in the light, seeing the human in the divine. Then in the final four lines of a poem of 14,233 lines, Dante has his climactic vision.

> O light supreme, more than conceivable
> by mortal mind, grant mine again
> some part
> of what you let me see, and give my
> tongue
> some power to leave a gleam of glory
> for my readers yet to come. Please
> give back
> a little of my memory, so that
> my poetry conveys your victory!
> So piercing was the splendour of
> that ray
> I am convinced that had I looked away
> even an instant, it had blinded me,
> but I sustained it until my gaze
> reached
> the central goodness. Bless abounding
> Grace!
> It let me dare to face infinite light
> So long that my whole mind was lost
> in it.

The scattered pages of the universe
were in that deepness, with its
substances,
accidents, relationships unified
and bound by love into a single book.
God by His light creates complexity,
yet sees it as one good grand simple
shape.
In writing this I feel my joy expand.
Twenty-five hundred centuries ago
the first ship was launched. A single
moment
gazing at that light seemed more. I
could not
look elsewhere. The good which is the
object
of all will was there. What exists
outside
is defective; all that exists within
is perfectly made. Now know that my
words
will tell even less of what I recall
than if my infant tongue still sucked a breast.
The living light remained the same, but I
began to change. My strengthened sight saw
more.
In the profoundest clear ground of the light
appeared three circles, different colours
and same size. Two reflected each other
as rainbows do, the third took fire from them.
Alas, such blethering cannot convey
the things I noticed in Eternal Light
fulfilling, knowing, loving its sweet self

in that reflecting, circling Trinity!
As my eyes dwelled on it I seemed to see
a human form. Like the geometer
battering his brain in vain to find how
circles are squared, I tried to see or feel
how such a human form could live in light
eternally. The wings of my fancy
could not fly so far, until in a flash
I saw desire and will, both are a pair
of finely balanced wheels kept turning by
the love that revolves sun, sky, and every star.
(Canto 33.48–97).

When Dante wrote these words in the early decades of
the fourteenth century, the Renaissance was about to begin,
and with it, the rise of the second great idea. We also may
be on the cusp of a revolution. It is interesting to speculate
whether someone is producing a literary work that will be
celebrated 700 years from now, as we are celebrating in 2021
the 700th anniversary of Dante's death.

Chapter 1. The Two Greatest Ideas

1. Albert Einstein (1950, 61).

2. Creation stories in ancient Egypt evolved into a cosmological system that may be a version of the first great idea. The creator is Atum, whose children are air and moisture, and their children are earth and sky. Other mythologies have a similar form, in which a story about personal gods is then interpreted as a story about all of nature from its beginning. See Frankfort et al. (1946) for a classic theory on the movement from what they call "mythopoeic thought" to "speculative thought" in the ancient world, presumably coinciding with what I call the rise of the first great idea. I will discuss Frankfort in chapter 2.

3. Karl Jaspers (1953) called this the Axial Age because the fundamental categories of human thought in philosophy and religion were begun independently in a number of different places at approximately the same time—in Persia, China, India, Palestine, and the Greco-Roman world. However, if we look at evidence in art rather than in writing, the origin of the first great idea may be earlier. In the next chapter I will mention possible evidence of the first great idea in China as early as 3500 BCE, long before the Axial Age.

4. Heraclitus is famous for allegedly saying, "You cannot step into the same river twice." But the line actually reads: "We step into and we do not step into the same rivers. We are and we are not" (Curd 2011, 45).

5. Curd (2011, 32). Putting these two fragments of Heraclitus together, it follows that being one in Heraclitus's sense is compatible with having temporal structure, permitting movement and change.

6. There are debates among ancient Greek scholars about whether the Pythagoreans thought that literally everything we call the material and non-material world is made of numbers and their relations, including perceptible objects. For an argument that the Pythagoreans' project was misunderstood by Aristotle and modern interpreters who mistakenly see them as the forerunners of modern materialism, see Rowett (2013).

7. See A. D. Nock (1933) for a fascinating interpretation of the psychology of conversion from 500 BCE to 400 CE, and an argument that conversion as a reorientation of the soul was not a component of early religions, but it was a component of Greek philosophy and became a major feature of Christianity. Nock did not look at Eastern religions, but I think it is interesting that the phenomenon of conversion was a component of the spread of Buddhism when the Mauryan Indian King Ashoka was converted to Buddhism in the third century BCE.

8. An even earlier expression of monotheism and the personal relationship between God and human beings may appear in Psalm 8, attributed to King David at the beginning of the tenth century BCE:

> Lord, our master,
> How majestic Your name in all the earth!
> Whose splendor was told over the heavens . . .
> When I see Your heavens, the work of Your fingers,
> The moon and the stars You fixed firm,
> What is man that You should note him,
> And the human creature, that You pay him heed,
> And You make him little less than the gods,
> With glory and grandeur You crown him. (Psalm 8:2, 4–6; translation
> in Alter 2007)

9. The doctrine of the cyclicality of all life and existence, or samsara, is a fundamental belief of Buddhism and Jainism and various schools of Hinduism from about the first millennium BCE. The Jewish idea that time is linear and events are contingent was, of course, inherited by Christian Europe. Pierre Duhem (1969) proposes that there is a historical connection between the rise of modern science and medieval Christian metaphysics and their view of time. Stanley Jaki has also argued in several places that it is not an accident that modern science had its origin in medieval Europe. See, for example, Jaki (1978, 21). For more recent arguments see Hannam (2010) and Stark (2004). For a popular book arguing that the Jewish view of the linearity of time played a critical role in shaping Western civilization, see Cahill (1998).

10. Unless otherwise stated, quotations from the Bible will be taken from the New Revised Standard translation.

11. Of course, this is not to say that the prophets always succeeded in transforming their behavior!

12. Jacques Maritain's contribution to drafting the Universal Declaration of Human Rights connected Thomistic natural law theory with the modern rights movement. The connection between medieval natural law theory and the rise of modern science was argued by Alfred North Whitehead, who writes, "There can be no living science unless there is a widespread instinctive conviction in the existence of an *Order of Things*, and in particular, of an *Order of Nature*, and that was the great contribution of the Middle Ages to the rise of modern science" (1925, 5 [italics in original]). See also the works mentioned in note 9.

13. The term "modern" has the unfortunate consequence that as centuries pass since the modern period began, the modern is no longer modern. The term "postmodern" was used for a while to mark a way of thinking that was new at the time, but it also has the problem that it names a period of history that presumably ends at some point. The term "contemporary" has the advantage of meaning "whatever is going on now," which can be carried forward indefinitely.

14. Although almost all commentators believe that Augustine stands apart in the literature of antiquity for his perceptive examination of his inner conscious

life, Mikhail Bakhtin (1981) does not see him as an exception. He writes, "It is significant that even today one cannot read Saint Augustine's *Confessions* 'to oneself'; it must be declaimed aloud—to such an extent is the spirit of the Greek public square still alive in it, that square upon which the self-consciousness of European man first coalesced" (134–135). I will discuss Bakhtin's interpretation of ancient literature in chapter 2.

15. See Martha Nussbaum (2001, 165–199) on the speech of Alcibiades in the *Symposium*. Nussbaum argues that unlike Socrates, Alcibiades knows what it is to love an individual person, not the imitation of a Platonic Form in a person. It is worth noticing that Plato wrote the speech of Alcibiades as well as the speech of Socrates, but there is very little in Plato's thought on the importance of personal uniqueness.

16. Of course, Descartes does not refer to what I call the first great idea, but he expresses skepticism about all the traditional sources of beliefs in almost all domains (*Discourse on Method*, part 1, and beginning of Meditation 1), and says he wants to start anew, accepting the possibility that his mind may not be able to attain certain knowledge of anything (beginning of Meditation 2).

17. William Egginton (2016) argues that Cervantes was one of the first to shape the modern world by creating the novel. The connection between the invention of the novel and the rise of the second great idea will be one of the topics of chapter 3.

18. It is interesting that in the twentieth century, philosophy of language was one of the first fields of philosophy to weaken the hold of the second great idea. In the second half of the century, the position that words refer to ideas in one's own mind, possibly inaccessible to others and possibly corresponding to nothing outside the mind, was attacked, leading to a decline in internalist views of the mind/world relation. Starting with Hilary Putnam (1975) and Saul Kripke (1980), externalist semantics became popular. Putnam explicitly used his semantical theory against skepticism in Putnam (1981).

19. I interpret ancient Pyrrhonian skepticism as based on epistemological arguments such as the problem of the infinite regress of reasons. That is the problem that no belief is justified unless it is based on a reason, which also needs a reason, and which in turn needs a reason, ad infinitum. The consequence seems to be that no belief is justified. Cartesian skepticism, in contrast, has a deeper metaphysical source in the way the boundary between mind and world is understood.

20. It is interesting that Descartes was much more historically influential in his method of doubt than in the positive part of his program in which he regains belief in an external world by the end of his *Meditations*. Everyone thinks of Descartes as the skeptic even though he ends up not being a skeptic. But the fact that Descartes thought he needed to prove the existence of a nondeceiving God to give a foundation to his belief in an external world has been particularly unpopular with subsequent readers.

21. There were exceptions such as Spinoza and Leibniz, but the decline of grand metaphysics was obvious in those places influenced by Hume's empirical

skepticism. In a famous passage at the end of his *Enquiries concerning Human Understanding* (1975), in the section called "Of the Academical or Skeptical Philosophy," Hume describes two kinds of "mitigated skepticism," the second of which is empiricism, which leads to "the limitation of our enquiries to such subjects as are best adapted to the narrow capacity of human understanding" (162). That led Hume to a negative judgment on "Divinity or Theology" and "morals and criticism," and to his famous rejection of metaphysics as "sophistry and illusion" (165).

22. The famous term "disenchanted" appears in Weber's essay "Science as a Vocation," originally given as a speech at Munich University in 1918 and published in English in Gerth and Mills (1946). See Josephson-Storm (2017) for an interesting argument that the cultural narrative of the disappearance of spirits and myths is seriously mistaken.

23. According to Dennett, consciousness as experienced by a subject is not part of reality. Dennett is an eliminativist about mental entities. The only things that exist are material entities. What science tells us about the brain and the nervous system is all there is to consciousness, which means that what I am calling the second great idea is fundamentally wrong. It is ironic that science reached the pinnacle of prestige because of the ascendance of the second great idea, and now Dennett is telling us that the idea is an illusion. As long as consciousness does not exist, science can give us a theory of everything. This is interesting for a number of reasons, one of which is confirmation of the strong human desire to have a theory of everything. I will return to Dennett and naturalism as an account of all of reality in chapter 5.

24. Nagel observes that atheists like himself have a disadvantage when compared with theists because the latter have a metaphysical picture of the world as a whole in which each person can find a meaningful place. The alternatives for atheists are less satisfying, in particular, the alternative of reductive naturalism, in which everything reduces to what is described in physics. Nagel says he desires a form of naturalism that also satisfies what he calls "the religious temperament" and what I am calling the sense of empowerment that came with both Judeo-Christian theism and other forms of the first great idea in the world religions.

25. An alternative to both scientific naturalism and Western theism has been proposed by John Schellenberg (2015, 2019), who describes what he calls religion for Western atheists. He argues that religion is still in its infancy in world civilization, and transcendentally oriented religions are immature. He believes that science should be welcomed as a positive force in the evolution of a humanistic religion.

26. It should be obvious that the theoretical acknowledgment of human rights was one thing, the recognition of rights in practice was another, as the painful history of slavery reveals.

27. Kant does not clearly make the self a category in the sense I mean, but his immediate successors did. In chapter 5 we will briefly look at how Fichte

intended to improve upon Kant's philosophy by making consciousness of the self central to philosophy.

28. See Foucault (1990, 1995).

## Chapter 2. The World Precedes the Mind

1. See Lagercrantz (2016) and Rochat (2003). Martha Bell (2015) suggests that current research methods make it unclear when infants have such an awareness; for instance, how long a baby looks in a certain direction or at a novel stimulus might not tell us much. But she does not deny that the awareness of the distinction between mind and world occurs naturally.

2. For the revolution in political structures, Burckhardt claims that the Renaissance began with reactions to the despotism of the fourteenth century, and he argues that political changes preceded the magnificent artistic revolution.

3. A central push in moving back the birth of the Scientific Revolution is the reexamination of medieval forms of science. Pierre Duhem's early work has made him widely regarded as the father of the history of medieval science. In 1914 he published a ten-volume work, *Le système du monde: histoire des doctrines cosmologiques de Platon à Copernic*, which has been translated into English in an abridged edition (Duhem 1985). For a collection of essays on precursors to Galileo, see Wallace (2014). In philosophy, Descartes is commonly identified as the first modern philosopher in the seventeenth century, but the skepticism of the sixteenth-century French philosopher Michel de Montaigne influenced Descartes. For essays on sixteenth- and seventeenth-century philosophy, see Popkin (1966). History books used to date the beginning of the Renaissance to the fifteenth century, but it is now widely held to have begun in the previous century.

4. This remark has been made many times by historians, philosophers, and literary scholars. Some examples include MacIntyre (1988, 2, 12–68); Raaflaub (2009, 566–571); Collobert (2009, 133–134); Burkert (1999, 88, 92); Hermann (2004, 15–16); Livingstone (2011, 133); Murray (2011, 188–189); Morgan (2000, 1–4).

5. Flaig (2013), Curl (2003), Jones (2014), Yunis (2013). Greek tragedies can be interpreted in more than one way, and it is interesting that Nietzsche insisted that Sophocles was an opponent of rationalism. See Gaukroger (1999).

6. Dimitri Gutas (2009, 18–21) traces the rise and development of Islamic philosophy through its benefits to concurrent developments in science, theology, and politics. Further connections can be found in Ettinghausen, Grabar, and Jenkins-Madina's (2001) work on medieval Islamic art and architecture. In China, we see the social import of the first great idea through the take of philosophers on social practice, the value of music for society, and in art. See Hung (1999), Nivison (1999), Brindley (2012).

7. Jaspers does not mention Islam, perhaps because it, like Christianity, is an Abrahamic faith.

8. Greece and Israel are presumably put together only because of the later historical confluence of the cultures. It is interesting that there was also a historical confluence of Greece with Islamic societies in the Middle Ages when Aristotle's works were studied and translated into Arabic at the time that they were lost in Europe. That suggests that the meaning of "the West" is read backwards from subsequent historical events.

9. Plato tells a different story about Thales that gives another impression of his personality. Reportedly, Thales was so entranced with looking up at the stars that he fell into a well and a serving girl laughed at him for being so absent-minded (*Theaetetus* 174b).

10. Rochberg (2016, chap. 2) gives an analysis of the Frankforts' work and describes the history of subsequent research. She shows the many potential elements of "speculative" thought already existing in ancient Near Eastern cultures and argues that the claim that the ancient Babylonians and Egyptians were thoroughly mythopoeic is dubious. Likewise, the Greeks did not give up their energetic myth-making when they became speculative. So as a historical claim the Frankforts' thesis is probably faulty, but their contrast between two ways of thinking is conceptually revealing.

11. Martin Buber's well-known book, *I and Thou* (1970), is a sustained critique of the idea that we improve by going towards speculative thought, separating subject from object. "[O]nce the sentence 'I see the tree' has been pronounced in such a way that it no longer relates a relation between a human *I* and a tree *You* but the perception of the tree object by the human consciousness, it has erected the crucial barrier between subject and object; the basic word *I-It*, the word of separation, has been spoken" (74–75).

12. Welch (2019, 16) argues that Native thought avoids oppositions between subject and object, reality and appearance, and reason and intuition, dichotomies that have produced numerous philosophical puzzles. Native people also utilize dreams as a way to close the gap between the internal connection to the energy of the universe in intuition and more explicit forms of knowing the world in speculative thought.

13. See Zhmud (2012, 81).

14. This appears explicitly in the work of the Pythagorean philosopher Philolaus (5th cent. BCE).

15. The idea that the mind grasps *only* numerical form is, of course, more extreme, but that depends upon whether we interpret a number as a formal relation or as an entity. The idea that what the mind grasps is form is not extreme and in fact was highly influential throughout Western history. I will mention examples of that below.

16. See Hopper ([1938] 2000) for a discussion of Pythagorean number theory in early Christian writers. Hopper says that Augustine is one of the most comprehensive sources for our information on Pythagorean number symbolism (79).

17. For an interesting book arguing that mathematics should be interpreted as the science of patterns, see Devlin (1997).

18. See *Republic* 521b–540a and the surrounding discussion.

19. The writing of the ancient Sumerians dates to the fourth millennium BCE, and the earliest artifact may be a Sumerian limestone tablet from 3500 BCE in the Ashmolean Museum, Oxford, containing pictographic writing. However, cave paintings found in recent years in Indonesia appear to be as much as 40,000 years old. For a description, see Vergano (2014). See also *Nature* magazine, fall 2018, for even earlier discoveries.

20. William G. Boltz (2000/2001) dates the invention of writing in China to 1200–1050 BCE.

21. There is an abundance of these disks and tubes in an exhibition in the National Palace Museum in Taipei, put on permanent display in 2011 in honor of the 100th year of the Republic of China. My information comes primarily from the exhibition book, *Art in Quest of Heaven and Truth: Chinese Jades through the Ages* (2012), particularly 47–52.

22. Panofsky published many important works. See particularly, Panofsky (1953) for a book that had a significant impact on studies of Renaissance art and the field of iconography.

23. Emile Mâle predated Panofsky. He first published his work in 1913 under the title *Religious Art in France of the Thirteenth Century: A Study in Medieval Iconography and Its Sources of Inspiration*. For a classic study of Christian iconography, see Andre Grabar (1968).

24. We see the same psychology today in responses to rough Christmas nativity scenes and unpolished patriotic songs. Art does not have to be good to serve the purpose of arousing emotion and giving people a sense of belonging.

25. In chapter 1, note 14, I mentioned Bakhtin's (1981) claim that the public square is alive even in Augustine's *Confessions*, which Bakhtin says must be "declaimed aloud" (135). Notice that it is nothing like Hamlet's soliloquy, much less the long reflections in modern novels such as those by Henry James, which go on for many more pages than the action the thoughts accompany.

26. For a treatment of Pythagorean numerology in *The Divine Comedy*, see Bigongiari and Paolucci (2005).

27. See, for instance, Newton-Fisher and Lee (2011) and Tombak et al. (2019).

28. The Code of Ur-Nammu was written in the Sumerian language 300 years earlier, around 2100 BCE. That code also traces the emperor's authority to the gods who declared that he should "set up equity in the land."

29. Hammurabi wrote: "When the lofty Anu, king of the Anunnaki, and Bel, lord of heaven and earth, he who determines the destiny of the land, committed the rule of all mankind to Marduk, the chief son of Ea; when they made him great among the Igigi; when they pronounced the lofty name of Babylon; when they made it famous among the quarters of the world and in its midst established an everlasting kingdom whose foundations were firm as heaven and earth—at that time, Anu and Bel called me, Hammurabi, the exalted prince, the worshiper of the gods, to cause justice to prevail in the land, to destroy the

wicked and the evil, to prevent the strong from oppressing the weak, to go forth like the Sun over the Black Head Race, to enlighten the land and to further the welfare of the people" (in Harper 1904).

30. See Scott MacDonald (1991), particularly his long introduction, which gives a history of the idea of the Good and its equation with Being from Greek philosophy through the medieval period, and his translation of Boethius's *De hebdomadibus* in the same volume.

31. I am treating the soul as it is discussed in traditional philosophies and religions as the same as the mind. The soul may extend beyond the mind, but I interpret the idea that the soul can unite with the universe as a version of the first great idea.

## *Chapter 3. The Mind Precedes the World*

1. In a frequently quoted letter to Mersenne (January 28, 1641), Descartes writes: "I may tell you, between ourselves, that these six *Meditations* contain the entire foundations of my physics. But, please, you must not say so; for partisans of Aristotle would find more difficulty, perhaps, in approving them; and what I hope is that readers will gradually get used to my principles, and recognize their truth, before observing that they destroy Aristotle's" (1971, 265).

2. From a letter to Guillaume Gibieuf (January 19, 1642), Descartes (1964–76, 3:474), translated by Smith (2018).

3. I say this mostly because of the seriousness with which radical skepticism was treated in the second half of the twentieth century in philosophy, using the assumption that the grasp of one's mind is primary.

4. See Descartes, *Principles of Philosophy*, in Descartes, *Philosophical Writings* (1971, 194–195).

5. Robert M. Adams discusses this background to Berkeley in a very useful introduction to his edition of Berkeley's *Three Dialogues between Hylas and Philonous*. He says it is doubtful that Berkeley knew the relevant passage in Leibniz, but he was aware of the argument by Bayle. Adams cites Leibniz's "On Nature Itself" (1698) in Leibniz (1951, 150–153). For the Bayle reference he cites a passage in Bayle's *Historical and Critical Dictionary*, mentioned in Popkin (1966, 348).

6. Hume's rejection of the primary/secondary quality distinction and his skeptical conclusion appears in *A Treatise of Human Nature*, book 1, part 4, sec. 4, "On the modern philosophy."

7. In *Critique of Pure Reason*, Transcendental Dialectic, chapter 2, Kant presents what he calls antinomies of reason, which are pairs of contradictions, both sides of which are equally rational, and which follow from the use of reason in an attempt to know transcendental reality.

8. It is interesting that in the eighteenth century, Kant's *Prolegomena to Any Future Metaphysics* was called *Prolegomena to Any Future Metaphysics that Will Be Able to Come Forth as a Science*. See Lewis White Beck's introduction

(in Kant 1950) to the *Prolegomena*, with remarks about Kant's dual aim: to give a defense of science and mathematics, and to avoid speculative metaphysics.

9. Williams ([1978] 2005) denies that it follows that philosophy gives absolute knowledge because even if philosophy can give us the absolute conception, philosophy would not have absolute status unless we not only have the absolute conception, but know that we have it, and it is asking too much to expect that (287).

10. Hans-Georg Gadamer (1981) discusses this point in his essay, "On the Philosophic Element in the Sciences and the Scientific Character of Philosophy" (7).

11. See Moszkowski (1921, 1), quoted by Stanley Jaki (1978, 126).

12. I will not attempt to define art, and I do not know whether telling a story is a work of literary art. Presumably sometimes it is and sometimes it isn't. When Homer told a story about the Trojan War, it was art; when I tell a story about my encounter at the auto body shop, it is not art, whether or not it expresses my personality. But I doubt that it is necessary to have a definition of art for my purposes in this book.

13. Brunelleschi set up a mirror about six feet inside the main door of Florence Cathedral, facing outwards, so that he could see the Baptistery in the mirror across the square. He then painted the mirror image onto a flat wooden tablet. Next, he drilled a hole in the center of the painting, and viewers walking around and facing the Baptistery could look through the hole in the back of the painting while holding the mirror at arm's length in front of the painting. They were then looking at a mirror image of a mirror-image painting. When the mirror was removed, the viewer could see the Baptistery and compare it to the image on the painting. Brunelleschi's painting was so accurate that viewers could see no difference between the painting and the real Baptistery. James Burke (1985, 72) uses this example in his argument that the discovery of perspective was a world-changing event.

14. It may sound strange to the modern ear to hear the term "corporation" used in medieval contexts, but Burckhardt used the term appropriately. Greif (2006) defines medieval corporations as bodies that were "intentionally created, voluntary, interest-based, and self-governed permanent association[s]," which included entities such as "guilds, fraternities, universities, communes, and city-states" (308).

15. In painting, there was the baroque, classicism, and the rococo, neoclassicism and Romanticism, impressionism, fauvism, expressionism, cubism, surrealism, and geometric abstract art, not to mention pop art, feminist art, and the combination of painting with other media and technology.

16. Reported by Reuters, May 8, 2002; reported the same day in the *New York Times* and the *Guardian*.

17. Cervantes rapidly became famous. The book was read by people who could read and heard by people who could not read. Egginton reports that the printed copies immediately sold out, and that it was read aloud in taverns and village

squares where it was an instant sensation (2016, xv). Among philosophers it was read and admired by Spinoza, Hume, Hegel, and the German Romantics (xxvii).

18. It is interesting that Bakhtin says that humor marked a transition from medieval literature to the novel (1981, 20–22).

19. Bakhtin does not mention East Asian examples of the novel in his essay. One of my early favorites was the Japanese novel, *The Tale of Genji*, written by Lady Murasaki in the eleventh century. Also predating *Don Quixote* is the first of the four classic Chinese novels, *Water Margin*, which was published in the fourteenth century. These works combine many of the features of the epic with some of the stylistic features of the novel.

20. Kant says in the Second Preface: "We here propose to do just what COPERNICUS did in attempting to explain the celestial movements. When he found that he could make no progress by assuming that all the heavenly bodies revolved round the spectator, he reversed the process, and tried the experiment of assuming that the spectator revolved, while the stars remained at rest. We may make the same experiment with regard to the intuition of objects. If the intuition must conform to the nature of the objects, I do not see how we can know anything of them *à priori*. If, on the other hand, the object conforms to the nature of our faculty of intuition, I can then easily conceive the possibility of such an *à priori* knowledge."

21. See Taylor (1995) for a defense of this interpretation of the rise of modern moral theory. I discuss this point in Zagzebski (1998).

22. In Zagzebski (2012), chapter 1, section 3, I give a more detailed historical narrative about the rise of autonomy in both the moral and epistemic domains.

23. In the fourteenth century, Duns Scotus and William of Ockham shifted the locus of moral authority from reason to the will by defending the view that moral prescriptions come from the divine will, not the divine reason. That led to theological controversies that paved the way for the emphasis on will rather than reason in the modern era.

24. *A Treatise of Human Nature*, book 3, part 1, section 1.

25. The fact/value distinction is so deeply entrenched in Western culture that there was a time when young schoolchildren were taught that sentences containing value terms do not express facts. In the 1980s my children were taught that this is a matter of standard English grammar. Imagine a metaphysical position, and a disputed one at that, being so ingrained in the culture that children are taught that if they do not accept it, they do not understand the English language. Many writers have attacked the fact/value dichotomy, for instance, C. S. Lewis in *The Abolition of Man* (2009). See also Hilary Putnam (2004), who accepted the distinction but attacked the idea that it is a dichotomy.

26. In the United States, subjectivism and relativism noticeably faded after September 11, 2001, when many people who formerly believed that morality is relative to an individual culture found that they could not sustain that position after the experience of the attacks. One event does not change an entire moral framework, but it appears to me that there is a cultural shift towards a version

of the objectivity of morality, focused on human rights. I will take that up in the next chapter.

27. For discussions of Freud's poetic and philosophical precursors and influences, see Finn (2017) and Hendrix (2015, 230–260).

28. See Foucault (2016), "Christianity and Confession," 215–219.

29. See Mallon (2004, 2006, 2007) for discussion of competing views on the ontological status of race in the recent literature.

## Chapter 4. The Moral Legacy

1. Pope Leo is most famous for personally meeting with Attila the Hun in 452 and stopping the attack on Rome. There is no record of what was said by either party at the meeting, only that Attila and his army departed. Both Leo and Attila must have been very impressive men.

2. Boethius actually says that God is not a person except in a metaphorical sense. But Boethius's reason for denying personhood to God has nothing to do with God's status, which is obviously at the top. His main concern as described by Aquinas seems to be that every person is a *hypostasis*, which signifies the subject of accidents, but God has no accidents. He also mentions the origin of "*persona*" in the masks worn on the stage, which does not apply to God except metaphorically (*ST* 1, q. 29, art. 3, obj. 2 and 3).

3. Aquinas is referring to Alan of Lille. Cf. Zagzebski (2016a, 61–62).

4. Apparently, the title "*Oration on the Dignity of Man*" was given to the work only after Pico's death (Copenhaver 2017).

5. This claim was made by Marcel Mauss, appearing in a book of essays reacting to him in Carrithers, Collins, and Lukes (1985, 22). This essay gives an interesting discussion of the replacement of the person by the self (see esp. 21). In the same book, Michael Carrithers (1985, 234–256) defends the view that the idea of the individual self was fully developed in India in the fifth century BCE.

6. See Neuhouser (1990) for an extended discussion of Fichte's theory of subjectivity as an attempt to solve the problem that Kant's philosophy needs a way to unify theoretical and practical rationality in the self. I will return to Fichte in the next chapter.

7. In Zagzebski (2016a) I argue that Kant identifies both senses of dignity in a famous passage of the *Groundwork*, but without noticing that they are two different kinds of value.

8. I discuss this process in some detail in Zagzebski (2012), chapter 2.

9. See Kateb (2014) for a view of human dignity that includes a focus on our responsibility to care for and protect nonhuman creatures.

10. It is interesting that John Rawls's classic book, *A Theory of Justice*, was often interpreted as both a political theory and a moral theory, although he objected that it was only intended to be a theory of a part of morality—justice (Rawls 2005, xv–xvi).

11. The seventeenth-century Dutch legal philosopher Hugo Grotius grounded natural rights in a secular natural law theory, an important example of a theory of natural rights that does not arise from social contract theory. See Geddert (2017) for an argument that we should rethink the legacy of Grotius's theory of rights as an alternative to the modern approach to rights, which ignores the ancient Greek and Christian ideal of human flourishing. For the contemporary approach, important defenses of human rights from a basis in human agency and autonomy include Alan Gewirth (1982) and James Griffin (2008).

12. Aaron Rhodes (2018) blames the almost endless expansion of rights claims to the problem that ever since the Universal Declaration of Human Rights, rights documents tend to mix natural rights guaranteeing fundamental freedoms with social and economic rights established by positive law. The consequence, he says, is the debasement of the idea of a human right. I do not have any objection to rights documents, but I think Rhodes is right about the endless expansion of rights claims. For instance, we see such phenomena as a state ballot question in 2016 that would have enshrined the right to farm and ranch in the Oklahoma state constitution. (It was defeated). In recent years, the right to internet access and the right to repair technology at third-party vendors have become popular causes. These might well be socially desirable causes, but calling them rights dilutes the moral force of the word "rights."

13. It is interesting that a recent book debating abortion is titled *Abortion Rights: For and Against* (Greasley and Kaczor 2018), with Kate Greasley taking the pro–abortion rights position, and Christopher Kaczor taking the anti-abortion rights position. The dialectic is the reverse of the older debate in which abortion defenders were the ones denying a right.

14. For an influential paper arguing for a shift from the rhetoric of rights and deontology to virtue ethics as a framework for discussion of abortion, see Hursthouse (1991).

15. For an interesting discussion of the dispute between Maritain and MacIntyre on human rights, see Deborah Wallace (1999).

16. The first book on virtue to make a major impact on philosophy in the United States in the later twentieth century was Alasdair MacIntyre's *After Virtue* (1981). Since then many books have been published on virtue, including intellectual virtue (see my 1996 book), civic virtue, and virtue in education. Nancy Snow currently edits a book series called "The Virtues" for Oxford University Press. The positive psychology movement, based at the University of Pennsylvania, focuses on character strengths and the good life. At my university, the Institute for the Study of Human Flourishing is devoted to advancing the science of virtue and promoting the flourishing of students and community. There are many other notable institutes, including the Jubilee Center for Character and Virtues in Birmingham, England, and the Aretai Center in Genoa, Italy.

17. I know of at least two. One is a big project at the University of Connecticut on humility and conviction in public life. The central question for

their research and engagement initiatives is how we can balance our deeply held convictions with humility and open-mindedness in civic life. See https://humilityandconviction.uconn.edu. The other is a major project at Saint Louis University on the Philosophy and Theology of Intellectual Humility. See humility.slu.edu.

18. For a large volume of current work on character from the perspectives of philosophy, theology, and psychology, see Miller et al. (2015). The John Templeton Foundation has funded a great number of projects in their funding area of Character Virtue Development. See their website at Templeton.org for recent and ongoing projects.

19. The Intellectual Virtues Academy in Long Beach, California, is a nonsectarian public charter school that was the first to offer an education based on an intellectual virtues model. It started with a middle school in 2013 and now has a public high school.

20. A nineteenth-century icon in the American conservation movement was John Muir, who was significant in raising public awareness of the need to protect wilderness areas and to prevent the exploitation of nature for commercial purposes.

21. This thought experiment was devised by Richard Sylvan (see Routley 1973). See also Rolston (1975) for an early argument that natural processes deserve respect because nature itself is sacred.

22. Of course, there are people who deny that there is any human-caused climate change or that the costs of ameliorating it are not worth the infringement on individual autonomy, and therefore we should merely accept it.

23. For a book proposing a virtue-based environmental ethics, see van Wensveen (2000).

24. Fukuyama (2018) calls this "the politics of resentment" in the subtitle of his book. Unfortunately, calling attention to feelings of resentment among people who believe they have been treated unjustly may make them sound petty. "Indignation" sounds morally high-minded, whereas "resentment" sounds like the whining of the weak. This is an example of the way in which the words we use to identify two sides of an emotionally laden issue can bias the discussion before it begins.

25. An obvious exception is women, who are only a slight minority in world population, but who have been treated as minorities in most societies for most of human history.

## Chapter 5. Can We Grasp All of Reality?

1. For empirical studies supporting the idea that it is natural to distinguish mind from world at a very early age, see note 1 to chapter 2 above.

2. The recognition of this problem is not unique to Western philosophy, and one possible response to it comes from Hinduism. The ancient *Brihadaranyaka Upanishad* says that we can know the world only so long as we insist on the separateness of the self and the world (chap. 2, 4.14): "As long as there is

separateness, one sees another as separated from oneself, smells another as separate from oneself, thinks of another as separate from oneself, knows another as separate from oneself. But when the Self is realized as the indivisible unity of life, who can be seen by whom, who can be heard by whom, who can be smelled by whom, who can be spoken to by whom, who can be thought of by whom, who can be known by whom? Maitryei, my beloved, how can the knower ever be known?" (Easwaran 2007, 103). Here the answer to the puzzle of how the knower can be known is turned on its head. The knower cannot be known because knowing requires separation, and the self is not separate from the world known. Once the knower realizes that, knowledge ceases.

3. This dialogue was universally ascribed to Plato in antiquity, but Plato's authorship was disputed in the nineteenth century by Friedrich Schleiermacher, and since then scholars have been divided, with some recent authors supporting the attribution to Plato. The dispute is mentioned by Richard Sorabji (2006, 51–52), who sides with those who ascribe the work to Plato.

4. See also Neuhouser (1990, chap. 3). As far as I can tell, neither the commentary by Henrich nor the one by Neuhouser mentions the similarity with Augustine.

5. Hume (2000), book 1, part 4, section 6.

6. Buddhist thought has also appeared in an important interdisciplinary and cross-cultural study relating Buddhist meditation and its no-self view to Hume's view of the self and the contemporary scientific evidence for the nonexistence of a self (Varela, Thompson, and Rosch 2016).

7. If our starting conception is one that precedes the era of the division between the subjective and the objective, it will not be called "objective," but it will nonetheless leave out subjectivity.

8. There is a dispute about whether physical entities are the entities posited by our current physics or instead an ideal physics in the future. The latter seems much more plausible, but this raises the problem that the entities endorsed in the future may be different in kind from current physical entities, perhaps even including mental entities, conflicting with the basic physicalist idea. This problem is called "Hempel's dilemma" because it was raised by Carl Hempel (1980).

9. See Zhong (2016) for an argument that the physicalist should accept the position that the same property is denoted by both a physical concept and a mental, nonphysical concept, which is intended to avoid problems with the physicalist view that all reality consists of entities that are physical. The entities are physical, but they can be correctly denoted by mental concepts.

10. This is an objection made by Thomas Nagel (2012), who argues that neither reductive materialism nor theism unifies reality. Nagel says, "Apart from the difficulty of believing in God, the disadvantage of theism as an answer to the desire for comprehensive understanding is not that it offers no explanations but that it does not do so in the form of a comprehensive account of the natural order. Theism pushes the quest for intelligibility outside the world" (25–26).

11. I do not know anyone who has explained this turn, and Nagel (2012) makes a similar observation when he says that for several centuries after Descartes, the desire for a unification of what we can know of the universe was expressed primarily through idealism, from the direction of mind first, but then "in a rapid historical shift whose causes are somewhat obscure, idealism was largely displaced in later twentieth century philosophy by attempts at unification in the opposite direction, starting from the physical" (37). I think that a possible explanation is that idealism had taken hold in Anglo-American philosophy primarily in the form of the logical positivists' verification principle, according to which a statement has meaning only if it is either tautologous or is verifiable by sense experience. That principle rapidly declined in influence after attacks by Karl Hempel (1950, 1951) and by Willard Quine in his famous 1951 paper, "Two Dogmas of Empiricism."

12. Dennett continues to use the word "consciousness" for something that exists, but objectors have pointed out that it is not what most philosophers and ordinary people mean by consciousness because he denies the existence of *qualia*—the subjective feel of what it is like to be in a certain conscious state. For a highly polemical exchange on Dennett's view of consciousness, see Dennett and Searle (1995).

13. One example is the traditional Japanese religion of Shinto, which does not make a sharp distinction between nature and the supernatural, incorporating the worship of ancestors and nature spirits and a belief in sacred power (*kami*) in both animate and inanimate things. Another example is Shona traditional religion, or Chivanhu, practiced in Zimbabwe, a part of the umbrella group of African traditional religions across the continent. It consists of a remote monotheistic God, Mwari or Musikavanhu (the creator of men), whose interactions with humans is mediated by ancestors, *vadzimu*. Communication with the ancestors is mediated by spirit mediums or *svikiro*, which are part of the natural world. I thank my student, Munashe Mataranyika, for describing to me the way the natural and the supernatural are understood in Shona traditional religion.

14. Arguments that purport to show that a position is self-defeating may not be terribly common in philosophy, but they are among the most powerful. Other examples include Plantinga's own criticism of Cartesian foundationalism (1983) and the now widely accepted criticism that verificationism—the view that only verifiable statements are meaningful—cannot be verified; see Creath (2017, §4.1) for discussion.

15. For a collection of papers responding to Plantinga's original argument for the self-defeat of naturalism, see Beilby (2002). Plantinga's argument is supported by Nagel (2012, 27).

16. I use the analogy of maps for my theory of theories and apply it to moral theories in Zagzebski (2017, chap. 1).

17. John Searle (1994, 96) argues that we must give up the visual model of the mind for similar reasons.

18. See Neuhouser (1990, chap. 3). The connection between Fichte's idea of the self-positing subject and the regress problem is discussed around page 75.

19. Richard Sorabji (2006, 206–207) discusses this passage in Aristotle as an answer to the regress problem, mentioning that the late-nineteenth-century philosopher Franz Brentano drew on Aristotle for his way out of the problem.

20. See Anscombe (1975) for a famous argument that the word "I" does not refer; in particular, it does not refer to the speaker.

21. Fichte discusses the identity of subject and object (what he calls "I = I") at length after he uses the argument I mention above as a reason to reject the representational view of the mind as applied to self-consciousness. See Fichte (1982, part 1).

22. This is not a proof of an enduring self, if such a proof is needed. It is the observation that the distinction between the self as subject and the self as object is bridged in memory. If memory cannot be trusted, and there is no enduring self, there is no reflective consciousness.

23. We have no trouble identifying the subjective *I* with the objective person publicly recognized and described. The situation is harder with the identification of individual subjective states with those same states objectively described. Any TOC that has a hope for success must be one in which the objective description of my mental states is something I can recognize myself in the same way I can recognize that the objectively described Linda Zagzebski is the same as *I*. One of the problems with identifying subjective conscious states with brain states is my lack of recognition of such an identity.

## Chapter 6. The Future

1. Wittgenstein (2009, § 243).

2. See, for instance, Simone de Beauvoir (2009); Held (2006).

3. A mirror neuron is one that fires both when an animal acts and when the animal observes the same action performed by another animal. In the late 1990s, neuroscientists at the University of Parma discovered that the same neurons fired when a monkey observed another animal reaching for a peanut as when the monkey reached for the peanut himself (Ramachandran 2011, 121–122). Although mirror neurons have not been observed in humans, there is conjecture that the neurological accompaniment to the awareness of another person's intentions or feelings is the same as the neurological accompaniment to the awareness of the same intentions or feelings in oneself (see Iacoboni et al. 2005). Iacoboni (2009) has also argued that the mirror neuron system is the basis for imitation, facilitating social behavior. V. S. Ramachandran (2011, 122) has speculated that the combination of the ability to read another's intentions and the ability to imitate their vocalizations, both of which seem to be connected with mirror neurons, may have shaped the evolution of human language.

4. A study of pediatric cancer patients and their parents found that more empathic parental responses to the children's pain during a medical procedure

was associated with less pain as reported by the children (Penner et al., 2008). In another study (Manczak et al., 2016), researchers looked at the effects of parental empathy on 247 pairs of parents and adolescent children. They found that parental empathy was correlated with better psychological and physiological well-being in their children, but the more empathic parents were also found to have a greater likelihood of experiencing chronic low-grade inflammation. Other physical problems have been reported in empathic health care workers. So apparently, the effects of empathy on the empathizer are not always positive.

5. Literature and film are by nature communicative of subjectivity. Literature focuses on the subjectivity of a fictional character, which raises some interesting puzzles about subjectivity. For instance, can a fictional character have the uniqueness of an actual person? Since the communication of subjectivity occurs in entertainment, there must be something fun or at least satisfying about it. Why do we like it so much?

6. Maxwell (2006), quoted in McGilchrist (2009, 250).

7. Husserl's argument is helpfully summarized by Dan Zahavi in an influential book bringing the work of phenomenology into conversation with analytic philosophy of mind and cognitive science (2005, chap. 6, sec. 2).

8. For discussions of Husserl's idea of double sensation, see Taipale (2014, 51), as well as Zahavi (2005, 157).

9. Husserl makes an interesting contrast with Aristotle, who at the beginning of his *Metaphysics* says that we love above all the sense of sight. "For not only with a view to action, but even when we are not going to do anything, we prefer seeing (one might say) to everything else. The reason is that this, most of all the senses, makes us know and brings to light many differences between things." Sight creates a greater distance between subject and object than does touch. Perhaps Western philosophy would have taken a different path if it had not put such a strong emphasis on sight.

10. For a recent paper giving a detailed account of the primacy of intersubjectivity in the works of Husserl and Merleau-Ponty, see Dermot Moran (2016).

11. Shaun Gallagher observes that phenomenology went into a decline in the 1960s but was reborn in the 1990s, particularly in works that connected it with cognitive science (2012, 14–15).

12. This point is related to the idea that propositions containing pure indexicals do not reduce to propositions in which the indexicals are eliminated, e.g., Castaneda (1966) and Perry (1979). Presumably, if "I" is a non-eliminable indexical, so is "you." I will not pursue that issue here. It is possible that first-person propositions are distinct from propositions in the third person. It is also possible that propositions are always objective, and the existence of subjectivity reveals that there is much in the world that propositions cannot express. No proposition fully expresses "I." The same point could apply to indexicals like "here" and "now."

13. My position is that first-person reasons for belief are conscious states in the person acquiring the belief. Other beliefs, emotions, and experiences

produce new beliefs, and a rational person reflects upon her conscious states in order to make them harmonious since lack of harmony shows that something is wrong—a belief is false, an emotion is inappropriate, a plan is misguided. A conscientiously self-governing agent adjudicates conflict within her conscious states in order to make her consciousness fit the world. In contrast, a third-person reason includes what we typically call evidence. It is a reason that can be offered to anybody, regardless of her personal experiences and previous beliefs. But if we accept the evidence, it is added to our set of beliefs and becomes first personal. In addition to Zagzebski (2012), I discuss this distinction in Zagzebski (2011) and Zagzebski (2014).

14. In several studies, Glenn Reeder and his colleagues (2005) have found that people tend to attribute negative motivations to people with whom they differ, and the more strongly they feel about an issue, the more suspicious they are of hidden motives on the other side. In the years since Reeder and his colleagues' study, this problem has become clear on social media where comments need to be very brief, eliminating subtlety, and making it even more likely that people give the worst interpretation to remarks by the opposing side. I think of the difference between reading a post on Twitter or Facebook and spending two hours watching a movie or two days reading a novel. When someone else spends a lot of time attempting to convey their view of the world, I take it seriously and I am much less suspicious of their motives, even if their viewpoint is contrary to my own.

15. Not every writer wants to encourage empathy. Paul Bloom's (2016) book, *Against Empathy,* defends what he calls "rational compassion," which is perspective-taking without the emotion-sharing. Bloom's view is not an objection to my point in this section since he is still defending a form of intersubjectivity.

16. Some writers argue that empathy is "affect matching" in which the empathic person experiences something close to the feelings of the target person (Snow 2000; De Vignemont and Singer 2006; De Vignemont and Jacob 2012), whereas other researchers argue that a cognitive component of taking on the perspective of the target person is necessary or sufficient for empathy (Goldie 1999; Rameson and Lieberman 2009; Ickes 2003). For a helpful summary of disagreement on the nature of empathy, see John Michael (2014). Michael argues that the main controversy concerns whether a few affective and cognitive phenomena are necessary conditions for empathy or instead its characteristic features or consequences. Michael argues that empathy can generate interpersonal understanding by virtue of these phenomena whether or not they are conceptualized as necessary conditions for empathy. That is reasonable. It should therefore be possible to reach consensus on the connection between these phenomena and interpersonal understanding, whether or not these phenomena are actually components of empathy.

17. See Talisse (2016, 80). He refers to Iyengar and Krupenkin (2018) and Williamson (2008).

18. The studies on sorting primarily pertain to the polarization of political beliefs, but I suspect that the sorting phenomenon applies much more widely than that, including the sorting of philosophical, moral, and religious viewpoints.

19. Talisse's proposal sounds reasonable, but one difficulty with his idea is that people sometimes become estranged from friends and family members *after* they discover their political viewpoints. The discovery of opposing viewpoints is enough to diminish previous sympathy and trust.

20. Dreams are rarely examined except in psychoanalytic studies. Freud's (2010) *The Interpretation of Dreams* is the landmark work. Jonathan Lear's (2008) book *Radical Hope* includes the way an important dream shaped the destiny of the Crow Indians. Lear has a background in psychoanalysis as well as philosophy, and this book is one of the exceptions in its serious treatment of dreams.

21. *ST* 3, supp. q. 72, a. 1; q. 92, a. 3.

Alexander, Stephon. (2016). *The Jazz of Physics: The Secret Link between Music and the Structure of the Universe*. New York: Basic Books.

Alter, Robert, transl. (2007). *The Book of Psalms*. New York: W. W. Norton.

Amodio, David M., and Jillian K. Swencionis. (2018). "Proactive Control of Implicit Bias: A Theoretical Model and Implications for Behavior Change." *Journal of Personality and Social Psychology* 115 (2): 255–275.

Anscombe, G.E.M. (1975). "The First Person." In *Mind and Language: Wolfson College Lectures*. Samuel D. Guttenplan, editor. Oxford: Oxford University Press, 45–65.

Aquinas, Thomas. (1922). *Summa Theologica* [*ST*]. Fathers of the English Dominican Province, translators. London: Burns, Oates and Washbourne.

———. (1954). *De Veritate*. R. W. Mulligan (Q. 1–9), J. V. McGlynn (Q. 10–20), and R. W. Schmidt (Q. 21–29), translators. Chicago: Henry Regnery.

———. (1975). *Summa Contra Gentiles*. A. C. Pegis (bk. 1), J. F. Anderson (bk. 2), V. J. Bourke (bks. 3 and 4), and C. J. O'Neil (bk. 5), translators. Notre Dame, IN: University of Notre Dame Press.

Aristotle. *De Anima*. J. A. Smith, translator. In Barnes (1984).

———. *Eudemian Ethics*. J. Solomon, translator. In Barnes (1984), vol. 2.

———. *Metaphysics*. W. D. Ross, translator. In Barnes (1984).

———. *Nicomachean Ethics* [*NE*]. W. D. Ross, translator. In Barnes (1984).

———. *Poetics*. Ingram Bywater, translator. In Barnes (1984).

———. *Politics*. Benjamin Jowett, translator. In Barnes (1984).

Armstrong, David M. (1961). *Perception and the Physical World*. London: Routledge and Kegan Paul.

Armstrong, Karen. (1994). *A History of God: A 4,000-Year Quest of Judaism, Christianity, and Islam*. New York: Ballantine Books.

*Art in Quest of Heaven and Truth*. (2012). Exhibit book for "Chinese Jades through the Ages." Taipei, Taiwan: National Palace Museum.

"Art through Time: A Global View." *Annenberg Learner*. Retrieved November 14, 2020, from https://www.learner.org/series/art-through-time-a-global-view/.

Augustine. (1993a). *Confessions*. E. J. Sheed, translator. Indianapolis: Hackett Publishing.

———. (1993b). *On the Free Choice of the Will*. Thomas Williams, translator. Indianapolis: Hackett Publishing.

———. (2002). *On the Trinity*. Gareth Matthews, editor; Stephen McKenna, translator. Cambridge: Cambridge University Press.

Baehr, Jason, ed. (2016). *Intellectual Virtues in Education: Essays in Applied Virtue Epistemology*. New York: Routledge.

Baker, Lynn Rudder. (2013). "Can Subjectivity Be Naturalized?" *International Studies in Phenomenology and Philosophy* 1 (2): 15–25.

Bakhtin, Mikhail. (1981). *The Dialogic Imagination: Four Essays*. Caryl Emerson and Michael Holquist, translators. Austin: University of Texas Press.

Ballantyne, Nathan. (2019). *Knowing Our Limits*. New York: Oxford University Press.

Balthasar, Hans Urs von. (1986). "On the Concept of Person." Peter Verhalen, translator. *Communio: International Catholic Review* 13 (1): 18–26.

Barnes, Jonathan, ed. (1984). *Complete Works of Aristotle*. 2 vols. Princeton, NJ: Princeton University Press.

Beauvoir, Simone de. (2009). *The Second Sex*. Constance Borde and Sheila Malovany-Chevallier, translators. New York: Alfred A. Knopf.

Beilby, James K., ed. (2002). *Naturalism Defeated? Essays on Plantinga's Evolutionary Argument against Naturalism*. Ithaca, NY: Cornell University Press.

Bell, Martha A. (2015). "Bringing the Field of Infant Cognition and Perception toward a Biopsychosocial Perspective." In *Handbook of Infant Biopsychosocial Development*. Susan D. Calkins, editor. New York: Guilford Press, 27–37.

Berkeley, George. (1979). *Three Dialogues between Hylas and Philonous*. Robert Merrihew Adams, editor. Indianapolis: Hackett Publishing.

Bigongiari, Dino, and Henry Paolucci. (2005). *Backgrounds of the Divine Comedy: A Series of Lectures*. Anne Paolucci, editor. Dover, DE: Griffon House.

Bloom, Paul. (2016). *Against Empathy: The Case for Rational Compassion*. New York: HarperCollins.

Boethius. (1973). *The Theological Tractates and The Consolation of Philosophy*. H. F. Stewart, E. K. Rand, and S. J. Tester, translators. Cambridge, MA: Harvard University Press (Loeb Classical Library).

Boltz, William G. (2000/2001). "The Invention of Writing in China." *Oriens Extremus* 42: 1–17.

Borges, Jorge Luis. (1998). *Collected Fictions*. Andrew Hurley, translator. New York: Viking Penguin.

Botvinick, Matthew, Amishi P. Jha, Lauren M. Bylsma, Sara A. Fabian, Patricia E. Solomon, and Kenneth M. Prkachin. (2005). "Viewing Facial Expressions of Pain Engages Cortical Areas Involved in the Direct Experience of Pain." *NeuroImage* 25 (1): 312–319.

Brennan, Andrew, and Y. S. Lo. (2010). "Two Conceptions of Dignity: Honour and Self-Determination." In *Perspectives on Human Dignity: A Conversation*. Jeff Malpas and Norelle Lickiss, editors. Dordrecht: Springer, 43–58.

Brindley, Erica. (2012). *Music, Cosmology, and the Politics of Harmony in Early China*. Albany: SUNY Press.

Buber, Martin. (1970). *I and Thou*. Walter Kaufmann, translator. New York: Simon and Schuster.

Burckhardt, Jacob. ([1860] 1954). *The Civilization of the Renaissance in Italy*. New York: Modern Library.

Burge, Tyler. (1979). "Individualism and the Mental." *Midwest Studies in Philosophy* 4: 73–121.

———. (1986). "Individualism and Psychology." *Philosophical Review* 95 (1): 3–45.

Burke, James. (1985). *The Day the Universe Changed*. London: London Writers.

Burkert, Walter. (1999). "The Logic of Cosmogony." In *From Myth to Reason? Studies in the Development of Greek Thought*. Richard Buxton, editor. Oxford: Oxford University Press, 87–106.

Butchvarov, Panayot. (1998). *Skepticism about the External World*. New York: Oxford University Press.

Butler, Judith. (1990). *Gender Trouble: Feminism and the Subversion of Identity*. London: Routledge.

Buxton, Richard. (1999). "Introduction." In *From Myth to Reason? Studies in the Development of Greek Thought*. Richard Buxton, editor. Oxford: Oxford University Press, 1–21.

Cahill, Thomas. (1998). *The Gifts of the Jews: How a Tribe of Desert Nomads Changed the Way Everyone Thinks and Feels*. Hinges of History. New York: Anchor Books.

Carrithers, Michael. (1985). "An Alternative Social History of the Self." In Carrithers et al. (1985), 234–256.

Carrithers, Michael, Steven Collins, and Steven Lukes, eds. (1985). *The Category of the Person: Anthropology, Philosophy, History*. Cambridge: Cambridge University Press.

Carruthers, Peter. (1996). "Simulation and Self-Knowledge: A Defence of Theory-Theory." In *Theories of Theories of Mind*. Peter Carruthers and Peter K. Smith, editors. Cambridge: Cambridge University Press, 22–38.

———. (2011). *The Opacity of Mind: An Integrative Theory of Self-Knowledge*. Oxford: Oxford University Press.

Carruthers, Peter, Logan Fletcher, and J. Brendan Ritchie. (2012). "The Evolution of Self-Knowledge." *Philosophical Topics* 40 (2): 13–37.

Castaneda, Hector-Neri. 1966, "'He': A Study in the Logic of Self-Consciousness." *Ratio* 8: 130–157.

Cervantes, Miguel de. (2003). *Don Quixote*. Edith Grossman, translator. New York: HarperCollins.

Cheng, Yawei, Chia-Yen Yang, Ching-Po Lin, Po-Lei Lee, and Jean Decety. (2008). "The Perception of Pain in Others Suppresses Somatosensory Oscillations: A Magnetoencephalography Study." *NeuroImage* 40 (4): 1833–1840.

Cicero, Marcus Tullius. (1887). *De Officiis*. Andrew P. Peabody, translator, with introduction and notes. Boston: Little, Brown.

Cohen, H. (2003). "Scientific Revolution." In *The Oxford Companion to the History of Modern Science*. J. L. Heilbron, editor. New York: Oxford University Press, 741–743.

Cooke, Elizabeth F. (2006). *Peirce's Pragmatic Theory of Inquiry: Fallibilism and Indeterminacy*. New York: Bloomsbury Continuum.

Collins, Steven. (1985). "Categories, Concepts, or Predicaments? Remarks on Mauss's Use of Philosophical Terminology." In Carrithers et al. (1985), 46–82.

Collobert, Catherine. (2009). "Philosophical Readings of Homer: Ancient and Contemporary Insights." In *Logos and Muthos: Philosophical Essays in Greek Literature*. William Wians, editor. Albany: SUNY Press, 133–157.

Copenhaver, Brian. (2016). "Giovanni Pico della Mirandola." *The Stanford Encyclopedia of Philosophy*. Edward Zalta, editor. https://plato.stanford.edu /archives/spr2017/entries/pico-della-mirandola/.

Coseru, Christian. (Spring 2017). "Mind in Indian Buddhist Philosophy." *The Stanford Encyclopedia of Philosophy*. Edward Zalta, editor. https://plato.stanford .edu/archives/spr2017/entries/mind-indian-buddhism/.

Creath, Richard. (Fall 2017). "Logical Empiricism." *The Stanford Encyclopedia of Philosophy*. Edward N. Zalta, editor. https://plato.stanford.edu/archives /fall2017/entries/logical-empiricism/.

Crick, Francis. (1981). *Life Itself: Its Origin and Nature*. New York: Simon and Shuster (Touchstone).

Crisp, Thomas M. (2004). "On Presentism and Triviality" and "Reply to Ludlow." In *Oxford Studies in Metaphysics*, vol. 1. Dean W. Zimmerman, editor. New York: Oxford University Press, 15–20 and 37–46.

Curd, Patricia, ed. (2011). *A Pre-Socratics Reader: Selected Fragments and Testimonia*. 2nd ed. Richard D. McKirahan and Patricia Curd, translators. Indianapolis: Hackett Publishing.

Curl, James S. (2003). *Classical Architecture: An Introduction to Its Vocabulary and Essentials, with a Select Glossary of Terms*. New York: Norton.

Dante Alighieri. (2020). *The Divine Comedy. Paradise*. Alasdair Gray, translator. Edinburgh, UK: Canongate Books.

Davidson, Donald. (2001a). "Knowing One's Own Mind." In *Subjective, Intersubjective, Objective*. Oxford: Clarendon Press.

———. (2001b). "The Myth of the Subjective." In *Subjective, Intersubjective, Objective*. Oxford: Clarendon Press.

Dawkins, Richard. (2006). *The Selfish Gene*. 30th anniv. ed. Oxford: Oxford University Press.

———. (2011). *The Magic of Reality: How We Know What's Really True*. New York: Free Press.

Dennett, Daniel. (1991). *Consciousness Explained*. Boston: Little, Brown.

———. (2017). *From Bacteria to Bach and Back: The Evolution of Minds*. New York: W. W. Norton.

Dennett, Daniel, and John Searle. (1995). " 'The Mystery of Consciousness': An Exchange." *New York Review of Books*, December 21.

Descartes, René. (1964–76). *Oeuvres de Descartes*. 11 vols. Charles Adam and Paul Tannery, editors. Paris: Vrin/CNRS.

———. (1971). *Philosophical Writings*. Elizabeth Anscombe and Peter Geach, translators. Indianapolis: Bobbs-Merrill.

———. (1984). *The Philosophical Writings of Descartes*, vol. 2. J. Cottingham, R. Stoothoff, and D. Murdoch, translators. Cambridge: Cambridge University Press.

———. (1998). *Discourse on Method and Meditations on First Philosophy*. D. Cress, translator. Indianapolis: Hackett Publishing.

———. (2006). *Meditations on First Philosophy*. R. Ariew and D. Cress, translators. Indianapolis: Hackett Publishing.

De Vignemont, F., and P. Jacob. (2012). "What Is It Like to Feel Another's Pain?" *Philosophy of Science* 79 (2): 295–316.

De Vignemont, F., and T. Singer. (2006). "The Empathic Brain: How, When and Why?" *Trends in Cognitive Sciences* 10 (10): 435–441.

Devlin, Keith. (1997). *Mathematics: The Science of Patterns: The Search for Order in Life, Mind and the Universe*. New York: Scientific American Paperback.

Duhem, Pierre. (1969). *To Save the Phenomena: An Essay on the Idea of Physical Theory from Plato to Galileo*. Edmund Dolan and Chaninah Maschler, translators. Chicago: University of Chicago Press.

———. (1985). *Medieval Cosmology: Theories of Infinity, Place, Time, Void, and the Plurality of Worlds*. Roger Ariew, translator. Chicago: University of Chicago Press.

Easwaran, Eknath, trans. (2007). *The Upanishads*. Tomales, CA: Nilgiri Press.

Egginton, William. (2016). *The Man Who Invented Fiction: How Cervantes Ushered in the Modern World*. New York: Bloomsbury.

Einstein, Albert. (1950). "Physics and Reality." In *Out of My Later Years*. New York: Philosophical Library.

Emerson, Ralph Waldo. (1982). "Self-Reliance." In *Nature and Selected Essays*. New York: Penguin Classics.

Ettinghausen, Richard, Oleg Grabar, and Marilyn Jenkins-Madina. (2001). *Islamic Art and Architecture, 650–1250*. Yale University Press Pelican History of Art. New Haven, CT: Yale University Press.

Feldman, Richard, and Ted A. Warfield. (2010). *Disagreement*. Oxford: Oxford University Press.

Fichte, Johann Gottlieb. (1982). *Science of Knowledge*. 2nd ed. Peter Heath and John Lachs, editors and translators. Cambridge: Cambridge University Press.

Finn, Michael R. (2017). *Figures of the Pre-Freudian Unconscious from Flaubert to Proust*. New York: Cambridge University Press.

Flaig, Egon. (2013). "To Act with Good Advice: Greek Tragedy and the Democratic Political Sphere." In *The Greek Polis and the Invention of Democracy: A Politico-Cultural Transformation and Its Interpretations*. Johann P. Arnason, Kurt A. Raaflaub, and Peter Wagner, editors. Chichester, UK: Wiley-Blackwell, 71–98.

Foucault, Michel. (1990). *A History of Sexuality*, vols. 1–3. Robert Hurley, translator. New York: Vintage Books.

———. (1995). *Discipline and Punish: The Birth of the Prison*. Alan Sheridan, translator. New York: Vintage Books.

——. (2016). *About the Beginnings of the Hermeneutics of the Self: Two Lectures at Dartmouth College.* In *Self and Subjectivity.* Kim Atkins, editor. Malden, MA: Blackwell Publishing, 211–219.

Frankfort, Henri, H. A. Frankfort, John A. Wilson, and Thorkild Jacobsen. (1946). *Before Philosophy.* Baltimore, MD: Penguin Books.

Freud, Sigmund. (2010). *The Interpretation of Dreams.* James Strachey, translator and editor. Basic Books.

Fry, Iris. (2000). *The Emergence of Life on Earth.* New Brunswick, NJ: Rutgers University Press.

Fukuyama, Francis. (2018). *Identity: The Demand for Dignity and the Politics of Resentment.* New York: Farrar, Straus and Giroux.

Gadamer, Hans-Georg. (1981). "On the Philosophic Element in the Sciences and the Scientific Character of Philosophy." In *Reason in the Age of Science.* Frederick G. Lawrence, translator. Cambridge, MA: MIT Press.

Gallagher, Shaun. (2012). *Phenomenology.* Basingstoke, UK: Palgrave Macmillan.

Gaukroger, S. (1999). "Beyond Reality: Nietzsche's Science of Appearances." In *Nietzsche, Theories of Knowledge, and Critical Theory: Nietzsche and the Sciences.* B. E. Babich, editor. Boston Studies in the Philosophy of Science, vol. 203. Dordrecht: Springer, 37–49.

——. (2006). *The Emergence of a Scientific Culture: Science and the Shaping of Modernity, 1210–1685.* Oxford: Oxford University Press.

Geddert, Jeremy S. (2017). *Hugo Grotius and the Modern Theology of Freedom: Transcending Natural Rights.* New York: Routledge.

Gewirth, Alan. (1982). *Human Rights: Essays on Justification and Applications.* Chicago: University of Chicago Press.

Goldie, Peter. (1999). "How We Think of Others' Emotions." *Mind and Language* 14 (4): 394–423.

Goodin, Robert E. (2003). *Reflective Democracy.* Oxford: Oxford University Press.

Grabar, Andre. (1968). *Christian Iconography: A Study of Its Origins.* A. W. Mellon Lectures in the Fine Arts. Princeton, NJ: Princeton University Press.

Greasley, Kate, and Christopher Kaczor. (2018). *Abortion Rights: For and Against.* New York: Cambridge University Press.

Gregory, Brad S. (2012). *The Unintended Reformation: How a Religious Revolution Secularized Society.* Cambridge, MA: Belknap Press.

Greif, Avner. (2006). "Family Structure, Institutions, and Growth: The Origins and Implications of Western Corporations." *American Economic Review* 96: 308–312.

Griffin, James. (2008). *On Human Rights.* New York: Oxford University Press.

Gutas, Dimitri. (2009). "Origins in Baghdad." In *The Cambridge History of Medieval Philosophy,* vol. 1. Robert Pasnau, editor. Cambridge: Cambridge University Press, 9–25.

Guthrie, Kenneth Sylvan. (1988). *The Pythagorean Sourcebook and Library.* David Fideler, editor; Kenneth Sylvan Guthrie, translator. Grand Rapids, MI: Phanes Press.

Gutmann, Amy, and Dennis Thompson. (1996). *Democracy and Disagreement*. Cambridge, MA: Belknap Press.

Haidt, Jonathan. (2012). *The Righteous Mind: Why Good People Are Divided by Politics and Religion*. New York: Vintage Books.

Hallam, Jennifer. (2017). "Cosmology and Belief." *Art through Time: A Global View*. https://www.learner.org/series/art-through-time-a-global-view /cosmology-and-belief/. St. Louis, MO: Annenberg Learner Media.

Hankinson, R. J. (2008). "Reason, Cause, and Explanation in Pre-Socratic Philosophy." In *The Oxford Handbook of Pre-Socratic Philosophy*. Patricia Curd and Daniel W. Graham, editors. Oxford: Oxford University Press.

Hannam, James. (2010). *God's Philosophers: How the Medieval World Laid the Foundations of Modern Science*. London: Icon Books.

Hardcastle, Valerie Gray, ed. (1999). *Where Biology Meets Psychology: Philosophical Essays*. Cambridge, MA: MIT Press.

Harman, Gilbert. (1996). "Explaining Objective Color in Terms of Subjective Reactions." *Philosophical Issues* 7 (Perception): 1–17.

Harper, Robert F. (1904). *The Code of Hammurabi: King of Babylon about 2250 B.C.* Chicago: University of Chicago Press.

Harré, Rom. (2006). "Resolving the Emergence-Reduction Debate." *Synthese* 151 (3): 499–509.

Hawking, Stephen W. (1988). *A Brief History of Time: From the Big Bang to Black Holes*. Toronto: Bantam Books.

Hegel, G.W.F. (1977). *Phenomenology of Spirit*. A. V. Miller, translator. Oxford: Oxford University Press.

———. (2020). *Lectures on the History of Philosophy*. E. S. Haldane and Frances H. Simson, translators. Delhi: Lector House.

Held, Virginia. (2006). *The Ethics of Care: Personal, Political, and Global*. New York: Oxford University Press.

Hempel, Carl. (1950) "Problems and Changes in the Empiricist Criterion of Meaning." *Revue Internationale de Philosophie* 41 (11): 41–63.

———. (1951) "The Concept of Cognitive Significance: A Reconsideration." *Proceedings of the American Academy of Arts and Sciences* 80 (1): 61–77.

———. (1980). "Comments on Goodman's Ways of Worldmaking," *Synthese* 45 (2) (October): 193–199.

Hendrix, John Shannon. (2015). "Unconscious Thought in Freud." In *Unconscious Thought in Philosophy and Psychoanalysis*. London: Palgrave Macmillan.

Henrich, Dieter. (1982). "Fichte's Original Insight." In *Contemporary German Philosophy*, vol. 1. D. E. Christensen, editor. University Park: Pennsylvania State University Press, 15–53.

Heraclitus. (2011). Untitled fragment. In *A Pre-Socratics Reader: Selected Fragments and Testimonia*. 2nd ed. Patricia Curd, editor; Richard D. McKirahan and Patricia Curd, translators. Indianapolis: Hackett Publishing.

Hermann, Arnold. (2004). *To Think Like God: Pythagoras and Parmenides: The Origins of Philosophy*. Las Vegas: Parmenides Publishing.

Hickok, Gregory. (2014). *The Myth of Mirror Neurons*. New York: W. W. Norton.

Hobbes, Thomas. (1994). *Leviathan*. Indianapolis: Hackett Publishing.

Hopper, V. F. ([1938] 2000). *Medieval Number Symbolism: Its Sources, Meaning, and Influence on Thought and Expression*. Reprint; Mineola, NY: Dover Publications.

Hume, David. (1975). *Enquiries concerning Human Understanding and concerning the Principles of Morals*. L. A. Selby-Bigge and Peter H. Nidditch, editors. Oxford: Clarendon Press.

———. (2000). *A Treatise of Human Nature*. Mary J. Norton and David F. Norton, editors. Oxford: Oxford University Press.

Hung, Wu. (1999). "The Art and Architecture of the Warring States Period." In *The Cambridge History of Ancient China: From Origins to Civilization to 221 B.C.* Michael Loewe and Edward Shaughnessy, editors. New York: Cambridge University Press, 651–744.

Hunter, James Davison. (1992). *Culture Wars: The Struggle to Define America*. New York: Basic Books.

Hursthouse, Rosalind. (1991). "Virtue Theory and Abortion." *Philosophy and Public Affairs* 20: 223–246.

Husserl, Edmund. (1960). *Cartesian Meditations*. Dorian Cairns, translator. The Hague: Martinus Nijhoff.

———. (1967) *Ideas*. W. R. Boyce Gibson, translator. New York: Collier.

Iacoboni, M. (2009). "Imitation, Empathy, and Mirror Neurons." In *Annual Review of Psychology* 60 (1): 653–670.

Iacoboni, M., I. Molnar-Szakacs, V. Gallese, G. Buccino, and J. C. Mazziotta. (2005). "Grasping the Intentions of Others with One's Own Mirror Neuron System." *PLOS Biology* 3 (3): e79.

Ickes, William. (2003). *Everyday Mind Reading: Understanding What Other People Think and Feel*. Amherst, NY: Prometheus Books.

Illingworth, John Richardson. (1902). *Personality, Human, and Divine: Being the Bampton Lectures for the Year 1894*. London: Macmillan.

Indich, William. (2000). *Consciousness in Advaita Vedanta*. New Delhi: Motilal Barnarsidass.

Iyengar, Shanto, and Masha Krupenkin. (2018). "The Strengthening of Partisan Affect." *Advances in Political Psychology* 39 (1): 201–218.

Jabbi, Mbemba, Marte Swart, and Christian Keysers. (2007). "Empathy for Positive and Negative Emotions in the Gustatory Cortex." *NeuroImage* 34 (4): 1744–1753.

Jaki, Stanley. (1978). *The Origin of Science and the Science of Its Origins*. South Bend, IN: Regnery Gateway.

Jaspers, Karl. (1951). *The Way to Wisdom: An Introduction to Philosophy*. R. Manheim, translator. New Haven, CT: Yale University Press.

———. (1953). *The Origin and Goal of History*. M. Bullock, translator. New Haven, CT: Yale University Press.

Jingo, Minoru (producer), and Akira Kurosawa (director). (1994). *Rashomon.* Japan: Daiei Film.

Johnson, Casey R. (2018). *Voicing Dissent: The Ethics and Epistemology of Making Disagreements Public.* New York: Routledge, Taylor and Francis.

———. (2019). "Intellectual Humility and Empathy by Analogy." *Topoi* 38: 221–228.

Jones, Mark Wilson. (2014). *Origins of Classical Architecture: Temples, Orders and Gifts to the Gods in Ancient Greece.* New Haven, CT: Yale University Press.

Joost-Gaugier, Christiane L. (2006). *Measuring Heaven: Pythagoras and His Influence on Thought and Art in Antiquity and the Middle Ages.* Ithaca, NY: Cornell University Press.

Josephson-Storm, Jason Ā. (2017). *The Myth of Disenchantment: Magic, Modernity, and the Birth of the Human Sciences.* Chicago: University of Chicago Press.

Kallestrup, Jesper. (2012). *Semantic Externalism.* New Problems of Philosophy Series. Abingdon, UK: Routledge.

Kant, Immanuel. (1950). *Prolegomena to Any Future Metaphysics.* Lewis White Beck, translator. Library of Liberal Arts Series 27. Indianapolis: Bobbs-Merrill.

———. (2007). *Critique of Pure Reason [CPR].* Marcus Weigelt, translator. London: Penguin Classics.

———. (2009). *Groundwork of the Metaphysic of Morals.* H. J. Paton, translator. Harper Perennial Modern Thought Series. New York: HarperCollins.

Kateb, George. (2014). *Human Dignity.* Cambridge, MA: Belknap Press.

Kepler, Johannes. [1619] (2014). *Harmonies of the World.* Charles Glenn Wallis, translator. Scotts Valley, CA: CreateSpace Independent Publishing Platform.

Ker, William Paton. (1922). *Epic and Romance: Essays on Medieval Literature.* London: Macmillan.

Kierkegaard, Søren. (1941). *Concluding Unscientific Postscript.* David F. Swenson and Walter Lowrie, translators. Princeton, NJ: Princeton University Press.

Kirk, Geoffrey Stephen. (1974). *The Nature of Greek Myths.* Harmondsworth: Penguin Books.

Klima, Gyula. (2015). "Semantic Content in Aquinas and Ockham." In *Linguistic Content: New Essays on the History of Philosophy of Language.* M. Cameron and R. J. Stainton, editors. Oxford: Oxford University Press, 121–135.

Konrath, S., and D. Grynberg. (2016). "The Positive (and Negative) Psychology of Empathy." In *The Neurobiology and Psychology of Empathy.* D. Watt and J. Panksepp, editors. Hauppauge, NY: Nova Science Publishers.

Korsgaard, Christine. (2009). *Self-Constitution: Agency, Identity, and Integrity.* Oxford: Oxford University Press.

Kripke, Saul. (1980). *Naming and Necessity.* Cambridge, MA: Harvard University Press.

Lagercrantz, H. (2016). *Infant Brain Development: Formation of the Mind and the Emergence of Consciousness.* New York: Springer.

Lamm, Claus, C. D. Batson, and Jean Decety. (2007). "The Neural Substrate of Human Empathy: Effects of Perspective-taking and Cognitive Appraisal." *Journal of Cognitive Neuroscience* 19 (1): 42–58.

Lao Tzu. (1963). *Tao Te Ching*. D. C. Lau, translator. London: Penguin Classics.

Lau, Joe, and Max Deutsch. (Winter 2016). "Externalism about Mental Content." *The Stanford Encyclopedia of Philosophy*. Edward Zalta, editor. https://plato .stanford.edu/archives/win2016/entries/content-externalism/.

Lear, Jonathan. (2008). *Radical Hope*. Cambridge, MA: Harvard University Press.

Le Bihan, D., R. Turner, T. A. Zeffiro, C. A. Cuénod, P. Jezzard, and V. Bonnerot. (1993). "Activation of Human Primary Visual Cortex during Visual Recall: A Magnetic Resonance Imaging Study." *Proceedings of the National Academy of Sciences of the USA* 90 (24): 11802–11805.

Leibniz, Gottfried Wilhelm. (1951). *Selections*. Philip Wiener, editor. New York: Scribner's.

Leo the Great (Pope). (1997). *Nicene and Post Nicene Fathers*. 2nd ser. Vol. 12, *Leo the Great, Gregory the Great*. Phillip Schaff and Rev. Henry Wallace, editors. New York: Cosimo Classics.

Leonardo da Vinci. (2008). *Notebooks*. I. A. Richter and M. Kemp, editors. New York: Oxford University Press.

Lewis, C. S. (1964). *The Discarded Image: An Introduction to Medieval and Renaissance Literature*. Cambridge: Cambridge University Press.

———. (2009). *The Abolition of Man*. San Francisco: HarperOne.

Lewis, Milton. (2010). "A Brief History of Human Dignity: Idea and Application." In *Perspectives on Human Dignity*. Jeff Malpas and Norelle Lickiss, editors. Dordrecht: Springer, 93–105.

Livingstone, Niall. (2011). "Instructing Myth: From Homer to the Sophists." In *A Companion to Greek Mythology*. Ken Dowden and Niall Livingstone, editors. Chichester, UK: Wiley-Blackwell, 125–140.

Locke, John. (1975). *An Essay concerning Human Understanding*. Oxford: Oxford World's Classics.

———. (2004). *An Essay concerning Human Understanding*. Alexander Campbell Fraser, editor. New York: Barnes and Noble.

Long, Anthony A. (2013). "Heraclitus on Measure and the Explicit Emergence of Rationality." In *Doctrine and Doxography: Studies on Heraclitus and Pythagoras*. D. Sider and D. Obbink, editors. Studies in the Recovery of Ancient Texts. Berlin: De Gruyter, 201–224.

Lopez, Donald S., Jr. (2009). *The Story of Buddhism: A Concise Guide to Its History and Teachings*. New York: HarperCollins.

Lugones, Maria. (1987). "Playfulness, 'World'-Travelling, and Loving Perception," *Hypatia* 2 (2) (Summer): 3–19.

Luther, Martin. (1957). *Christian Liberty*. Harold J. Grimm, editor. Philadelphia: Fortress Press.

Lyotard, Jean-François. (1984). *The Postmodern Condition: A Report on Knowledge*. Geoff Bennington and Brian Massumi, translators. Minneapolis: University of Minnesota Press.

MacDonald, Scott, editor. (1991). *Being and Goodness: The Concept of the Good in Metaphysics and Philosophical Theology*. Ithaca, NY: Cornell University Press.

MacIntyre, Alasdair. (1981). *After Virtue*. Notre Dame, IN: University of Notre Dame Press.

———. (1988). *Whose Justice? Which Rationality?* Notre Dame, IN: University of Notre Dame Press.

———. (1991). "Community, Law, and the Idiom and Rhetoric of Rights." *Listening: Journal of Religion and Culture* 55: 96–110.

———. (1999). *Dependent Rational Animals: Why Human Beings Need the Virtues*. Chicago: Open Court Press.

———. (2016). *Ethics in the Conflict of Modernity: An Essay on Desire, Practical Reasoning, and Narrative*. Cambridge: Cambridge University Press.

Mâle, Emile. (1972). *The Gothic Image: Religious Art in France of the Thirteenth Century*. Dora Nussey, translator. Icon Edition. New York: Harper and Row.

Malevich, Kazimir. (1968). "From Cubism and Futurism to Suprematism: The New Realism in Painting." In *Essays on Art 1915–1928*. Copenhagen: Borgens Forlag, 1968, 33.

Mallon, Ron. (2004). "Passing, Traveling and Reality: Social Constructionism and the Metaphysics of Race." *Noûs* 38 (4): 644–673.

———. (2006). "Race: Normative, Not Metaphysical or Semantic," *Ethics*, 116 (3): 525–551.

———. (2007). "A Field Guide to Social Construction." *Philosophy Compass* 2 (1): 93–108.

Manczak E. M., A. DeLongis, and E. Chen. (2016). "Does Empathy Have a Cost? Diverging Psychological and Physiological Effects within Families." *Health Psychology* 35 (3): 211–218.

Mandik, Peter. (2013). "The Neurophilosophy of Subjectivity." In *Oxford Handbook of Philosophy and Neuroscience*. John Bickel, editor. New York: Oxford University Press.

Mann, Charles (2011). "The Birth of Religion." *National Geographic* (June), 39–59.

Maritain, Jacques. (1943). *The Rights of Man and the Natural Law*. New York: Scribner.

———. (1949). *Human Rights: Comments and Interpretations*. UNESCO, editor. New York: Columbia University Press.

Markosian, Ned (2004). "A Defense of Presentism." In Zimmerman (2004), 47–82.

Martin, Linette. (2002). *Sacred Doorways: A Beginner's Guide to Icons*. Brewster, MA: Paraclete Press.

Mauss, Marcel. (1985). "A Category of the Human Mind: The Notion of Person; the Notion of Self." In Carrithers et al. (1985), 1–25.

Maxwell, I. (2006) *Animal Tracks, ID and Techniques*. Falmouth, UK: Flame Lilly Press.

McDowell, John. (1994). *Mind and World*. Cambridge, MA: Harvard University Press.

McGilchrist, Iain. (2009). *The Master and His Emissary: The Divided Brain and the Making of the Western World*. New Haven, CT: Yale University Press.

Merleau-Ponty, Maurice. (2012). *The Phenomenology of Perception*. Donald A. Landes, translator. New York: Routledge Classics.

Michael, J. (2014). "Towards a Consensus about the Role of Empathy in Interpersonal Understanding." *Topoi* 33 (1): 157–172.

Miller, Christian B., R. Michael Furr, Angela Knobel, and William Fleeson, editors. (2015). *Character: New Directions from Philosophy, Psychology, and Theology*. New York: Oxford University Press.

Mirra, Nicole. (2018). *Educating for Empathy: Literacy, Learning, and Civic Engagement*. New York: Teachers College Press.

Mooney, James. (1995). *Myths of the Cherokee*. New York: Dover Publications.

Moran, Dermot. (2016). "*Ineinandersein* and *L'interlacs*: The Constitution of the Social World or 'We-World' (*Wir-Welt*) in Edmund Husserl and Maurice Merleau-Ponty." In *Phenomenology of Sociality*. Thomas Szanto and Dermot Moran, editors. New York: Routledge.

Morgan, Kathryn A. (2000). *Myth and Philosophy from the Presocratics to Plato*. Cambridge: Cambridge University Press.

Morrell, Michael E. (2007). "Empathy and Democratic Education." *Public Affairs Quarterly* 21 (4): 381–403.

———. (2010). *Empathy and Democracy*. University Park: Pennsylvania State University Press.

Morrison, India, Donna Lloyd, Giuseppe Di Pellegrino, and Neil Roberts. (2004). "Vicarious Responses to Pain in Anterior Cingulate Cortex: Is Empathy a Multisensory Issue?" *Cognitive, Affective & Behavioral Neuroscience* 4 (2): 270–278.

Moszkowski, Alexander. (1921). *Einstein the Searcher: His Work Explained from Dialogues with Einstein*. H. L. Brose, translator. London: Methuen.

Mueller, Gustav E. (1948). *Philosophy of Literature*. New York: Philosophical Library.

Murray, Penelope. (2011). "Platonic 'Myths.'" In *A Companion to Greek Mythology*. Ken Dowden and Niall Livingstone, editors. Chichester, UK: Wiley-Blackwell, 179–194.

Næss, A. (1973). "The Shallow and the Deep, Long-Range Ecology Movement: A Summary," *Inquiry* 16:95–100.

Nagel, Thomas. (1986). *The View from Nowhere*. New York: Oxford University Press.

———. (2009). "Secular Philosophy and the Religious Temperament." In *Secular Philosophy and the Religious Temperament: Essays 2002–2008*. New York: Oxford University Press.

———. (2012). *Mind and Cosmos: Why the Materialist Neo-Darwinian Conception of Nature Is Almost Certainly False*. New York: Oxford University Press.

———. (2017). "Is Consciousness an Illusion?" *New York Review of Books* (March 9). https://www.nybooks.com/articles/2017/03/09/is-consciousness-an-illusion-dennett-evolution/.

Neta, Ram. (2018). "External World Skepticism." In *Skepticism: From Antiquity to the Present*. Baron Reed and Diego Machuca, editors. New York: Bloomsbury Academic, 634–651.

Neuhouser, Frederick. (1990). *Fichte's Theory of Subjectivity*. Cambridge: Cambridge University Press.

Newton-Fisher, Nicholas E., and Phyllis C Lee. (2011). "Grooming Reciprocity in Wild Male Chimpanzees." *Animal Behaviour* 81 (2): 439–446.

Nivison, David Shepherd. (1999). "The Classical Philosophical Writings." In *The Cambridge History of Ancient China: From Origins to Civilization to 221 B.C.* Michael Loewe and Edward Shaughnessy, editors. New York: Cambridge University Press, 745–812.

Nock, A. D. (1933). *Conversion: The Old and the New in Religion from Alexander the Great to Augustine of Hippo*. Baltimore, MD: Johns Hopkins University Press.

Nussbaum, Martha C. (2001). *The Fragility of Goodness*. Cambridge: Cambridge University Press.

Olberding, Amy. (2019). *The Wrong of Rudeness: Learning Modern Civility from Ancient Chinese Philosophy*. New York: Oxford University Press.

Osler, Margaret J. (2000). "The Canonical Imperative: Rethinking the Scientific Revolution." In *Rethinking the Scientific Revolution*. Margaret J. Osler, editor. Cambridge: Cambridge University Press, 3–22.

Pächt, Otto. (1999). *The Practice of Art History: Reflections on Method*. David Britt, translator. London: Harvey Miller Publishers.

Panofsky, Erwin. (1953). *Early Netherlandish Painting: Its Origins and Character*. Cambridge, MA: Harvard University Press.

Park, Katharine, and Daston, Lorraine. (2003). "Introduction: The Age of the New." In *The Cambridge History of Science*. Vol. 3, *Early Modern Science*. Roy Porter, editor. New York: Cambridge University Press, 1–17.

Paul, L. A. (2014). *Transformative Experience*. New York: Oxford University Press.

Peirce, Charles S. (1966). *Selected Writings (Values in a World of Chance)*. Philip P. Wiener, editor. New York: Dover.

———. (1982). *Writings of Charles S. Peirce: A Chronological Edition*. Max H. Fisch and Christian J. W. Kloesel, editors. Bloomington: Indiana University Press.

Penner, L. A., R. J. Cline, T. L. Albrecht, F. W. Harper, A. M. Peterson, J. M. Taub, et al. (2008). "Parents' Empathic Responses and Pain and Distress in Pediatric Patients." *Basic and Applied Social Psychology* 30 (2), 102–113.

Perry, John. (1979). "The Problem of the Essential Indexical." *Noûs* 13 (1): 3–21.

Pico della Mirandola, Giovanni. ([1486] 2012). *Oration on the Dignity of Man: A New Translation and Commentary*. F. Borghesi, M. Papio, and M. Riva, editors. Cambridge: Cambridge University Press.

Pieper, Josef. (1963). *Leisure: The Basis of Culture*. New York: Random House.

———. (1998). *Happiness and Contemplation*. Richard and Clara Winston, translators. South Bend, IN: St. Augustine's Press.

Plantinga, Alvin. (1983). "Reason and Belief in God." In *Faith and Rationality*. Alvin Plantinga and Nicholas Wolterstorff, editors. Notre Dame, IN: University of Notre Dame Press.

———. (1993). *Warrant and Proper Function*. New York: Oxford University Press.

———. (2000). *Warranted Christian Belief*. New York: Oxford University Press.

———. (2011). *Where the Conflict Really Lies: Science, Religion, and Naturalism.* New York: Oxford University Press.

Plato. (1997). *Plato: Complete Works.* John M. Cooper, editor. Indianapolis: Hackett Publishing.

Plotinus. (2018). *The Enneads.* Lloyd P. Gerson, editor; G. Boys-Stones, J. M. Dillon, L. P. Gerson, R.A.H. King, A. Smith, and J. Wilberding, translators. Cambridge: Cambridge University Press.

Pope-Hennessy, John. (1989). *The Portrait in the Renaissance: The A. W. Mellon Lectures in the Fine Arts 12.* Bollingen Series 35. Princeton, NJ: Princeton University Press.

Popkin, Richard, ed. (1966). *The Philosophy of the Sixteenth and Seventeenth Centuries.* New York: Free Press.

Porphyry of Tyre. (2018) *On the Life of Plotinus and the Order of His Books.* In *The Enneads.* Lloyd P. Gerson, editor; G. Boys-Stones, J. M. Dillon, L. P. Gerson, R.A.H. King, A. Smith, and J. Wilberding, translators. Cambridge: Cambridge University Press.

*A Presocratics Reader: Selected Fragments and Testimonia* (2011). 2nd ed. Patricia Curd, editor; Richard D. McKirahan and Patricia Curd, translators. Indianapolis: Hackett Publishing.

Putnam, Hilary. (1973). "Meaning and Reference." *Journal of Philosophy* 70 (19), Seventieth Annual Meeting of the American Philosophical Association Eastern Division. (November 8, 1973): 699–711.

———. (1975). "The Meaning of 'Meaning.'" *Minnesota Studies in the Philosophy of Science* 7: 131–193. Reprinted in *Philosophical Papers.* Vol. 2, *Mind, Language, and Reality.* Hilary Putnam, editor. Cambridge: Cambridge University Press, 1975.

———. (1981). "Brains in a Vat." *Reason, Truth, and History.* Cambridge: Cambridge University Press.

———. (1982). "Why Reason Can't Be Naturalized." *Synthese* 52: 3–23.

———. (1999). *The Threefold Cord: Mind, Body, and World.* New York: Columbia University Press.

———. (2004). *The Collapse of the Fact/Value Dichotomy and Other Essays.* Cambridge, MA: Harvard University Press.

Quine, Willard V. O. (1951). "Two Dogmas of Empiricism." *Philosophical Review.* 60 (1): 20–43.

Raaflaub, Kurt. (2009). "Intellectual Achievements." In *A Companion to Archaic Greece.* Kurt Raaflaub and Hans van Wees, editors. Chichester, UK: Wiley-Blackwell, 564–584.

Ramachandran, V. S. (2007). "The Neurology of Self-Awareness." Edge Foundation 10th Anniversary Essay. John Brockman, editor. London: Edge Foundation.

———. (2011). *The Tell-Tale Brain: A Neuroscientist's Quest for What Makes Us Human.* New York: W. W. Norton.

Rameson, Lian T., and Matthew D. Lieberman. (2009). "Empathy: A Social Cognitive Neuroscience Approach." *Social and Personality Psychology Compass* 3 (1): 94–110.

Rawls, John. (1971). *A Theory of Justice*. Cambridge, MA: Belknap Press.
———. (1996). *Political Liberalism*. New York: Columbia University Press.
———. (1999). *A Theory of Justice*. Rev. ed. Oxford: Oxford University Press.
———. (2005). *Political Liberalism*. New York: Columbia University Press.
Reeder, Glenn. John B. Pryor, Michael J. A. Wohl, and Michael L. Griswell. (2005). "On Attributing Negative Emotions to Others Who Disagree with Our Opinions." *Personality and Social Psychology Bulletin* 31 (11): 1498–1510.
Rheinfelder, Hans. (1928). *Das Wort "Persona": Geschichte seiner Bedeutungen mit besonderer Berücksichtigung des französischen und italienischen Mittelalters*. Beihefte zur Zeitschrift für romanische Philologie 77. Halle: Niemeyer.
Rhodes, Aaron. (2018). *The Debasement of Human Rights: How Politics Sabotage the Ideal of Freedom*. New York: Encounter Books.
Rochat, P. (2003). "Five Levels of Self-Awareness as They Unfold Early in Life." *Conscious and Cognition* 12 (4): 717–731.
Rochberg, Francesca. (2016). *Before Nature: Cuneiform Knowledge and the History of Science*. Chicago: University of Chicago Press.
Rolston, H. (1975). "Is There an Ecological Ethic?" *Ethics* 85: 93–109.
Rosen, Michael. (2012). *Dignity: Its History and Meaning*. Cambridge, MA: Harvard University Press.
Roth, Harold D. (2004). *Original Tao: Inward Training (Nei-yeh) and the Foundations of Taoist Mysticism*. New York: Columbia University Press.
Routley, Richard. (1973). "Is There a Need for a New, an Environmental, Ethic?" *Proceedings of the 15th World Congress of Philosophy* 1: 205–210.
Rowett, Catherine. (2013). "Philosophy's Numerical Turn: Why the Pythagoreans' Interest in Numbers Is Truly Awesome." In *Doctrine and Doxography: Studies on Heraclitus and Pythagoras*. D. Sider and D. Obbink, editors. Sozomena: Studies in the Recovery of Ancient Texts. Berlin: De Gruyter, 3–32.
Ruff, Willie, and John Rodgers. (2011). *The Harmony of the World: A Realization for the Ear of Johannes Kepler's Astronomical Data from Harmonices Mundi 1619*. Audio recording. Guilford, CT: Kepler Records.
Russell, Bertrand. (1959). *The Problems of Philosophy*. Oxford: Oxford University Press.
Sagan, Carl, et al. (writers), Adrian Malone et al. (directors), and Gregory Andorfer et al. (producers). (1980). *Cosmos: A Personal Journey*. Episode 1, "The Shores of the Cosmic Ocean." Aired September 28 on PBS.
Sartre, Jean-Paul. (1948). "Existentialism Is a Humanism." Philip Mairet, translator. London: Methuen.
———. (1960). *The Transcendence of the Ego: A Sketch for a Phenomenological Description*. New York: Hill and Wang.
———. (1993). *Being and Nothingness*. Hazel E. Barnes, translator. New York: Washington Square Press.
Schellenberg, J. L. (2015). *The Hiddenness Argument: Philosophy's New Challenge to Belief in God*. New York: Oxford University Press.
———. (2019). *Progressive Atheism: How Moral Evolution Changes the God Debate*. London: Bloomsbury Publishing.

Schmitz, Kenneth L. (1986). "The Geography of the Human Person." *Communio: International Catholic Review* 13 (1): 27–48.

Schneewind, J. B. (1997). *The Invention of Autonomy: A History of Modern Moral Philosophy*. Cambridge: Cambridge University Press.

Schopenhauer, Arthur. (2004). "On Some Forms of Literature." In *The Art of Literature*. T. Bailey Saunders, translator. Mineola, NY: Dover Publications. Replica of 6ᵗʰ ed. (New York: Macmillan, 1891).

Searle, John. (1994). *The Rediscovery of the Mind*. Cambridge, Mass.: MIT Press.

———. (2015). *Seeing Things as They Are: A Theory of Perception*. New York: Oxford University Press.

Sibley, Chris G., and Fiona Kate Barlow. (2017). *The Cambridge Handbook of the Psychology of Prejudice*. Cambridge: Cambridge University Press.

Siderits, Mark. (2011). "Buddhist Non-Self: The No-Owner's Manual." In *The Oxford Handbook of the Self*. Shaun Gallagher, editor. Oxford: Oxford University Press

Singer, Peter. (2011). *Practical Ethics*. 3ʳᵈ ed. Cambridge: Cambridge University Press.

Slote, Michael A. (2007). *The Ethics of Care and Empathy*. New York: Routledge University Press.

Smith, Kurt. (Winter 2018). "Descartes' Theory of Ideas." *The Stanford Encyclopedia of Philosophy*. Edward N. Zalta, editor. https://plato.stanford.edu/archives/win2018/entries/descartes-ideas/.

Snow, N. E. (2000). "Empathy." *American Philosophical Quarterly* 37(1): 65–78.

Sorabji, Richard. (2006). *Self: Ancient and Modern Insights about Individuality, Life, and Death*. Chicago: University of Chicago Press.

Spinoza, Benedict. (1994). *A Spinoza Reader: The* Ethics *and Other Works*. Edwin Curley, editor and translator. Princeton, NJ: Princeton University Press.

Stark, Rodney. (2004). *For the Glory of God: How Monotheism Led to Reformations, Science, Witch-Hunts, and the End of Slavery*. Princeton, NJ: Princeton University Press.

Sulmasy, Daniel P. (2010). "Human Dignity and Human Worth." In *Perspectives on Human Dignity*. J. Malpas and N. Lickiss, editors. Dordrecht, Netherlands: Springer, 9–25.

Sunstein, Cass R. (2017). *Republic: Divided Democracy in the Age of Social Media*. Princeton, NJ: Princeton University Press.

Taipale, Joona. (2014). *Phenomenology and Embodiment: Husserl and the Constitution of Subjectivity*. Chicago: Northwestern University Press.

Talisse, Robert. (2016). *Engaging Political Philosophy: An Introduction*. Abingdon: Routledge.

———. (2019). *Overdoing Democracy: Why We Must Put Politics in Its Place*. Oxford: Oxford University Press.

Taylor, Charles. (1991). *The Ethics of Authenticity*. Cambridge, MA: Harvard University Press.

———. (1995). "A Most Peculiar Institution." In *World, Mind, and Ethics: Essays on the Ethical Philosophy of Bernard Williams*. J.E.J. Altham and Ross Harrison, editors. Cambridge: Cambridge University Press.

Theon of Smyrna. (1978). *Mathematics Useful for Understanding Plato: Or, Pythagorean Arithmetic, Music, Astronomy, Spiritual Disciplines*. Robert and Deborah Lawlor, translators. San Diego, CA: Wizards Bookshelf.

Tombak, Kaia J., Eva C. Wikberg, Daniel I. Rubenstein, and Colin A. Chapman. (2019). "Reciprocity and Rotating Social Advantage among Females in Egalitarian Primate Societies." *Animal Behaviour* 157: 189–200.

Tooley, Michael. (1972). "Abortion and Infanticide." *Philosophy and Public Affairs* 2 (1), 37–65.

———. (1983). *Abortion and Infanticide*. Oxford: Clarendon Press.

van Wensveen, Louke. (2000). *Dirty Virtues: The Emergence of Ecological Virtue Ethics*. New York: Humanity Books.

Varela, Francisco J., Evan Thompson, and Eleanor Rosch. (2016). *The Embodied Mind: Cognitive Science and Human Experience*. Rev. ed. Cambridge, MA: MIT Press.

Vergano, Dan. (2014). "Cave Paintings in Indonesia Redraw Picture of Earliest Art." *National Geographic*, October.

Waldron, Jeremy. (2012). "Dignity and Rank." In *Dignity, Rank, and Rights: The Berkeley Tanner Lectures*. Meir Dan-Cohen, editor. Oxford: Oxford University Press, 2–27.

Wallace, Deborah. (1999). "Jacques Maritain and Alasdair MacIntyre: The Person, the Common Good and Human Rights." In *The Failure of Modernism: The Cartesian Legacy and Contemporary Pluralism*. B. Sweetman, editor. Washington, DC: Catholic University of America Press, 127–140.

Wallace, William A. (1981). *Prelude to Galileo: Essays on Medieval and Sixteenth Century Sources of Galileo's Thought*. New York: Springer.

Weber, Max. (1919). *Science as a Vocation*. Munich: Duncker & Humblot. Reprinted in Weber (1946), 129–156.

———. (1946). *From Max Weber: Essays in Sociology*. H. H. Gerth and C. Wright Mills, translators and editors. New York: Oxford University Press.

Weithman, Paul. (2016). *Rawls, Political Liberalism, and Reasonable Faith*. Cambridge: Cambridge University Press.

Welch, Shay. (2019). *The Phenomenology of a Performative Knowledge System: Dancing with Native American Epistemology*. London: Palgrave MacMillan.

Whitehead, Alfred North. (1925). *Science and the Modern World*. New York: Free Press.

Wians, William Robert. (2009). "Introduction." In *Logos and Mythos: Philosophical Essays in Greek Literature*. William Wians, editor. Albany: SUNY Press, 1–10.

Williams, Bernard. ([1978] 2005). *Descartes: The Project of Pure Enquiry*. London: Routledge.

———. (2006). *Ethics and the Limits of Philosophy*. London: Routledge.

Williams, Daniel K. (2016). *Defenders of the Unborn: The Pro-Life Movement before Roe v. Wade*. New York: Oxford University Press.

Williamson, Thad. (2008). "Sprawl, Spatial Location, and Politics: How Ideological Identification Tracks the Built Environment." *American Politics Research* 36 (6): 903–933.

Wilshire, Bruce. 2000. *The Primal Roots of American Philosophy: Pragmatism, Phenomenology, and Native American Thought*. University Park: Pennsylvania State University Press.

Wittgenstein, Ludwig. (1961). *Tractatus Logico-Philosophicus*. D. F. Pears and B. F. McGuinness, translators. London: Routledge and Kegan Paul.

———. (2009). *Philosophical Investigations*. 4th ed. P.M.S. Hacker and Joachim Schulte, editors. Oxford: Blackwell.

Wojtyla, Karol (Pope St. John Paul II). (2008). *Person and Community: Selected Essays*. 2nd ed. Theresa Sandok, OSM, translator. Catholic Thought from Lublin. New York: Peter Lang.

Yunis, Harvey. (2013). "Political Uses of Rhetoric in Democratic Athens." In *The Greek Polis and the Invention of Democracy: A Politico-cultural Transformation and Its Interpretations*. Johann P. Arnason, Kurt A. Raaflaub, and Peter Wagner, editors. Chichester, UK: Wiley-Blackwell, 144–162.

Zagzebski, Linda. (1996). *Virtues of the Mind*. Cambridge: Cambridge University Press.

———. (1998). "Virtue in Ethics and Epistemology." Presidential address to the American Catholic Philosophical Association. *Proceedings of the 1997 American Catholic Philosophical Association*. 17: 1–17.

———. (1999). "*Phronesis* and Christian Belief." In *The Rationality of Theism*. Godehard Bruntrup, editor. Dordrecht, Netherlands: Kluwer.

———. (2000). "*Phronesis* and Religious Belief." In *Knowledge, Belief, and Character*. Guy Axtell, editor. Lanham, MD: Rowman and Littlefield.

———. (2008a). "Ethical and Epistemic Egoism and the Ideal of Autonomy." *Episteme: A Journal of Social Epistemology*. 4: 252–263.

———. (2008b). "Omnisubjectivity." In *Oxford Studies in Philosophy of Religion*. Jonathan Kvanvig, editor. Oxford: Oxford University Press, 231–248.

———. (2010). "Exemplarist Virtue Theory." *Metaphilosophy* 41: 41–57. Reprinted in Heather Battaly, ed. (2010), *Virtue and Vice: Moral and Epistemic*. Oxford: Wiley-Blackwell.

———. (2011). "First Person and Third Person Epistemic Reasons and Religious Epistemology." *European Journal of Philosophy of Religion* (Fall). Reprinted in Sebastian Kolodziejczyk and Janusz Salamon, eds. (2013). *Knowledge, Action, Pluralism*. Frankfurt am Main: Peter Lang.

———. (2012). *Epistemic Authority: A Theory of Trust, Authority, and Autonomy in Belief*. New York: Oxford University Press.

———. (2013). *Omnisubjectivity: A Defense of a Divine Attribute*. Milwaukee: Marquette University Press.

——. (2014). "First Person and Third Person Reasons and the Regress Problem." In *Ad Infinitum: New Essays on Epistemological Infinitism*. John Turri and Peter Klein, editors. New York: Oxford University Press, 243–255.

——. (2016a). "The Dignity of Persons and the Value of Uniqueness." Presidential address to the Central Division of the American Philosophical Association. In *Proceedings and Addresses of the American Philosophical Association* 90 (November): 55–70.

——. (2016b). "Omnisubjectivity: Why It Is a Divine Attribute." *Nova et Vetera* 14 (2): 435–450.

——. (2017). *Exemplarist Moral Theory*. New York: Oxford University Press.

——. (2019). "Intellectual Virtue Terms and the Division of Linguistic Labor. In *Virtue and Voice: Habits of Mind for a Return to Civil Discourse*. Gregg Ten Elshof and Evan Rosa, editors. Abilene, TX: Abilene Christian University Press.

Zahavi, Dan. (2005). *Subjectivity and Selfhood: Investigating the First-Person Perspective*. Cambridge, MA: MIT Press.

Zhong, Lei. 2016. "Physicalism, Psychism, and Phenomenalism." *Journal of Philosophy* 113 (11): 572–590.

Zhmud, Leonid. (2012). *Pythagoras and the Early Pythagoreans*. Kevin Windle and Rosh Ireland, translators. Oxford: Oxford University Press.

Zimmerman, Dean, ed. (2004). *Oxford Studies in Metaphysics*, vol. 1. New York: Oxford University Press.

A NOTE ON THE TYPE

THIS BOOK has been composed in Miller, a Scotch Roman typeface designed by Matthew Carter and first released by Font Bureau in 1997. It resembles Monticello, the typeface developed for The Papers of Thomas Jefferson in the 1940s by C. H. Griffith and P. J. Conkwright and reinterpreted in digital form by Carter in 2003.

Pleasant Jefferson ("P. J.") Conkwright (1905–1986) was Typographer at Princeton University Press from 1939 to 1970. He was an acclaimed book designer and AIGA Medalist.

The ornament used throughout this book was designed by Pierre Simon Fournier (1712–1768) and was a favorite of Conkwright's, used in his design of the *Princeton University Library Chronicle*.